FAITH AND FORTUNE

In Memory of Father Michael Napier, Cong. Orat.
15th February 1929–22nd August 1996

Requiescat in Pace

FAITH AND FORTUNE

Madeleine Beard

First published in 1997

Gracewing
Fowler Wright Books
2 Southern Ave, Leominster
Herefordshire HR6 0QF

ISBN 0 85244 392 7

Typesetting by Action Typesetting Ltd,
Gloucester, GL1 1SP

Printed by Cromwell Press
Broughton Gifford, Wiltshire, SN12 8PH

Contents

Introduction

Intrinsic to the nature of Roman Catholicism is the belief that one cannot disentangle the physical from the spiritual. I have chosen, therefore, to paint an impression of both the actual journeys and the hidden journeys to Rome made by particular English men and women during the nineteenth century. The first part of the book, 'Off to Rome', sets the scene by drawing together accounts of travels through the Continent of which some were sympathetic to Catholicism and others not. The second part, 'Over to Rome', attempts to describe the intangible and mysterious promptings which led many to become Roman Catholics, some without having set foot in the Eternal City at all. *Visibilium et invisibilium.* Such is the mysterious nature of Faith.

List of Illustrations

14. Dominic Barberi, photograph taken from a prayer card in church in Rome on the Coelian Hill!

15. L. Wolf, 'Life of the First Marquess of Ripon', London, John Murray, 1921
   456.c.92.213 Photographed in the garden at Studley

16. H. Vickers, 'Gladys, Duchess of Marlborough', London, Weidenfeld & Nicolson, 1979
   9450.c.1142 Photographed outside entrance to Blenheim

PART I – OFF TO ROME

Chapter One

The Catholic's hunger for the land of Faith

I am writing these pages in an English village. I see a low line of pale, misty hills to my left. A venerable church-tower peeps from amid large elms and red brick cottage chimneys. In front of my trim garden is a green meadow. The white butterflies are courting each other in the noontide warmth, and the village children have crowned themselves with tall paper caps, and are holding some jubilee of their own, the mysteries of which are indiscernible to older minds. The clematis which climbs my porch breathes soft, perfumed sighs at my open window. But between this and the dreamlike beauty of Amalfi there lies far more than the distance of many hundreds of miles. There lie the yearning of the soul for the best of God's beautiful creation – for the warmth of the sun – that natural god of life and gladness – the thirst of the artist's eye for colour, and the poet's love of the language of song; there lie the Catholic's hunger for the land of Faith and the longing for the regions of old memories and heroic sanctities.[1]

The Hon. Mrs Alfred Montgomery, daughter of Lord Leconfield, was expressing a yearning for Italy which had taken hold of many an English heart. Her childhood had been spent in what was a reconstruction of Italy. Petworth Park's Sussex soil had been chiselled, dredged and drained to recapture the romantic Italian scenes first viewed on the

Grand Tour. The Palladian bridge, the gentle hills, the lake, statues and planted trees were all an extravagant monument to classical Italy, which had bitten deep into the aristocratic Grand Tourist's mind. The classical uniformity of pillars, porticoes and domes had appealed to the ordered English outlook. But not to all. The tiny Victorian church dedicated to St. Antony and St. George not far from Petworth and built in the Gothic style of the thirteenth century was a deliberate reconstruction of England's Catholic past. But the child who had once played in Petworth's halls herself later travelled to Rome as a Roman Catholic.

Travelling to Rome through Tuscany, the Hon. Mrs Alfred Montgomery had had a mystical sense that what she was seeing from a speedy train she had seen before. Twenty five years earlier she had viewed the same Tuscan landscape from a slow carriage. Since then the journey had recurred to her in dreams. Now it was as if her soul spoke to her. Here at last was what had haunted her for so long, reconstructed before her piece by piece in the same way that the broken and half-forgotten fragments of her life would be pieced together when the barrier of death was passed.

Since the Hon. Mrs Alfred Montgomery had first visited Italy, many other English men and women had found solace in Mediterranean lands and stayed there. Their coroneted carriages and sleek horses were seen throughout Italian towns. In residences along the French and Italian rivieras, in Florentine villas and in Roman palaces, guests were received with Mayfair magnificence. Liveried gondoliers ferried passengers with names in Debrett's along the canals of Venice; crested dice were thrown in the casinos in Monte Carlo.[2] Cut off from the Continent at the beginning of the century by the Napoleonic wars, the English returned to gather spiritual and physical strength from the lands they thought they had left for good.

The Marquess of Normanby recalled that the power of Napoleon 'became as by a miracle dissolved … and the Continent opened up to our insular curiosity.' With 'the dull and newsless state of peace', foreign travel supplied the need for new adventure.³ The Channel crossing was not for the faint-hearted. While the political climate might change on the Continent, the barrier of the stormy Channel was ever there. The Hon. Edward Legge had made numerous journeys to the Continent since his undergraduate days. Twenty years after his first crossing he found himself at Folkestone again, this time with his wife and two small children. He struggled along the pier in the full blast of the wind, trying to protect his child and keep on his hat. In the stormy crossing in a small and crowded vessel Legge found a place for his family to huddle below while he sat on deck bearing the full brunt of the wind and waves. Soaked to the skin and sea-sick, he stepped ashore at Boulogne and established his party at the Hotel Imperial du Pavillon.⁴

Rising early on a dark December morning Charles Richard Weld drove through London when the inhabitants of the 'mighty metropolis were still hushed in slumber'. He and his party caught the train to Folkestone. 'Dawn breaks through the heavy lead-hued mist that curtains the earth' and in the tumbling Channel 'waves dashed beneath the bows of the steamer in glittering sheets of foam'.⁵ Some stayed in Boulogne and never moved any further. Others journeyed to Paris and then on to the Riviera, where a small colony of northern Europeans had established themselves to improve their health. After the long journey through France it was a delight 'to find oneself upon the blue Mediterranean with a sky above us that tells we are fast approaching the sweet south!'⁶ Medical opinion then deemed the warmth of the Mediterranean climate an antidote for consumption and bronchitis. By 1860 Hyères, Cannes and Nice were well-known health-resorts, followed a few years later by Menton, Bordighera and San Remo. The climates of Pisa and Rome were thought best for throat and bronchial afflictions, gout and rheumatism. Cannes, San Remo and Menton had a more bracing air, and Nice and Naples had the most bracing air of all. It was in the moderately bracing air of Menton that Anglican clergymen, Nonconformist ministers and Evangelicals created a niche of quiet Protestant protest.[7]

Before the Presbyterian church was opened at Menton, Miss Dudgeon's villa 'Les Grottes' was a venue for prayer meetings and Bible classes. By the 1880s the sophisticated Monte Carlo contingent had moved in and so the religious contingent moved to Bordighera and San Remo, 'where ecclesiastical repose remained intact for another generation'.[8] Yet the author of *Wintering on the Riviera. A 'Compagnon de Voyage' with hints to invalids*, informed his readers that among local inhabitants they would find much religious devotion, carried out 'with a medieval charm which our exclusive islanders but dream or read of in romance'. In the land of his temporary sojourn, the invalid would be touched to observe a faith and devotion more deeply rooted than at home.[9]

Some English travelled for medical cures only to experience miraculous cures – once they had taken the leap of faith into a Church where miracles had never ceased. Lady Feilding suffered from sciatica and Lord Feilding had managed to track down a man not far from Rome whose family had tilled the ground since the time of St. Peter and St. Paul and had received from the two apostles the gift of healing rheumatic disorders. The young Lady Feilding was in agony. Praying and laying on hands by the holy Roman resulted in her cure. She walked instantly and remained cured for six weeks. Thus encouraged, Lord Feilding set off for Strasbourg to visit a nun in direct communion with Christ and reknowned for answering prayers. All this was related by Mrs John Ruskin, who just managed to disguise her irritation at the Feildings' persistent attempts to convert her and her husband, finding it odd that so elegantly dressed a young man should talk of 'miracles, the gifts of the Spirit, Penance and crucifying the flesh'.[10] The Feildings were more successful in their being instrumental in the conversion of Augustus Hare's mother, who had long lived in Rome. Augustus Hare recorded the miracle in greater detail than the equally sceptical Mrs Ruskin. According to him, Lady Feilding had been advised by Pope Pius IX to apply to a family living in the mountains above Foligno. St. Peter had once passed by that way and lodged with them, and on leaving had said he had neither silver nor gold to give them, but the gift of healing. A messenger was despatched and he returned with an old peasant who stood in front of Lady Feilding and recited the Our Father, Hail Mary and Apostles' Creed. He then said: 'Per l'intercessione dei SS. Apostoli Pietro e Paolo siate guarita da tutti i mali come speriamo'. He quickly ran his hands over her limbs and made the Sign of the Cross saying 'In nomine Patris et Filii et Spiritus Sancti', adding 'E finito.' Lady Feilding felt her limbs suddenly strengthen. Rising, she walked upstairs, something she had not done for many months. That same afternoon she went to St. Peter's to give thanks, walking all around the enormous basilica free from pain.[11] Rome could indeed provide a cure for rheumatism, but not quite in the way English Victorian doctors might have anticipated.

Converts such as the Feildings did not socialise with their Protestant compatriots in the Eternal City. They did not appear at the five o'clock teas or the dinner parties or the receptions. They stayed in different hotels from the rest, stuck together and followed their own objects and pursuits, experiencing an inner life 'utterly and inevitably invisible to the sightseers and the societarians who bring the manners of Mayfair into the Piazza di Spagna'.[12] For twelve weeks, between Christmas and Easter, the Corso seemed like Piccadilly, such were the numbers of English who spent the winter in Rome. Why did they come? Because life was easy, they were never bored, they slept well at night, the Romans were civil, they could do what they liked. Existence was cheap; idleness was not accounted a crime. Yet they still carried England with them. An American traveller observed that as an island nation the English formed an insular community, upon which 'the waves of foreign influence beat in vain'. In restaurants the French or the Germans created 'a social continent; but an English coffee room, at the hour of dinner, is an archipelago of islets, with deep straits of reserve and exclusiveness flowing between'.[13]

So too in worship the Protestants retained their exclusive island of non-conformity in papal Rome. With no colour, no organ, no singing, everything was as plain and simple as possible. 'Never did I feel so grateful to the Reformers of the Church of England, that at the cost of their own lives they had bequeathed to us primitive purity', wrote one clergyman in 1847. He likened this apparent purity of worship to the early Christians, hidden away from the heathen ritual of old Rome.

The Protestant perception of Roman Catholicism was reinforced by what they saw as the plain superstition and mummery of liturgical practice. At last the long years of anti-Catholic prejudice could be confirmed at first hand. Some treated the spectacle with disdain, likening High Mass to a trip to the opera, jostling and talking, gossiping and laughing. Clergymen who came to observe with open eyes and closed minds recorded their impressions in journals and letters, using the pen as an outlet for their horrified fascination. One such parson returned to England in 1855 to set down his thoughts on paper. They were that the Papal world was quite simply 'a wriggling mass of corruption and suffering'.

> The whine of mendicants, the curses, groans and shrieks of victims, and the demoniacal laughter of tyrants co-mingle in one hoarse roar ... What is to be done with the carcass? We cannot dwell in its neighbourhood. It would be impossible long to inhabit the same globe with it: its stench were enough to pollute and poison the atmosphere of our planet. It must be buried or burned. It cannot be allowed to remain on the surface of the earth: it would breed a plague, which would infect, not a world only, but a universe.[14]

Romanism was 'the idolatrous apostasy from the purer, holier Faith', destined to receive God's judgement with fire, volcano or earthquake. Looking back on the domes, the turrets, the cupolas, the palaces, the Vatican and St. Peter's, rendered magnificent by the morning sun, a Doctor of Divinity exclaimed 'Farewell, farewell to Rome! What will convert thee?' To the Protestant mind, earthly beauty was a corruption of the Gospel; blank simplicity was not.[15] The purity of the faith of St. Peter and the simplicity of ancient worship had been deformed, the Gospel had been mingled with strange legends from old mythology. Ritual was pagan. St. Peter himself with a 'lofty rebuke' would have startled the thousands kneeling in the shrine dedicated to him, he who wished for his name only to be written in heaven. The kneeling worshippers would be summoned away by St. Peter 'from cunningly devised fables to changeless and immutable truths'.[16] And visitors to Rome could see St. Peter's elected successor – elected by old gentlemen in scarlet robes and white petticoats – driving out daily in a coach and four or out on the Pincian hills dressed in a white flannel dressing gown. Darkly, furtively and somewhat vengefully, fervent Protestants gloried in Rome. Shocked, they took copious notes.

> He is horror-struck at the very idea of the Pope, but he is not averse to throwing himself in his way; and with the pride of conscious rectitude he relates (when he reaches Clapham) how resolutely he refused to uncover and kneel as the idolatrous crowds around him did, when the Pope alighted from his carriage ...[17]

When Newman travelled to Italy in 1833, his imagination was powerfully affected by witnessing at first hand the Church which he had long thought was the Church of the Anti-Christ. On the Feast of the Annunciation he went to High Mass at the church of Santa Maria sopra Minerva. He could not discern whether what he saw was falsehood or reality. 'Who can separate the light from the darkness but the Greater Word who prophesied their union?' But in Rome he perceived from afar for the first time the 'timidity, indolence and that secular spirit which creeps on established religion everywhere'.[18]

In Italy, Protestants were themselves viewed with suspicion. One traveller was amused at the 'prying interest with which we were surveyed'. When on entering a church it was observed that Mrs George Gretton and her companion took no holy water nor made the Sign of the Cross, an old woman whispered 'Peccato, non sono Christiane!', while the children gazed inquisitively. Spending three months living near Rome, Lady Calcot was questioned by her Italian hosts who, 'never having seen heretics before, except struggling in flames in a picture, questioned us very minutely as to our faith'.[19] An Anglican clergyman travelling through France and Italy recalled, 'I believed myself a priest, yet I could not say so to strangers without qualifying clauses.'[20]

⚬❦⚬

How did Anglican clergy view Catholic priests? The common point of reference was the sermon, the only part of the Mass not in Latin. G.M. Musgrave, a clergyman travelling from his Kent vicarage to Paris, observed the priest in the pulpit in the church of St. Roch. The priest leaned on one elbow, then on the other, then leaned over the pulpit. With one hand wide open he struck its palm with the fingers of the other, producing a sound 'that would have cleared a cherry-orchard of twenty tribes of birds in a moment of time'. [21] The sermon ended abruptly and with a rapid descent of the pulpit steps the priest scuffled back to the altar, to undertake more urgent matters in the sanctuary. Nine years later Mr Musgrave was still distressed to observe a priest preaching in Orleans Cathedral with an easy familiarity, one moment holding up his hands as if he were playing castanets, the next leaning on them on the pulpit ledge as if he were at a shop counter in angry confrontation with a purchaser asking for a lower price.[22]

Lord Teignmouth observed priests who walked rapidly within the limits of their pulpits, who sat down suddenly in their chair or rose just as suddenly from it. One, who attempted to describe the heart agitated by passions as if it were a net of venomous reptiles, stretched forth his hands and turned his head aside as if in horror. But Lord Teignmouth remarked that the content of the sermons was 'excellent'. He heard sound morality and denunciations of those who attended Mass in the morning and spent the rest of the day in unholy pursuits.[23] At the Gèsu in Rome medi-

tations on the Passion during Holy Week were delivered by
a Jesuit who after ten minutes of frenzied speech suddenly
dropped on his knees and prayed in silence for two
minutes. Resuming his sermon he clasped his hands
together, gesticulating and waving. To illustrate the
carrying of the cross he knelt down and walked on his
knees. The attentive congregation was then moved to tears
as the priest depicted an old lady at prayer. 'As he went on,
he waxed warmer and warmer, and carried us all along
with him, while he spoke of the short-lived nature of
earthly sorrow, and drew a picture of the happiness in
Heaven.'[24]

A Jesuit preaching at St. Ambrogio in Genoa sat on a
large armchair on a platform near the altar. He appeared
tired, wiped his face and began with a trembling voice:

> 'Cari auditori, before all things, it is necessary for us
> continually to establish the fact – that out of the
> Catholic church there is no salvation – the creed of
> this church must be retained in every particular, and
> faithfully believed by all, who would be saved: – and
> having stated this very first article necessary to be
> remembered by all the children of the only infallible
> church – I shall proceed to shew you – that, without
> the shedding of blood, there is no remission of sin.'[25]

During the course of his sermon he warmed to his subject
and stood up, enumerating God's goodness in the gifts of
nature and providence and grace. As if exhausted he sat
down again and went on in a subdued voice that Christ's
sacrifice was due to the generosity of the Blessed Virgin.
Rising again from the chair he turned to her image on the
altar and, weeping, agonised for her compassion, addressing
her by every endearing name. The congregation joined in
the litany of praise. To the English woman who stood among
them 'there seemed no more of *Christianity* in the multitude
than in that of Ephesus, when they exclaimed, "Great is
Diana of the Ephesians." '[26]

The Blessed Virgin Mary was venerated in a more
contemporary vein following her appearance to two young

children high up in the mountains near Grenoble in 1846, in a little hamlet called La Salette. An English traveller met a priest in a carriage who had travelled for five days and five nights in order to reach the shrine. Crossing himself as he spoke, the priest told his companion that, following the apparition, a fountain overflowing with crystalline water had appeared on the mountain rock where none had ever been before. Having climbed the precipices on a donkey the priest's feet had at once been cured and all fatigue left him. He had collected water from the fountain which he carried in a tin container. 'I could scarcely forebear smiling, but the solemnity of the priest's manner curbed my rising levity', observed Charles Weld.[27]

An encounter with a priest in a carriage might tip the balance between prejudice and grudging respect. The priest who had made the pilgrimage to La Salette asked if it were true that in England the aristocratic Protestant government forbade the erection of crosses in England. He was assured that there was no such hindrance and that if he visited England he would find a large class of Protestants as fond of this symbol as Roman Catholics. At La Salette the priest had himself seen the Blessed Virgin Mary seated on a stone wearing white robes trimmed with lace. Asked whether he considered himself privileged to have seen the mother of Jesus, a careless 'Oui' was his modest answer.

Devotion to Mary was an aspect of Catholicism which to the Protestant mind was one of the hardest to take. It had overtones of idolatry, a tawdry peasant culture, pagan ceremonial, bad taste. The processions and the statues, the miracles, apparitions and shrines appeared unfathomable to inhabitants of a land where statues and pilgrimages had long since been swept away. This was Mediterranean Catholicism, viewed with distaste by the subjects of a country once known as the Dowry of Mary. This title dated from 1061 when St. Edward the Confessor had offered England to Mary after her appearance to the Lady of the Manor of Walsingham, Richeldis de Faverches, in that same year. The miraculous appearance of the replica of the Holy House of Nazareth in the Norfolk fields following this apparition turned

Walsingham into a place of pilgrimage for almost five hundred years. The shrine was destroyed on 4th August 1538 when its famous statue of Our Lady of Walsingham was burned. Walsingham had ranked alongside Santiago de Compostella, Jerusalem and Rome as a place of pilgrimage and was the only one dedicated to the Mother of God. On the Continent there was a statue of the Blessed Virgin Mary in every church, candles were lit in front of her image, flowers placed at her feet. For Roman Catholics it was perfectly logical to pay homage to the Mother of God, Queen of Heaven and Our Lady of Victories. Such devotion was often misunderstood by the subjects of Queen Victoria.

Notes

[1] Hon. Mrs Alfred Montgomery, *On the Wing: A Southern Flight*, London, Hurst & Blackett, 1875, p. 313.

[2] J. Pemble, *The Mediterranean Passion. Victorians and Edwardians in the South*, Oxford, Clarendon Press, 1987, p. 2.

[3] Marquis of Normanby, *The English in Italy, Vol. I*, London, Saunders and Otley, 1825, p. 12.

[4] Greater London Record Office, Papers of Hon. Edward Legge, 11th Oct. 1876, F/LEG/902.

[5] C.R. Weld, *Last Winter in Rome*, London, Longman Green, 1865, pp. 1–3.

[6] Rev. M. Vicary, B.A., *Notes of a Residence at Rome in 1846*, London, Richard Bentley, 1847, p. 1.

[7] Pemble, op. cit., pp. 45, 85, 88, 93.

[8] Ibid.

[9] A.M. Brown, *Wintering at Menton on the Riviera. A Compagnon de Voyage with hints to invalids*, London, J. & A. Churchill, 1872, p. 29.

[10] M. Lutyens (ed.), *Effie in Venice. Unpublished letters of Mrs John Ruskin written from Venice between 1849–1852*, London, John Murray, 1963, p. 330.

[11] A.J.C. Hare, *The Story of My Life. Vol. I*, London, George Allen, 1896, p. 341.

[12] G.A. Sala, *A Journey Due South: Travels in Search of Sunshine*, London, Vizetelly & Co., 1885, p. 265.

[13] G.S. Hillard, *Six Months in Italy. Vol. II*, London, John Murray, 1853, pp. 211, 212.

[14] Rev. J.A. Wylie, *Pilgrimage from the Alps to the Tiber or the Influence of Romanism on Trade, Justice and Knowledge*, Edinburgh, Shepherd & Elliot, 1855, p. 4.

15   G. Townsend, D.D., *Journal of a Tour in Italy in 1850, with an account of an interview with the Pope, at the Vatican*, London, Francis & John Rivington, 1850, p. 250.

16   Rev. W.I. Kip, M.A., *The Christmas Holydays in Rome*, London, Longman, Brown, Green & Longmans, 1847, p. 37.

17   G.A. Sala, *Rome and Venice, with other wanderings in Italy, 1866–7*, London, Tinsley, 1869, p. 314.

18   I. Ker, 'Newman and the Mediterranean' in M. Costell (ed.), *Creditable Warriors 1830–1876*, London, Atlantic Highlands N.J., The Ashfield Press, 1990, pp. 73–5.

19   Mrs G. Gretton, *The Englishwoman in Italy. Impressions of Life in the Roman States and Sardinia, during a ten years' residence*, London, Hurst & Blackett, 1861, p. 88. M. Graham, *Three Months passed in the mountains East of Rome, during the year 1819*, London, Longman, Hurst, Rees, Orme and Brown, 1820, p. 33.

20   R.H. Benson, *Confessions of a Convert*, London, Longmans, Green & Co., 1913, p. 44.

21   G.M. Musgrave, *The Parson, Pen and Pencil: or, Reminiscences and Illustrations of an Excursion to Paris, Tours and Rouen, in the Summer of 1847; with a few memoranda on French farming*, London, Richard Bentley, 1848, p. 248.

22   G.M. Musgrave, *A.Pilgrimage into Dauphiné; comprising a visit to the monastery of the Grande Chartreuse; with anecdotes, incidents and sketches from twenty departments of France, Vol. II*, London, Hurst and Blackett, 1857, p. 263.

23   Lord Teignmouth, *Reminiscences of Many Years. Vol. I*, Edinburgh, David Douglas, 1878, p. 161.

24   Rev. J.W. Burgon, *Letters from Rome to Friends in England*, London, John Murray, 1862, pp. 69, 82.

25   H. Morton, *Protestant Vigils; or, Evening Records of a journey in Italy in the years 1826 and 1827, Vol. II*, London, Seeley and Burnside, 1829, pp. 214–6.

26   Ibid.

27   C.R. Weld, *Auvergne, Piedmont and Savoy: A Summer Ramble*, London, John W. Parker, 1850, p. 220.

Chapter Two

A sound which one seemed to understand

'I saw crowds come pouring into the town to do homage to the Virgin, who in consequence of the recent astounding Papal dogma is now regarded as apparently more worthy of worship than God himself.'[1] Charles Richard Weld was recalling his visit to Brittany in 1856 and protesting about the 1854 definition of the Immaculate Conception of Mary. In 1854 it was infallibly declared that like Eve, the Blessed Virgin Mary was created sinless at the moment of her conception. Like Eve, she was also given free will to follow God and co-operate with His divine plan. Free from sin, she was a normal human being in which God would dwell.

The crowds who poured into the church at St. Brieuc in Brittany were lighting candles to a normal human being who had perfectly fulfilled the will of God. Inside the church were depictions of her appearance at La Salette which C.R. Weld had visited some years before. He took the opportunity to apologise to his readers for devoting so much space to the apparition in his previous volume describing his travels in the Auvergne, Piedmont and Savoy. 'But results have shown that the little cloud first seen on La Salette had overshadowed all France, and, if the Vatican would have its way, would darken the face of the entire world.'[2] The equally sceptical Evangelical minister, the Hon. Baptist Noel, travelling in Piedmont in 1854, also remarked upon the superstitious tale of La Salette. Nevertheless he listed accounts of sore eyes being cured, a baker's wife bedridden and paralyzed who got up and walked after her neighbours prayed by the holy fountain, and a fragment of stone which the Queen of Heaven touched discovered to contain a portrait of Christ.[3]

Two years after Weld's apology to his readers for mentioning the apparitions of La Salette, the Blessed Virgin Mary appeared in another part of France, at Lourdes. This was four years after the declaration of the Immaculate Conception. Indeed it was the young and illiterate Bernadette's statement that the Blessed Virgin Mary had said in the local patois that she was the Immaculate Conception which convinced the ecclesiastical authorities that the visions were genuine. Here too a healing fountain flowed, visited on innumerable occasions by the fourteenth Duke of Norfolk, whose wife and father-in-law, the first Baron Donington, were both converts. They brought with them their blind epileptic son. On one occasion the Duchess encountered a procession chanting the *Magnificat.* Hearing 'Esurientes implevit bonis et divites dimisit inanes' the Duchess could not keep back her tears, saying '*We* shall get nothing.' The Duke was devoted to his incurably ill son, saying that it was a delight to wake in the morning knowing that he was in the same house as his afflicted heir. After his son's death the Duke's fortitude almost gave way.[4] But he lived for another fifty seven years, dying on the Feast of Our Lady of Lourdes in 1917.

While Lourdes became France's most famous shrine, Italians had for centuries been proud of their Holy House on the Adriatic coast. It was believed that the house in Nazareth had been miraculously transferred from Palestine to Italy, where from the end of the thirteenth century it was venerated in its final resting place of Loreto. The Holy House, or Santa Casa, was conveyed by angels from Galilee to Tersatto, thence to Recanati, where the trees and shrubs bowed. After a duel between the owners of the site at Reccanati, it reached its final dwelling place at Loreto. On the outside the house was encrusted with marble and richly decorated with sculpture, but inside the walls were left in their original state. The sanctuary was separated from the rest of the church by a silver trellised screen in front of which was an image of the Blessed Virgin Mary said to be the work of St. Luke. The image was arrayed in glittering robes, dressed in a triple crown, holding a globe and the Infant Jesus. 'The face is of an Ethiopian hue, and looks like that of some Eastern idol adorned with barbaric pomp, rather than that of the meek and lowly mother of Christ', observed the Countess of Blessington.[5] There was another altar opposite the sanctuary under the window through which the Angel Gabriel entered the house at the Annunciation.

The Chaplain to the Earl of Leven and Melvill was at Loreto for the Feast of the Annunciation in 1791. On the vigil of the Feast the clergy assembled 'most gorgeously arrayed in vestments of flowered silk richly and superbly embroidered with gold'. Later that night fireworks and crackers 'blazed and bounced' and cannons roared all over the town. Between three and four in the morning 'the cannonading was so incessant and so loud, that we felt our beds shake under us'. The following morning the Reverend Hill observed that one of the beams of the ceiling of the inn in which he was staying had been dislodged. He made a hasty departure from Loreto that day on hearing that the fireworks that were to follow would exceed those that had gone before. He and his party left Loreto wondering not only at the clergy being able to 'keep up the farce with such demure looks' but at 'the amazing folly of so many kings, queens, emperors and empresses (among whom the bigoted Mary of England cuts no mean figure) in sending such an immense profusion of gold, silver and precious stones ... to a parcel of mouldering bricks and an old black wooden idol'.[6]

Feast Days and festivals caught most travellers by surprise, when towns erupted in carnival for several days in the celebration of their patron saint. Visiting Sicily in 1810, Sir George Cockburn described one Feast Day in Álcamo when an immense fire was lit in the centre of the town into which were thrown combustible objects and fireworks. Hundreds of flambeaux were distributed to the townspeople and thrown into the flames. To Sir George it seemed like a picture of Hell, as the gaiety was accompanied by beating drums. Sir George travelled on to Palermo, where he witnessed the Feast of St. Rosolia, a celebration which lasted five days. It began with a carnival led by an orchestra on a horse-drawn platform, beneath a dome supported by Corinthian columns. On top of the dome was a giant silver statue of St. Rosolia decorated with orange branches. After interruptions for hymns the procession eventually reached the sea front at Porto Nuovo where a façade of a palace had been erected to which fireworks were attached. These were let off while the ships in the bay discharged their artillery, the sound of which re-echoed from the mountains. The palatial structure itself was set alight with water-rockets and bombs and the artillery ceased. When the palace had destroyed itself thousands of rockets erupted in a vast explosion. Horse races through the town started the next day, and the day after that were more fireworks. On the fourth day were more street races. The interior of the church at Palermo was covered with mirrors, gold and silver paper and flowers, all illuminated with twenty thousand wax tapers. On the final day the great procession started again in the evening, with priests, friars and religious preceding a carnival of temples and tabernacles each containing a wax model of an angel or saint dressed in robes of gold and tissue. A great silver box containing the bones of St. Rosolia closed the procession, behind which walked the Archbishop. No sooner had the procession finished its tour of the great square than its fountain had been turned into a fountain of fire. This lasted only a few minutes before it was extinguished with a vast explosion.[7]

Far away from Sicily in the north-west of Europe, the relics of St. Kerdevot were venerated at Kerdevot in Brittany. The interior of the church was covered in flowers, statues of the Saints were clothed in Breton costume and the church bells tolled. Thousands of peasants in colourful costume gathered in a meadow and made their way along a narrow lane to the church, where standing outside they paced about saying the rosary, some women circulating the outside of the church on their knees. A Calvary received some interest, but the tobacco stall next to it received more attention. The prayers being over, drinking began, 'and though the day was not far spent, many men were already in a hopeless state of horizontal inebriety'.[8] Soon the beginning of the procession appeared at the doors of the church where, inside, psalms were being sung which were repeated by the crowd outside. From the church a procession of priests emerged followed by the congregation of several hundred, all carrying flags and banners. A frame covered in satin upon which the relics of the Saint lay was carried by young girls dressed in white. The relics were carried round the church three times amidst loud singing, the spectators falling on their knees each time the relics passed them. Despite the onlookers' inebriated state, as soon as they saw the relics 'religious awe seemed to obtain mastery over them; their steps became steadier, and, doffing their huge hats they stared with a half-crazed expression at the show, but, when the relics had passed, resumed their boisterous merriment'. As evening fell and 'the moon silvered the exquisite finials of the lofty spire' there were scenes of 'broken vows and wild revelry, penitence, groans, shouts and imprecations.'[9]

Relics of saints were a source of morbid fascination for English onlookers. One church in Le Puy had a fragment of the lance that pierced the side of Christ, a piece of the True Cross, a shoe of the Blessed Virgin Mary, a tooth of St. Mary Magdalene, a bone of Lazarus, and the finger of St. John the Baptist which he pointed to say 'Behold the Lord!'[10] The cathedral in Amiens contained a fragment of the skull of St. John the Baptist in a crystal casket on an octagonal gold dish placed on crimson velvet. This was on an altar surrounded by railings in the northern transept before which tapers burned continuously. Children climbed the railing and kissed the casket, crossed themselves and went away.[11]

Relics of St. Agnes were kissed and money placed in a golden orb on the Feast of St. Agnes in the tiny chapel of Menton on the Riviera.[12] On the same Feast Day at the church of S. Agnese fuori le Mura in Rome two blessed lambs were carried in from the sacristy in baskets and placed on either side of the altar. Red bows were tied

round their necks and on their heads were wreaths of
roses. The lambs sat quite still except for one or two startled looks of mild questioning. At the end of the Mass as
they were carried back the congregation rushed to touch
them. The archbishops' palliums were made from their
consecrated wool.[13]

A religion of reliquaries was a living symbol of consecration. Although Rome did not possess the relics of St. Agnes
the city contained a nail and portion of the Cross, the reed
on which the sponge was offered to Christ on the Cross,
the inscription over the Cross, a fragment of the rock upon
which God rested when he wrote the Laws for Moses, a vial
containing Christ's Precious Blood, a piece of the rock on
which Christ stood when He ascended, some manna which
fed the Israelites, the finger which Thomas thrust into the
side of Jesus, some ashes of St. Laurence and the cross-
beam of the good thief.[14] There was consternation in Rome
when the head of St. Andrew was stolen in March 1848, but
it was found on the last day of March buried in a vineyard
outside the city walls. The clue to its whereabouts had been
given in the Confessional.

⚘

Confessions were another source of Protestant discomfort.
One vicar observed a priest in Amiens Cathedral waiting to
hear Confessions and saw a woman kneel down on the
steps leading to the iron grille which enclosed a side
chapel. The priest put aside his book, advanced towards
her and placed the end of his stole on her head and
repeated some words rapidly in French. He then put the
end of the stole to his lips and devoutly kissed the embroidered gold cross. He then held a cap to her into which she
dropped some coins before departing.[15] Reverend
Musgrave was spending ten days in a French parsonage
and the local priest tried to describe the feeling of consolation, confidence, hope, strength and positive happiness
which he invariably experienced on leaving his Confessor.
'How you Anglicans can throw away these Christian privi-
leges as you do, and deny yourselves the enjoyment of the

sense of reconciliation and acceptance with God, is to us beyond comprehension.'[16]

In Rome the Hon. Mrs Alfred Montgomery saw the priests in their Confessionals give a tap with a long wand to passers-by who wished to receive an Indulgence. This meant disturbing the priest saying his Office who then reached for the stick to tap the penitent a yard or two away. This was a source of some embarrassment for English Catholics, one of whom managed to overcome his natural undemonstrativeness enough to kneel down for the little blow, rising hurriedly. On Maundy Thursday a Grand Penitentiary sat on a raised platform in purple vestments on a crimson velvet chair, near a low stool on which penitents knelt. One such was a known criminal and by degrees the prelate was seen to bend his ear closer and closer to the confessing penitent. His countenance was compassionate and paternal and the man's forehead almost touched the priest's shoulder as he poured out his long history of error and shame. At length the priest raised his arm to give absolution and a murmur of relief and congratulation ran through the crowd. The priest rested his hand on the man's head who then rose from his knees and hurried down the steps.[17]

At the Scala Santa in Rome women ascended the flight of steps on their knees as an act of penance – the sight of which distressed the Anglican clergyman who viewed the scene.[18] A retreatant at the friary of St. Eusebio observed through the window of his cell a candlelit procession of penitents passing through the gates of the Porta San Lorenzo. The breeze wafted across the Campagna from the Tivoli hills. In the soft balmy night the sublime prayers recited in solemn unison mingled with the lugubrious sound of the bells in the quiet gloom of the nightly air along the deserted roads.[19]

Cloaked and hooded noble members of confraternities dedicated to the searching out of the un-claimed dead and their burial, followed priests and monks in funeral processions. English visitors to Rome might be startled in the street by such a figure with a collection box, little realising that the eyes behind the hood had met theirs at a conver-

sazione, or ball. It was hard to imagine 'London gentlemen
leaving their fire-side on a winter's night to bring in a
corpse from Plaistow marshes or Wimbledon Common to a
city church'.[20] The Arciconfraternità degl' Agonizzanti
gave spiritual succour to those in their last agony to help
them obtain a happy passage into eternity. They continually offered up prayers for those who every moment, all
over the world, were agonizing in the pangs of death,
seeing themselves as pilgrims walking upon the earth in
one vast funeral procession to the tomb. For them it was
the height of folly to think that this earthly pilgrimage
would last forever and that when death came everyone
would be prepared for 'the marriage feast in His blissful
kingdom of light and light everlasting.'[21]

The Fratelli del Suffragio assembled in the oratory in the
Via Giulia to pray for the souls of all who were destitute of
friends. During the Octave of All Souls they procured an
eloquent preacher to plead the cause of the suffering souls
in purgatory. The Arciconfraternità de S. Maria dell'
Orazione was dedicated to the Christian burial of peasants
and others found dead from fatigue or other causes on the
high roads and fields of the desolate Campagna near
Rome, while the Confraternità de S. Giovanni Decollato
spent time praying with criminals awaiting execution.[22]

In the meditative prayer of the Stations of the Cross the
road to Calvary was reconstructed step by step. One unsus-
pecting visitor to the Coliseum was looking up at the
Apennines as they rose through the tracery of foliage and
broken arches when her attention was caught by the
solemn and devout air of a priest in the arena below as he
slowly advanced to the foot of the cross, knelt and kissed it
and passed on. Then a widow with a small child knelt and
kissed the foot of the cross and bathed it in her tears. One
man dragged himself round the arena on his knees,
casting up a look of entreaty at every station. Then a
procession of monks, capuccini and sacconi each with
burning torches and preceded by a crucifix, slowly filed
through the high entrance arches to the chapel. There
followed 'l'esercizio della via crucis' and they all advanced
to the central crucifix before assembling by a small pulpit.

A Capuchin friar in his brown cloak and cowl ascended the steps and planted his crucifix on the ledge with his right hand. The sacconi stood in two long lines and listened, their tapers burning.[23] Forty years later the same ceremony was observed, when the impassioned friar who meditated on the bleeding wounds of Christ moved the people to tears.

The soft sunlight fell in a flood on the mighty ruin, making it look exceedingly beautiful as well as exceedingly grand. More than half was in shadow. The wild flowers were all in bloom and the birds were singing as in England; a colony of rooks in particular kept up a continual cawing – a sound which one seemed to understand.[24]

Notes

[1]   C.R. Weld, *A Vacation in Brittany*, London, Chapman & Hall, 1856, p. 92.

[2]   Ibid., p. 95.

[3]   B.W. Noel, M.A., *Notes of a Tour in the Valleys of Piedmont in the Summer of 1854*, London, James Nisbet, 1855, p. 37.

[4]   J.M. Robinson, *The Dukes of Norfolk. A Quincentennial History*, Oxford, O.U.P., 1982, pp. 21, 224.

[5]   Countess of Blessington, *An Idler in Italy. Vol. III*, London, Henry Colburn, 1840, pp. 17–18.

[6]   Rev. B. Hill, *Observations and Remarks in a journey through Sicily and Calabria, in the year 1791*, 1792, pp. 303–4.

[7]   Lt. Gen. Sir George Cockburn, *A Voyage to Cadiz and Gibraltar up the Mediterranean to Sicily and Malta in 1810 & 11, Vol. II*, London, J. Harding, 1815, pp. 14, 286–91 *passim*.

[8]   C.R. Weld, *A Vacation in Brittany*, London, Chapman & Hall, 1856, p. 213.

[9]   Ibid., p. 221.

[10]   C.R. Weld, *Auvergne, Piedmont and Savoy: A Summer Ramble*, London, John W. Parker, 1850, p. 166.

[11]   G.M. Musgrave, *The Parson, Pen and Pencil: or, Reminiscences and Illustrations of an Excursion to Paris, Tours and Rouen, in the Summer of 1847; with a few memoranda on French farming. Vol. I*, London, Richard Bentley, 1848, p. 109.

[12]   A.M. Brown, *Wintering at Menton on the Riviera. A Compagnon de voyage with hints to invalids*, London, J. & A. Churchill, 1872, p. 72.

[13]   J.G. Cox, *Jubilee-Tide in Rome*, London, Burns & Oates, 1888, p. 55.

[14]   C.R. Weld, *Last Winter in Rome*, London, Longman Green, 1865, p. 450.

[15]   Musgrave, op. cit., p. 118.

[16]   G.M. Musgrave, *Ten Days in a French Parsonage in the Summer of 1863, Vol. II*, London, Sampson, Low, Son & Marston, 1864, p. 63.

[17]   Hon. Mrs Alfred Montgomery, *On the Wing: A Southern Flight*, London, Hurst & Blackett, 1875, p. 78.

[18]   Rev. John W. Burgon, *Letters from Rome to Friends in England*, London, John Murray, 1862, p. 75.

[19]   Olinthus, *Reminiscences of Rome: or, a religious moral, and literary view of the Eternal City; in a series of letters addressed to a friend in England, by a member of the Arcadian Academy*, London, Paternoster Row, 1838, p. 52.

[20]   Weld, op. cit., pp. 322–4.

[21]   Olinthus, op. cit., p. 76.

[22]   Ibid., pp. 72, 75.

[23]   H. Morton, *Protestant Vigils; or, Evening Records of a journey in Italy in the years 1826 and 1827, Vol. I*, London, Seeley & Burnside, 1829, pp. 70–1.

[24]   Burgon, op. cit., pp. 43, 44.

Chapter Three

City of Rome, source of eternal mysteries

No person who has been abroad, and heard and seen and investigated for himself, would credit the extensive system of lying pursued by English travel writers, religious tract compilers, and Exeter Hall speech makers, respecting the Roman Church abroad; and whether the lies be those of wilfulness or of prejudice, ignorance and indolence, I do not see much to distinguish in the guilt.[1]

Such were the thoughts of Frederick Faber, the convert Oratorian. Some of the strongest of these anti-Catholic prejudices centred on the monastic life which still flourished in Europe. Monks, nuns, convents and monasteries: the very words conjured up corrupt images swept away by the Reformation. The hooded Capuchin friars who followed the Stations of the Cross with candles in the Coliseum were a living testimonial to a reality which had never been extinguished. Nevertheless, by 1858 Capuchin friars were already walking the lanes of Flintshire – a friary at Pantasaph near Holywell having been founded there by the Earl of Denbigh. For those who did not make the pilgrimage to Holywell and went instead to Rome, Capuchins were but one of the many Orders in the Eternal City. Throughout its streets was seen 'a motley show of gowns, cloaks, cowls, scapulars and veils, of cords, crosses, shaven heads and naked feet – provoking the reflection what a vast deal of curious gear it takes to teach Christianity.'[2]

For a Jesuit neither 'cowl nor scapular fetters his motions; a plain black gown, not unlike a frock-coat, envelopes his person'. As a lake hides dark caverns beneath it 'so does the calm, impassable face the workings of the heart beneath'.[3] Jesuits could unlock the cabinets of statesmen and enter unobserved the closets of princes. They could take their seats in synods and assemblies and dive into the secrets of noble families. In the Jesuit House in Rome with its galleries lighted by tall windows which overlooked a cloister and an orange grove, splendid pictures of the history of the Society of Jesus hung in the chapel next to the massive library. Amongst such splendour the priests themselves lived in low bare-walled rooms, with just a chair, a bookshelf and a bed. Nevertheless their demeanour combined humility and stillness with a certain 'practical, restless, unsatisfied imperiousness'.[4]

The Jesuits, Capuchins and Carmelites, Passionists, Dominicans and Oratorians were priests living in community who ministered to the world in the Roman parishes. Others retired from the world entirely – Benedictines, Cistercians, Trappists and Carthusians. In 1868 Trappists returned to a site outside Rome where traditionally St. Paul had been beheaded. Where his head had landed three fountains had appeared, each with different properties: one with soft and sweet water, another that was hard and cold, and the third icy cold. It was called S. Paolo alle Tre Fontane. Once a desert of ruin and decay, the Trappists returned once more to create an atmosphere of work, cheerfulness and peace amidst the eucalyptus. The monastery was situated in a humid hollow of the Campagna, surrounded by desolate hills. An English visitor conceded that perhaps 'the wholesome rule of living by the labour of their own hands, the quiet retirement and peaceful thoughts nourished thereby, may enable these recluses to support so uncircumstantial an existence even with pleasure and satisfaction'.[5]

Such an existence for Camaldoli monks consisted of rising an hour after midnight for Matins and Lauds. Prime was at five in the morning followed by Mass. Then followed manual labour for two hours, Terce at nine, Sext at half past ten, None at half past eleven, Vespers at four, Compline at half past six, spiritual reading for three quarters of an hour, then study for an hour and a half. They kept silence for every day of the week except Tuesday and Thursday. The pillared cloister enclosed a sunny quadrangle in the centre of which was a wall and some cedar trees. Sauntering along the cloisters there was 'a civil word of greeting from every one you meet; until you emerge into a quiet little garden full of orange trees, which commands an enchanting view'. The hard and inoffensive life of the monks 'disarms your prejudices and conciliates your goodwill'.[6]

At the Carthusian church and monastery of San Martino, on the same summit as the Castle of St. Elmo, the white marble Doric columns gleamed in the sunshine. Inside the abbey church, with its altar rail of lace marble, its multicoloured walls, floor and roof and lavish precious stones, all had been created out of the leisure of perpetual silence. The cloister breathed the very spirit of peace, the result of 'digging deep down into the minds of thought, consequent in all but unbroken solitude'.[7] Crossing the Apennines in 1802, Earl Mount Cashell caught a glimpse of a monastery shaded by tall dark Cypress, with 'black cowl'd Monks wandering through the Courts and meditating in long Avenues of cedar and cypress trees terminated by crucifixes' surrounded by poultry and sheep, gardens and vineyards.[8] Further north was the most famous of Carthusian monasteries, the Grande Chartreuse.

> At length, as my eager gaze began to rest on a crescent shaped agglomeration of forest trees and a range of rampart-like grey and white rocks to the right of them, which descended to a prodigious depth, till it reached a valley of hundreds of acres covered with grass of luxuriant growth, brightening a still richer verdure as it sloped, mile after mile, towards the lowlands, – I espied the roofs and pinnacles of the monastery.[9]

Visitors were received at the monastery gates by a monk in

a pale habit. Inside, he led them towards a cupboard out of which he took a dark green bottle from which he poured a liquid into a small glass. One sip countered the icy winds that blew through the kitchens, cellars and vaults below. Walking through the quiet library a monk was seen at a desk bending over a volume, the rays of the setting sun falling on his close-shaven head. 'He spoke not, stirred not, and we entered and left the apartment quite unheeded by him'. Supper consisted of thin watery soup, potatoes, an omelette and herbs. After two or three glasses of green Chartreuse the visitors stood by the fire, which blazed with aromatic pine, and discussed religion and philosophy. Then lamp in hand they passed along the cold dark corridors. Pushing open a door they entered a gallery overlooking the abbey church. In the stalls each monk carried a lantern. They were chanting the psalms, 'a long lugubrious chant, rarely interrupted, which the most rigid, Genevan Calvinist could not have found fault with'. At certain times in the Office the monks threw back their cowls and knelt and the light from the lanterns lit up their faces. 'Long after I had laid down, the chanting was borne with the sighs of the night through the corridors; and it was still in my ears when I passed from the Grande Chartreuse into the land of dreams.'[10]

☙❧

The departure of young women from the world into enclosed religious life was marked with dramatic ceremony. Lord Mount Cashell observed a crowd of two hundred Neapolitans witnessing the entrance of a novice into a life in the cloister. Dazzling in diamonds she appeared amongst them with downcast eyes, her hands folded across her breast. Slowly she walked towards the convent gates and the crowd made way for her. She knelt down at the gate and knocked. The gates were flung open to reveal veiled nuns waiting inside and 'one of the sweetest looking creatures' the Earl had ever seen was received by the Mother Abbess with welcoming arms. Inside the convent chapel 'the most sweet and solemn musick echo'd throughout the vaulted roofs'. The church seemed to be made of 'lapis lazuli and stain'd glass, with frankincense perfum'd all around'. When the novice appeared behind the grille which separated the community from the congregation, not only the Italian women but one young Englishman was in indignant tears. He instinctively reached for his sword, saying under his breath that 'such heart rending superstitious cruelties ought to be extirpated from off the face of the earth'.[11] In a silent ceremony the novice's hair was then shorn off, her jewellery removed, her temples bound with sack-cloth and a black gown thrown over her ball dress. On her head was placed a crown of thorns and at her side was placed a branch of white lilies and a crucifix. She disappeared among the black procession of veiled nuns each carrying a lighted torch, and followed the raised monstrance. The Mass, the music, the ceremony and the procession took four hours; Lord Mount Cashell thought he had spent a life among the cloisters.

One hundred years later another Irishman, Aubrey De Vere, was present at another 'clothing'. The novice sat alone by the altar in a white ball dress covered with jewels, her long hair wreathed with pearls. After the hymns and prayers the presiding Cardinal cut her hair and placed it in her hand, which she then threw 'contemptuously into a basket, as if glad to get rid of all worldly vanities'. Two old nuns cut off the rest of the hair, she was covered with a black habit and presented with a missal, a rosary, and a little figure of the Infant Jesus. She kissed each in turn, the Cardinal pronounced a benediction and the novice disappeared behind the altar.[12] One parson was left to ponder that a nun entering a convent would never look again upon the beautiful landscape of her youth, 'the blue mountain, the rapid Tiber and the classic ruins of her native land'.[13] The breeze from the Apennines would never more fan her cheek and she was separated from acquaintances and companions and parents. Mabel Sharman Crawford, sister of the novelist and convert Frances Marion Crawford, admitted that she had seen faces beneath the shade of the white spotless lawn cornettes of the Sisters of

Charity which spoke of purity and peace, of a quiet conscience and a mind 'that knew no shadow of regret, and a heart weaned truly from the vanities of this world'. Such nuns had consecrated the flower of their youth and the prime of their life to the relief of suffering humanity.[14]

In the heart of the Auvergne 'La Societé de la Sainte Famille', known as the Soeurs Bleues, were in a convent with elegant small towers, oriel-windows and winding stairs half covered with clustering vines. A young nun greeted the visitor, wearing a coarse black robe with blue sleeves and a rosary with a large silver cross hung from her waist. She asked the English visitor if he was a good Catholic. On being told that he was not a member of the Catholic Church she sighed and asked how he could remain a Protestant when outside 'la religion Catholique on ne peut être sauvé'. She said she lived not for this world but to merit a better one. 'Then you do not love the world?' she was asked. 'No, indeed, for it is full of deceit', she replied. In her conversation she dwelt much on the fascinations of Roman Catholicism.[15] At about this time Lady Herbert was visiting the Cistercian convent at Las Huelgas in Spain. Here the Mother Abbess was a Princess Palatine with feudal power over all the lands and villages around. She appointed her own priests and confessors and was in charge of a hospital a mile from the convent. Behind a grille, Lady Herbert glimpsed a beautiful old nun dressed in wimple and coif as in the time of Chaucer. In the convent hospital at the end of each room was an altar, where Mass was said every day.[16]

In Cadiz the Casa de Misericordia was under the care of the Carmelites de la Caridad. Stations of the Cross in blue and white ceramic lined the lofty white-washed dormitories and an image of the Blessed Virgin Mary was embroidered on each bed cover. Every wall and bed, every nook and corner, had some religious motto, picture or image.

And then I said farewell to this model hospital. As I passed through the outer door in the tiny vestibule quite open to the street, a young Spanish lady was kneeling, evidently in fervent prayer. Not until then had I noticed that a little altar was there, lighted up with much taste, barely removed from the street. A heap of aromatic boughs was lying in the street as I stepped out. I said to the guide 'What are these?' – 'Those', said he in broken English, 'are the scented shrubs we use on the good night. Don't you know? – The night God came down with the good news for us all.' Truly, I thought, religion here is not thrust into a corner, but speaks for itself at every turn.[17]

An English vicar in Rome observed a countrywoman who knelt down in the nave in the middle of the church of S. Carlo, raised her eyes, crossed herself, slowly bowed and kissed the floor. She rose, genuflected to the Tabernacle and crossed herself again before dipping her finger in the holy water stoup and making the Sign of the Cross before her departure. 'It was very heathenish – but it was very beautiful.'[18] Mrs George Gretton was disturbed to see a man kneeling in front of a small discoloured picture of the Blessed Virgin Mary who cradled in her hands a heart from which came flames. The man who prayed in front of this image knelt with an expression of such fervour in his upturned face that Mrs George Gretton felt sure he was praying heart and soul for her rescue from Protestant perdition.[19]

The Countess of Blessington was walking along the beach at Ventimiglia on the Italian Riviera when seeing an open church close to the sea she walked inside. The church was lighted by a single lamp which casting a dim light distinguished several veiled women. There was a deep silence, broken only by the breaking of the waves against the shore and the murmured prayers of the women, who did not notice the English party enter.[20]

Some observers who came to scoff, remained to pray. The conviction gradually dawned on them that they had truly entered the House of God, containing 'the Tabernacle 'which the Word that was made flesh still deigns to choose for His dwelling among the sons of men'.[21] One parson was impressed that unlike in England he saw no one asleep nor any lounging in the corner of a cushioned pew. Although there was undoubtedly more 'sound sense, solid comfort, enlightening doctrine and consistent and 'reasonable service' in one hour of Protestant ritual than in twenty-four hours of erring Rome's', the devotion of Catholic congregations who endured long hours of physical discomfort kneeling on stone in silence and adoration, put the assemblies of the Church of England to shame. Inside Catholic churches one clergyman was surprised never to discover apples and pears, walnuts and blackberries, filberts and gingerbread, pencils or knives for carving names. Such acts of slight and indifference, 'revolting to witness as they are perilous to commit' were entirely absent from French rural congregations.[22] But not from Italian urban congregations. To enter a fashionable church in Florence at a fashionable hour was to witness 'a display of vanity, of show and irreligiousness, and to behold a sanctuary, built for communion with God, degraded to a theatre, a lounge, a haunt of idleness'.[23] Gentlemen gazed on the face of every lady and talked in loud whispers. They made no pretence to pray. They just about bowed their heads at the elevation of the Host. The Marquess of Normanby recalled the rustle of silks, the sliding of slippers and the chatter of gossip between psalms and 'inquiries for health and propagation of anecdote carried on in the temple in the very face of religion'.[24] Irreverent behaviour was not confined only to the fashionable Florentines. In Rome the pushing and jostling accompanying free and easy remarks in the English tongue 'are not exactly the best means of persuading foreigners that we are Christians, or indeed that we have any religion at all.'[25]

On Pope Pius IX's Jubilee as a priest, a particularly rare congregation gathered in the Pope's private chapel in the Vatican. A Bishop from northern Italy found himself next to a Maronite from the Lebanon. Next to him a prelate from Munster sat next to a Spaniard. A tall Capuchin Archbishop who had been to South America 'was rolling out his impressions in a sonorous bass to a mild looking Benedictine abbot'. The Bishop of Cork was speaking in fluent Italian to a Swiss Guard. Some little stir was created by the arrival of the Grand Duchess of Tuscany, who took her seat to the right of the papal throne. The five hundred English pilgrims who came to pay their respects to the Pope were received one by one, including a woman of 90 who had become a Catholic at the age of 82. 'The meeting between this old lady, still erect beneath her burden of years, and the Sovereign Pontiff, bowed beneath burdens of other kinds, was a most touching spectacle'. Students at the College of Propaganda gave speeches in honour of the Papal Jubilee in English, Hebrew, Chaldean, Gaelic, Bulgarian, Norwegian, Blackhawk, Hungarian, Syriac, Persian, Arabic, Tamil, Turkish, Greek, Chinese, Danish, Spanish, Slav and Polish. An African delivered an address with an accent straight from County Cork; his father had been a soldier in India.[26] The Church of Rome was indeed a universal church, and the City of Rome the source of eternal mysteries.

Notes

1   J.E. Bowden, *The Life and Letters of Frederick William Faber, D.D.*, London, Thomas Richardson & Son, 1869, p. 166.
2   Rev. J.E. Wylie, *Pilgrimage from the Alps to the Tiber or the Influence of Romanism on Trade, Justice and Knowledge*, Edinburgh, Shepherd & Elliot, 1855, p. 285.
3   Ibid., p. 428.
4   W. Ward, *Aubrey De Vere. A Memoir*, London, Longmans, Green & Co., 1904, p. 38.
5   G.A. Sala, *A Journey Due South: Travels in Search of Sunshine*, London, Vizetelly & Co., 1885, p. 295. W. Davies, *The Pilgrimage of the Tiber, from its Mouth to its Source: with some account of its tributaries*, London, Sampson Low, 1873, p. 25.
6   Rev. John W. Burgon, *Letters from Rome to Friends in England*, London, John Murray, 1862, pp. 96, 97.
7   Hon. Mrs Alfred Montgomery, *On the Wing: A Southern Flight*, London, Hurst & Blackett, 1875, p. 275.
8   T.U. Sadleir (ed.), *An Irish Peer on the Continent (1801–1803). Being a narrative of the tour of Stephen, 2nd Earl Mount Cashell, through France, Italy etc.*, London, Williams & Norgate, 1920, p. 125.

[9]   Rev. G.M. Musgrave, *A Pilgrimage into Dauphiné; comprising a visit to the monastery of the Grande Chartreuse; with anecdotes, incidents and sketches from twenty departments of France, Vol. II*, London, Hurst and Blackett, 1857, p. 164.

[10]   C.R. Weld, *Auvergne, Piedmont and Savoy: A Summer Ramble*, London, John W. Parker, 1850, pp. 229, 232–4, 247–8.

[11]   Sadler, op. cit., p. 154.

[12]   W. Ward, op. cit., p. 39.

[13]   Rev. M. Vicary, B.A., *Notes of a Residence at Rome in 1846*, London, Richard Bentley, 1847, p. 78.

[14]   M.S. Crawford, *Life in Tuscany*, London, Smith, Elder & Co., 1859, pp. 276, 279.

[15]   Weld, op. cit., pp. 45, 47.

[16]   Lady Herbert, *Impressions of Spain in 1866*, London, Richard Bentley, 1867, p. 29.

[17]   H.J. Rose, *Untrodden Spain, and her Black Country; being sketches of the life and character of the Spaniard of the interior, Vol. I*, London, Samuel Tinsley, 1875, pp. 111–113.

[18]   Burgon, op. cit., p. 62.

[19]   Mrs G. Gretton, *The Englishwoman in Italy. Impressions of life in the Roman States and Sardinia, during a ten years' residence*, London, Hurst & Blackett, 1861, p. 89.

[20]   Countess of Blessington, *The Idler in Italy Vol. I*, London, Henry Colburn, 1839, p. 374.

[21]   'Olinthus', *Reminiscences of Rome: or, a religious, moral and literary view of the Eternal City; in a series of letters addressed to a friend in England, by a member of the Arcadian Academy*, London, Paternoster Row, 1838, p. 90.

[22]   G.M. Musgrave, *A Ramble through Normandy; or Scenes, Characters and Incidents in a sketching excursion through Calvados*, London, David Bogue, 1865, pp. 294, 6.

[23]   Crawford, op. cit., pp. 253–4.

[24]   Marquis of Normanby, *The English in Italy Vol. II*, London, Saunders and Otley, 1825, p. 195.

[25]   G.A. Sala, *Rome and Venice, with other wanderings in Italy, 1866–7*, London, Tinsley, 1869, p. 388.

[26]   J.G. Cox, *Jubilee-Tide in Rome*, London, Burns & Oates, 1888, pp. 19, 51–4.

Chapter Four

An inability to cross the threshold

The glittering rays of the morning sun revealed a beautiful scene, different in character from the neighbourhood of Rome. To the right, the curved shore of Gaeta, as the light fell upon the rippling line of the breaking waves, shone like a sickle of silver, and the gulf which it clasped was of the darkest blue. It was pleasant to be so near the sea once more – to catch again the deep respirations of its mighty heart, and to hear the sound of oars, and of keels grating upon pebbles.[1]

English visitors to Rome crossed the grey Channel, travelled through France to the startling blue of the Mediterranean and took a boat to Civita Vécchia, the port closest to Rome. 'The parting bell rings, shrill sounds the steam whistle, the paddle-wheels revolve, we glide between many ships and lateen-rigged barks and in a few minutes are out in the Mediterranean.' Travelling on this particular journey was the Cardinal Archbishop of Lyons, Monsignor Bonald. As soon as they saw him passengers knelt on deck for his blessing and the cardinal described with outstretched hand the monogram of Christ, ICXC, for which was gained one hundred days' Indulgence. On arrival at Civita Vécchia his Eminence was greeted by the roar of cannon and puffs of white smoke from a warship in the harbour. The cardinal, scarlet hat in hand, bowed his farewell to his fellow passengers before descending the steamer's side to the boat which took him ashore.[2]

Nicholas Wiseman's first visit to Rome as a young seminarian was less auspicious. It was in 1818, long before steamers had appeared in the Mediterranean and he made the voyage from Liverpool to Livorno. It took a fortnight to get from Savona to Genoa and another week to get from Genoa to Livorno. A man fell overboard and drowned off Cape St. Vincent, a dog went mad and jumped into the sea and the vessel caught fire at least once. All the passengers were almost lost in a sudden squall. But on land at last they made their way across a few miles of weary hills each giving a clearer view of Rome, the cupola of St. Peter's cutting into the winter's sky.[3]

The same dome was viewed from the east of the city by an English party ten years later. The country round about was dreary and uncultivated, and they all exclaimed at once when they caught a glimpse of the dome. They climbed the red rocks behind the inn at Storta and in the dim distance beheld the imperial city and beyond it the great line of the sea. Walking at sunset in the Pincian hills the tints of the sky were such as never seen in northern climes. Against the clear circle of the horizon 'lit up by the brilliant departing beams of day, St. Peter's reposes its magnificent dark cupola and St. Angelo its mighty angel ...' Vesper bells rang throughout the city at the moment of sunset.[4] 'And St. Peter's softly lit dome follows us with a mild yet insistent glare, right up to the Alban hills.'[5] From the Alban hills a narrow lane bordered with violets led into wide fields towards the fortifications of the Castle of St. Angelo. The white walls of Rome stood glittering in the sunshine. 'Darkly looming against the blue-white sky, the bronze figure of Rome's guardian angel forever holds his weapon half-way out of his scabbard, like the suspending threat of an avenging power.'[6]

Shots were fired from the Castle of St. Angelo when a procession of cardinals crossed the Ponte St. Angelo. Dressed in red, riding on mules, they were accompanied by gentlemen and prelates on horseback. The occasion was a visit by Pope Pius IX to the Minerva chapel. Prelates and clergy, treasurers, clerks of the chamber, penitentiaries, prebendaries, notaries, protonotaries, the double cross, the sword, the imperial hat, cardinals, ambassadors were followed by the Bishop of Rome himself, blessing the parish and carried in his chair by men in scarlet robes. The procession was a quarter of a mile long and on the Pope's arrival in the Piazza della Minerva, showers of what seemed like discs of gold came quivering down from the windows. 'And when the cardinals were set, the chapel choir began the offertory of the mass, and sang so sweetly that one thought I had never heard the like.'[7]

One parson first arrived in Rome at night. No lights, no sound except the moaning wind, he glimpsed some high columns, not realising that this was the piazza of St. Peter's, whose dome he saw in the lightning. Soon he was riding under the walls of an immense fortress, whose battlements were lost in the darkness. He crossed a long bridge 'with shade-like statues looking down upon us from either parapet, and a dark silent river flowing underneath'.[8] For R. H. Benson, Rome was where 'the air is like water and the water like wine'.

> Morning by morning I awoke to the crying of the swifts outside, drawing long icy breaths of freshness, seeing the netted sunshine strike on the ceiling from the jug of water on the floor, hearing the rustle of leaves below my window. There, in Italy, the morning struck the key of the day; the world was alive there, and as good as God made it, and everything was in His hand.[9]

Marble columns, rich friezes, balustrades, statues, fountains, arcades and galleries mingled with terraced gardens in which bloomed orange, myrtle and oleander 'with a luxuriance unknown even in the conservatories of our cold clime'.[10] In the Vatican Gardens at every turn there was a statue, a fountain, a summer house, a grotto or a stream. Parts of the garden were of an elaborate plan, others were overgrown. Vines, oaks, olives, ilexes, palms, eucalyptus, deordoras, orange trees, pines, cactuses, aloes and prickly-pear trees provided shade for white peacocks, white

fantails, turtle doves, and Indian pheasants.[11] The art lover
Anna Jameson, who re-discovered the hidden frescoes of
Renaissance art and brought them to the Grand Tourists'
eye, loved the 'rich delicious skies' and the genial
sunshine, which even in December revived the soul. She
loved the pure atmosphere 'which not only brings the
distant landscape, but almost Heaven itself nearer the
eye'.[12] The balmy air and blue skies were appreciated all
the more keenly after having spent an hour or two in the
dim religious light of a church. Sitting on the steps outside
the Basilica of St. John Lateran the Hon. Mrs Alfred
Montgomery recalled that it was enough to be alive on
such a day and in such a scene, scattering the skins of
chestnuts on the pavement at her feet, silently drinking in
the balmy air.[13]

ᏬᏖᎧ

Entering a Roman Catholic church for the first time, the
statues and ornaments, candles and images could prove to
some that the Church of Rome was a church of idols.
Relics, hearts pierced with swords, darkness and mumbled
Latin spoke of a pagan age thought to be long swept away
yet still disconcertingly alive. One traveller described the
church of S. Pedro in Piedra Buena in Spain.

> Take King's College Chapel, block up all the windows
> in 1620, put up altars every six years from 1720 to
> 1845, paint all the stalls green in 1820, blue in 1850
> and yellow and red in 1870 but never scrape off the
> colours, paint the roof pink and the background pale
> blue with gold stars, open one of the blocked windows
> in 1848 and fill with English stained glass, hang
> pictures of hell and martyrdoms of Saint Lawrence on
> the walls beyond the reach of a duster ...[14]

On one of the altars there was a statue in a sheet which
looked like a corpse, there was a life-sized crucifix with real
hair and blood which shone in the flickering lamp, and in a
glass case a statue of the Blessed Virgin Mary in a black crino-

line with tears on her cheeks. Every spare corner was filled with candlesticks, vases, lecterns, benches. All the chairs in the nave were cleared away and replaced by rush matting.[15]

Lady Lovat decided she wanted to look inside the cathedral at Seville. A priest lifted the heavy curtain and ushered her in. 'My first impression was that of peace.' Leaving behind the heat and the crowds her admiration was hushed into silence, except to say 'Indeed this is the house of God, and the gate of heaven, and shall be called the court of the Most High!' The cathedral was an act of faith immortalised in stone, the impression deepening as time went on. 'Wherever the eye soared it was delighted: nay more, the mind was soothed and rested.'[16] But Lady Elizabeth Grosvenor's impression of Seville Cathedral was that of 'an awful and gloomy beauty' and she spoke of 'this vast interior, which is very impressive, and quite indescribable'. At its eighty altars five hundred Masses were said every day.[17]

On the other side of the Mediterranean, the cathedral at Milan was 'a vision of surpassing beauty'. One parson gazed entranced. 'The lovely creation before me was white as the Alpine snows, and shot up in a glorious cluster of towers, spires and pinnacles, which flashed back the splendours of the mid-day sun.' Thousands of statues and hundreds of seraphs perched on the loftier pinnacles. Entering by the western doorway, the curtain was pulled back and then

> the obscurity that wrapped pillar and aisle gradually brightened up, and the temple around me began to develop into the noblest proportions and most impressive grandeur ... a spirit of tranquility and calm seemed to breathe on you.[18]

One traveller was forced to admit that it was difficult to be insensible to the spirit which pervaded every church, however small. Always open, no cold official stood at their entrance. 'The deep stillness, felt like a palpable presence, falls with a hushing power upon worldly emotions ...' Worshippers either knelt in silence or moved about with noiseless steps. 'In the windless air, the very flames of the tapers do not tremble, but burn like painted flames upon painted candles.'[19] Not everyone agreed. To some a Roman Catholic church was simply 'a few common people kneeling before the candle-lighted shrines ... a priest mumbling at a side altar, bad pictures, gilt, marble, the odour of stale incense and mouldy cloth, and a dim dust-coloured light'.[20] Nevertheless in the Basilica of St. Paul's a mile from Rome, 'the open, airy look communicated by the abundant light falling everywhere on objects of splendour, fill the mind with amazement and defy description'.[21] Here was a nave surmounted by mosaic portraits of the popes from the earliest times, four ranges of polished granite columns on either side, supporting a ceiling of carved and gilded woodwork; a floor of polished marble on which the pillars were reflected. The alabaster pillars of the baldaccino, mosaics from an ancient church in the apse, precious stones; all this was but an introduction to St. Peter's.

A Doctor of Divinity observed after entering St. Peter's that if the intention of Michaelangelo had been to cause breathlessness, astonishment, an inability to cross the threshold, the silent pointing of a finger towards the High Altar and dome, and to continue that silence while walking from one end of the basilica to the other, then he had been successful.[22] The Hon. Edward Legge wrote in his diary that the spectacle was far too grand to describe, the basilica needing two or three visits to appreciate its immensity. It took two hours for him even to take a cursory view of the interior, just quietly walking up and down.[23] The Marquess of Normanby recalled that it was like walking from beneath a blue sky into a golden one.[24] When the golden tints of the Italian sun entered the sanctuary, the evening beams of the dusty sun passing through the high windows, the figures in the paintings seemed to come alive. It fell on the gorgeous mosaics which glittered with prismatic hues. It fell on marble and gilding. The whole edifice seemed illuminated by the glorious orb of day. No-one in the Countess of Blessington's party uttered a single word; the greatest anticipations of their imagination were realized. 'The eyes drink in the wondrous *coup d'oeil* and the mind luxuriates in the delicious draft.'[25] The eye was led from the beauty of the marble of the nave towards the golden vault of the dome up above. 'The lofty Corinthian pilasters with their bold entablature, the niches with their statues, the arcades with graceful figures that reclined on the curve of the arches, charm your eye in succession as you pass along.' Having contemplated the four superb vistas from the foot of the altar the pilgrim looked up to see a firmament of gold, 'presenting, in glowing mosaic, the companies of the just, the choirs of celestial spirits and the whole hierarchy of heaven arrayed in the presence of the Eternal ...'[26]

Having contemplated such magnificence, one parson was struck by the saddening thought that 'this pile, unrivalled as it is among temples made with hands, is literally useless'.[27] For others the sad history of ages was exemplified by the kissing of the toe of St. Peter, a huge bronze statue beneath a canopy, before which a light flickered continually.

> What I am about to tell you is, I am aware, almost incredible: it is nevertheless true that, in this *nineteenth century*, in a temple of a city calling itself the head and seat of Christendom, I saw all ranks and ages, priests and people, pay apparently the most solemn adoration to this figure. They knelt to it – kissed it – rubbed their heads under its foot – mothers lifted up their babies to kiss its toe – they stroked it: in short, every demonstration of adoration and love was poured out before it – a cold statue of bronze, that sits with the stern majesty of a heathen Jupiter, having the keys thrust in to its powerless hand.[28]

From the 'tasteless column of the Immaculate Conception in the Piazza di Spagna', tablets inscribed with the names of bishops and cardinals reminiscent of those in English churches recording donors to charities, to Pugin's impression that St. Peter's was far more ugly than he expected, 'vilely constructed and a mass of bad taste run riot – I assure you I have felt quite depressed and miserable here; I shall be quite glad to get away' – Rome was for some a monstrous disappointment.[29] St. Peter's was a temple, a museum, a gallery of art and a mausoleum. But were not the galleries and porticoes like all-embracing arms of invitation extended by the Church to the whole Christian world, summoning them to come and worship under the roof of the most majestic place of worship ever created? 'When we dream of the climate of heaven, we make it warmth without heat and coolness without cold, like that of St. Peter's.'[30]

It was with a beating heat that Dom Bede Camm first pushed aside the great leather curtain and entered the tomb of the fisherman. As he entered, he heard the sound of a distant chanting from the chapel of the choir. The Canons were singing the First Vespers of the Feast of St. Gregory the Great. 'And I venture to believe that the great Pope who loved our land so well, looked down from Heaven with compassion upon the young stranger from the "Isle of the Angles"'.[31] When the Reverend William Ingram Kip drew aside the curtain of St. Peter's, the next few minutes were 'worth a year of common-place life'.[32] Forty years later Lady Clare Feilding recalled that 'it quite took my breath away as we lifted the great curtain before the door... one cannot compare it with any other impression whatever'. Lady Clare's father, the Earl of Denbigh, wrote to his sister after first entering St. Peter's as a Catholic:

> O the delight to feel that at length this glorious building really belonged to one, that here everything was in harmony with our feelings, that now we were in the eternal, the holy city where so many martyrs had shed their best blood for the faith delivered to them not as aliens, not as strangers, but as children. The thought was quite overpowering. I cannot describe the happiness we feel at being in this holy city where everything, turn which way you will, reminds one of the Christian religion; where churches are open all day and never empty of devout worshippers.[33]

The Earl of Denbigh was in Rome for the occasion of the Jubilee of Pope Pius IX, who was celebrating fifty years as a priest. The Pope's entrance into St. Peter's on this occasion was greeted with a sound of silver trumpets in the dome, drowned by the deafening shout of fifty thousand voices, applause and excited cries of 'Vivat!'. Men and women were sobbing, until a hushed stillness preceded the papal benediction. As the Holy Father returned to the Vatican the shout of fifty thousand voices demonstrated their loyalty again.

When Pope Pius VI gave his blessing from the balcony of St. Peter's on Easter Day, 1791, crowds gathered in the piazza and beneath the colonnades the cavalry appeared with colours flying. When they reached the centre of the square the soldiers dismounted to the sound of drums and trumpets and simultaneously fell on their knees, remaining in silence along with the vast assembly. At that moment a cannon was fired from the Castle of St. Angelo and all Rome's inhabitants knelt low in the same attitude of devotion. 'Pius the Sixth waved his hand and showered on the heads of the attending multitudes those blessings which they so ardently expected.'[34] Elizabeth, Lady Holland observed the same scene, but with a cynical eye. 'The sight was imposing. He is an excellent actor; Garrick could not have represented the part with more theatrical effect than his present Holiness.'[35] Pope Pius IX was viewed with equal disdain by the Reverend Wylie. Here was the successor of St. Peter about to enter a rather shabby coach with red wheels led by four black horses, two of which were ridden by postillions while a fat coachman sat in the box. Workmen digging in the piazza fell prostrate when the Pope appeared while a group of Englishmen stood and gazed. Pope Pius IX was a 'portly, good-looking gentleman' and the Reverend Wylie was impressed enough to imagine him entering the pulpit of a Presbyterian or Methodist congregation. The Holy Father stooped slightly and ambled towards the waiting carriage. With a benevolent smile he waved his hand in a careless way towards the prostrate onlookers and made a profound bow to the English party.[36]

When the same Pope received visitors at a private audience in the Vatican 'No Quaker could have received us with more simplicity than Pio Nono – no sovereign with more dignified courtesy, – no Presbyterian with more plainness.' There were no Lords-in-Waiting, no ceremony, the Pontiff was alone, standing in a room the size of a London drawing-room. 'We approached him as to a temporal prince, with the courtesies we should have paid to our own Queen; bowing three times ... He gazed at us, as we might have expected, with intense curiosity as we approached him.'[37] The procedure for such audiences with Pope Benedict XIV was that, after the ringing of a bell and the opening of the door to the pontifical apartment, the visitor then knelt at the threshold, knelt again in the middle of the room and once more at the feet of the Pope, who would allow the embroidered cross on his shoe to be kissed or would present his hand. The Pontiff would then converse, the audience being brought to an end with a gift of a rosary or holy medal. The ceremony of genuflection was then carried out in reverse.[38]

At Christmas 1847, Pope Pius IX entered St. Peter's on the sedatorial chair held high on the shoulders of men in violet-coloured robes. He was borne above the heads of the kneeling multitudes, falling drapery half concealing those who carried him. Wearing the sparkling papal tiara, his robes were encrusted with jewels. On each side of him great ostrich fans swept back and forth and fifty Roman noblemen preceded him, followed by his court of cardinals and bishops from Greek, Armenian and Eastern churches in their most gorgeous array. Priests dressed in purple and white, some bearing the great crucifix and lighted tapers, others with golden censers, sang the anthem in procession. In front of the altar the Pope was lowered, and the guard of noblemen stood on his side of the throne. The cardinals in scarlet, their trains gliding over the surface of the gleaming marble, ascended the steps and one by one kissed the Pontiff's hand and the hem of his garment. In the High Mass that followed sweet incense floated through the air, breathed by the thousands who gathered under the golden dome. The priests crossed and re-crossed the steps, censers clinked back and forth, candles were lighted and extinguished, vestments were changed and re-changed, until some observers in the congregation became utterly bewildered.[39]

Notes

1   G.S. Hillard, *Six Months in Italy, Vol. II*, London, John Murray, 1853, p. 80.
2   C.R. Weld, *Last Winter in Rome*, London, Longman Green, 1865, p. 7.
3   Cardinal Wiseman, *Recollections of the Last Four Popes*, London, Hurst and Blackett, 1858, pp. 3, 5.
4   H. Morton, *Protestant Vigils; or, Evening Records of a journey in Italy in the years 1826 and 1827*, London, Seeley and Burnside, 1829, pp. 66, 134.
5   J. Sully, *Italian Travel Sketches*, London, Constable, 1912, p. 93.
6   Hon. Mrs Alfred Montgomery, *On the Wing: A Southern Flight*, London, Hurst and Blackett, 1875, p. 58.
7   Weld, op. cit., pp. 434–6.
8   Rev. J.A. Wylie, *Pilgrimage from the Alps to the Tiber or the Influence of Romanism on Trade, Justice & Knowledge*, Edinburgh, Shepherd and Elliot, 1855, p. 273.
9   C.C. Martindale, *The Life of Monsignor Robert Hugh Benson*, London, Longmans, 1916, p. 302.
10 Countess of Blessington, *An Idler in Italy. Vol. II*, London, Henry Colburn, 1839, p. 2.
11 J.G. Cox, *Jubilee-Tide in Rome*, London, Burns and Oates, 1888, p. 70.
12 C. Thomas, *Love and Work Enough. The Life of Anna Jameson*, London, Macdonald, 1967, p. 35.
13 Montgomery, op. cit., p. 85.
14 S. Leslie, *Mark Sykes, His Life and Letters*, London, Cassell, 1923, p. 135.
15 Ibid., p. 136.
16 Lady Lovat, *The Catholic Church from Within*, London, Longmans, 1901, pp. xiv–xv.
17 Lady Elizabeth Grosvenor, *Narrative of a Yacht Voyage in the Mediterranean during the years 1840–41, Vol. I*, London, John Murray, 1842, p. 32.
18 Wylie, op. cit., pp. 103, 127.
19 G.S. Hillard, *Six Months in Italy, Vol. I*, London, John Murray, 1853, p. 259.
20 E. Dicey, *Rome in 1860*, London, Macmillan, 1861, p. 12.
21 W. Davies, *The Pilgrimage of the Tiber, from its Mouth to its Source: with some account of its tributaries*, London, Sampson Low, 1873, p. 25.

22   G. Townsend, D.D. *Journal of a Tour in Italy, in 1850, with an account of an interview with the Pope, at the Vatican*, London, Francis & John Rivington, 1850, pp. 72–3.

23   Papers of Hon. Edward Legge, Greater London Record Office, 4th March 1862, F/LEG/902.

24   Marquis of Normanby, *The English in Italy, Vol. II*, London, Saunders and Otley, 1825, p. 193.

25   Blessington, op. cit., p. 171. Rev. M. Vicary, *Notes of a Residence at Rome in 1846*, London, Richard Bentley, 1847, p. 83.

26   Rev. John Chetwode Eustace, *A Classical Tour through Italy*, London, J. Mawman, 1819, p. 130.

27   Wylie, op. cit., p. 317.

28   Morton, op. cit., p. 74.

29   Weld, op. cit., p. 50. M. Trappes-Lomax, *Pugin. A Medieval Victorian*, London, Sheed and Ward, 1932, p. 112.

30   Hillard, op. cit., pp. 162, 179.

31   B. Camm, 'Memoirs of a Benedictine monk', in *The City of Peace by those who have entered it*, Dublin, C.T.S., Sealy, Bryers and Walker, 1903, p. 12.

32   Rev. W.I. Kip, *The Christmas Holydays in Rome*, London, Longman, Brown, Green and Longmans, 1847, p. 21.

33   W. Elwes, *The Feilding Album*, London, Geoffrey Bles, 1950, pp. 66, 138.

34   Rev. B. Hill, *Observations and Remarks in a journey through Sicily and Calabria, in the year 1791*, 1792, p. 294.

35   Earl of Ilchester (ed.), *The Journal of Elizabeth Lady Holland Vol. I 1791–1811*, London, Longmans, 1908, p. 125.

36   Wylie, op. cit., p. 316.

37   Townsend, op. cit., pp. 162–3.

38   Eustace, op. cit., Vol. IV, p. 374.

39   Kip, op. cit., pp. 45–7.

Chapter Five

Therein he at last found peace

The English were in Rome for the winter, where for mete-
orological and medical reasons they spun out their time in
the relative warmth of the Italian sun. It so happened that
the cold months in England began in Rome with the liturgical splendours of Christmas and culminated with Holy
Week and Easter, with perhaps some canonisations in
between. 'What does one miss of Christmas?', asked one
traveller. He missed the joyous peal of bells clashing over
frosty English fields, sitting down to Christmas dinner with
the rector or squire, a roaring fire and a 'good hearty
Church Service in the old church, decked with holly and
mistletoe and dark green ivy.'[1] In Rome, Christmas was not
accompanied by the sudden merriment of northern
Europe but was more a spontaneous interruption in an
already joyous atmosphere. Dawn in St. Peter's on
Christmas Day 1888 found the Bishop of Newport, just
distinguished through the gloom, celebrating Mass at the
chapel of the *Cathedra*. From the scattered altars in the
huge Basilica the candles shed their light while every few
minutes the great silence was broken by tinkling bells as
priest after priest in chapel after chapel held up the Body
of Christ. At High Mass later in the morning there was a
break in the sound of the organ and some simple notes
reminiscent of the thin reed-music of shepherds were
heard.[2] On the same day in a church in the hills of
Provence an old man sitting at the front of the congregation held a white lamb, emblem of the innocence of the

new-born God. The lamb, taken from its field in the mountains was content to be kissed and hugged by the poor
children who huddled around. Their attention then
turned to the *bambino*, the Child Jesus lying in the crib.[3] A
silver *bambino* was carried into the church of St. Maria
Maggiore in Rome on a silver cradle beneath a white satin
canopy, preceded by a crucifix and immense ostrich
feather fans. Soldiers cleared the way, standing in line
between the western door and the High Altar, letting
through a procession of solemn chanting cardinals and
priests carrying tapers. Nobles in court dress mixed with
the congregation while at the High Altar the Pope in white
vestments prepared to celebrate High Mass.[4]

Visitors to Rome in 1888 witnessed the canonisation of
ten saints in one ceremony; St. John Berchmans, St.
Alphonsus Rodriquez, St. Peter Claver and the seven thirteenth century Florentine founders of the Order of
Servites. The canonisation was held in a small chapel high
up above the façade of St. Peter's, to which three hundred
people climbed up the narrow stairs. There was a crush at
the narrow entrance to the chapel, where there were as
many bishops and cardinals inside. The Pope, carried in
his chair beneath a canopy 'looked dear and sweet and
blessed the people as he was borne slowly along'. The High
Mass took three hours, the canonisation an hour and a
half. At the Offertory ten cardinals presented the offerings
to represent the newly canonised saints – two small birds,
two pairs of doves, a gold and a silver loaf, and a gold and a
silver cask of wine. The loggia was lit up and hung with
pictures, banners and tapestry, the proceedings lasting
from nine in the morning until two. As everyone had
arrived an hour early to ensure a place, there was some
opportunity for patience.[5]

Opportunities for patience abounded during the Holy
Week ceremonies in Rome. Lent was preceded by the cele-
brations for Mardi Gras, which to Lady Georgiana
Fullerton seemed like a dream. Confetti and military music
in the afternoon were followed by horse-racing in the
Corso at five. Inside the Gèsu church the altar was magnifi-

cently illuminated, the rest of the church being lit by just a few lamps. With what seemed extraordinary versatility the crowds who had been in high celebration outside were soon inside the church deep in prayer. At the elevation of the Host at Mass every head bowed low in adoration. Then out in the streets there was uproar and the Corso was one blaze of light. At windows and in carriages everyone carried candles. 'The whole scene, the noise, the brilliancy, the confusion, is unimaginable when one has not seen it. Yet there was no fighting. At a given signal all the lights were extinguished and everything was quiet again.'[6]

When midnight chimed on Shrove Tuesday in Ancona, silence and darkness enveloped the whole town so lately surrendered to feasting and enjoyment in preparation for Lent.[7] And in Rome on Ash Wednesday the Hon. Edward Legge saw twenty five cardinals in red stockings, purple silk gowns, white cottas and red skull caps and long silk purple trains gathering in the Sistine chapel before the arrival of the Pope, dressed in scarlet with a gold chasuble and a white mitre. From his throne on the north side of the chapel he received obeisance from each cardinal, whose head was sprinkled with ashes by His Holiness. The cardinals were followed by friars, monks, abbots, priests, laymen and army officers, who did not kiss the Pope's hand but prostrated themselves to kiss his foot. The cardinals changed vestments for the Lenten season and Mass followed, the Pope moving from the stool in front of the altar back to his throne and back again amidst the burning incense, each time having his mitre taken off and replaced by his attendant priests. The chanting stopped at the elevation of the Host when there was a deep silence.[8]

A light shining in the darkness of Passion Week was the commemoration of the Last Supper on Maundy Thursday. In Venice, flags flew on all the ships at the quay near St. Mark's Square. The Mass was the first witnessed by Frederick Faber since his arrival on the Continent and he searched in vain for 'the mummery, disgusting repetition, childish arrangements, and so forth, which one reads of in modern travellers'.[9] In Rome the traditional washing of the feet was performed by the Pope, twelve pilgrims representing the disciples. They were seated on a bench in one of the Vatican chapels and the Pope, bare-foot and wearing a white apron, held a basin of water with napkins over his arm. Attended by all the cardinals, he knelt down to wash the pilgrims' feet, giving each an embroidered napkin and a bouquet of flowers. 'The agitation these poor Pilgrims undergo in seeing the Pope on his knees before them is quite apparent and one of them I really thought would have fainted dead away.'[10] When Lord Mount Cashell visited Rome in the first year of the nineteenth century the pilgrims were served at table by the Pope. Bare-foot, taking away their plates and offering them wine, the Pope performed the role of a servant.

At Mass on Maundy Thursday two hosts were consecrated, one of which was placed in the ciborium, a chalice of rock crystal mounted in silver and covered with a lid. The Pope carried the ciborium under a canopy accompanied by the cardinals who advanced in pairs, each carrying a taper and a mitre. The choristers sang the *Pange lingua* as they advanced towards the Pauline chapel, which was brilliantly illuminated. When the Pope reached the altar *Verbum caro* was sung and a cardinal knelt, took the chalice from the Pope and placed it on the altar. The consecrated Host was then placed in a monstrance which was placed in the Tabernacle and the door left open. The Pope then knelt and censed the Host. The door was then shut, the Tabernacle locked and the key given to the Cardinal. The Pope then proceeded to the balcony of St. Peter's to give the triple benediction. The altars in St. Peter's were stripped of all ornament and washed with wine, remaining quite bare; the candlesticks and flowers were taken away. The flickering sanctuary lamp was extinguished. All was darkness and desolation. The Tabernacle above the High Altar was empty, the veil drawn aside, the door open.[11]

Tenebrae was sung in the Sistine Chapel in the morning of Thursday, Friday and Saturday. Allegri's *Miserere* – 'melancholy beyond all that I could have thought it possible to produce in sweet sounds, but at the same time so unearthly that you might fancy it the wailing of angels after their fall' – caused more than one man to weep bitterly as he became imbued with the spirit of the hour which commemorated the silent anguish and death of the Saviour.[12] These were the 'Lamentations of Jeremiah', the immemorial cry of sorrow and desolation. They were sung while the candles were extinguished one by one, leaving just one lighted behind the altar, when the congregation knelt in silence. During this timeless ceremony 'the great Past was not dead in Rome – rather does it at times make the present seem shadowy and ephemeral; we become part of the stream of life that has flowed for many centuries past those same temples, arches of triumph, porticoes and palaces'.[13] Not everyone was so impressed; for one observer 'a dirge which goes on for three hours and a chandelier which takes the same time to have its lights snuffed out, become an intolerable nuisance'.[14]

In the south of France at Menton, life-size figures of the disciples at the Last Supper were illuminated, and on Good Friday a procession made its way up to the cathedral led by the Order of White Penitents, carrying banners, lamps and tapers. A tomb-like silence pervaded the church which was draped in black and at the moment when the veil of the Temple was rent, the wailing music of the worshippers was of grief and fear. The crush of the crowd made the heat over-powering and the body of the crucified Redeemer with a crown of thorns, a wound from the spear, bleeding hands and feet, lay stretched on a bier before the altar, illuminated by candles. Then the procession left the church in darkness, the body of the Saviour on the bier being carried beneath a black canopy. Arriving at the Place du Cap the procession halted. In the gloom the star-like double line of lights lit up the faces, costume and insignia of the bearers. The sacred bier was placed on an ornamental catafalque and at a given signal the body was slightly raised, the faithful knelt, the band struck up and the procession went back to the church.[15]

At Linares, a mining town in Spain, a wild wailing chant telling of the sufferings of Christ was heard every night in Lent until one or two in the morning. Holy Week dawned upon a land utterly scorched, on brown crops of barley and wheat, plains of beans hanging as if they had been scalded, and withered and discoloured wild flowers.

As the sun sank below the horizon, shedding a ray of
parting glory over the rocky, purple moorland and
making the distant Sierra look quite blue and sombre,
the band struck up the Dead March in 'Saul' and
eight men, bare-footed, in long robes of sackcloth,
girdled around the waist with a knotted cord of
esparto grass, in which was stuck a small black cross,
each one bearing a huge wax candle on his left hand,
staggered down the church steps, bearing on their
shoulders the image of the Saviour.[16]

As the image was lowered on to the ground in front of the
church, a crowd of two hundred knelt in silence. A bare-
foot man in a black robe descended from the church door.
Putting a long trumpet to his mouth he blew four discordant notes. The image of Christ was carried again, and the
long line of men in sackcloth marched forward slowly. A
banner of purple velvet, borne by two men carrying long
candles, depicting a picture of Christ whose tears fell on
rough ground, was carried behind the image. The masked
penitents were followed by an image of Mary Magdalene
borne aloft, seated and robed in a long dark cloak, her
head between her hands. Down the slanting unpaved
street, crammed with thousands, the beginning of the
procession moved slowly, the candles glowing gently in the
setting sun, the dark images standing out in bold relief
against the steely-blue darkening sky. Then came the
image of the Blessed Virgin Mary, robed in black velvet,
bordered with gold. At the sight of her everyone knelt,
their heads buried in their hands. Then came St. John,
then came St. Luke. More penitents, a brass band playing
mournfully, priests robed in black and white, one in dark
purple, made their way across the market square. The
procession went up one street and down another for two
weary hours and returned to the dark and silent church,
the images placed around the dimly lit altar. The crowds
quietly dispersed.

On the morning of Maundy Thursday the same fierce
sun shone, the same rainless wind was blowing. At half past
six in the evening the same procession resumed but now

the penitents were dressed in black, with high peaked hoods on which were placed a crown of thorns. Hundreds of children wore the same costume. Added to this procession were twelve men in tunics and steel helmets, accompanied by a strange trumpet and the rattle of a muffled kettle-drum, representing the Roman soldiers of Palestine. Good Friday morning was bitterly cold and two thousand people stood outside the church. This time the penitents each carried a black-stained cross of wood, four feet long. Inside the church of San Francisco the exchange of money was acted out and the arm of Christ was raised as if in a silent appeal against the treachery. The crowd cried out 'Aqua, aqua!' and soon afterwards there fell a light shower. That evening one more procession carried the dead Christ under a glass case to the church where it was guarded by two angels and the Roman soldiers kept a vigil. The doors were closed but from outside the soldiers' measured tramp could be heard, keeping watch. Saturday morning dawned with clouds and darkness and the rain poured down in tropical torrents. A few guns were fired off, and there were a few explosions which signified the ceremony known as 'shooting Judas'.[17]

In the cathedral town of Baeza not far from Linares Good Friday dawned upon the barren Campo with a chill east wind and a cloudless sky. On the way from Linares across hills of vines and olives overlooked by the sharp blue jagged outline of the Sierra Morena, wooden crosses on the spot where a man had died a violent death were propped up against a loose stone wall or nailed against olive and ilex trees. Men and women gaily dressed made their way on horseback towards Baeza. Tethering their horses and mules the crowd entered the enclosed Plaza with its overhanging upper storeys, where solemn Passion music was being played. Men dressed in long robes and hoods, carrying lighted candles, appeared, followed by an image of Christ in a flowing robe of claret red, embroidered with gold. A crown of thorns pierced the temples entwined with real hair and there was blood on the shoulders. The expression was one of utter weariness. At the sight of this, every hand beat its breast, every knee was bent. One hundred Roman soldiers followed in pairs with flashing steel helmets, some on fiery Andalucian chargers. The Roman soldiery gathered round the suffering Christ and then the figure of Veronica appeared, holding in her hands a white handkerchief. She was lowered as if to curtsey and approached Christ. Stooping down, she was made to wipe the sweat, blood and dirt from the Saviour's brow. By means of a spring mechanism the handkerchief was rolled up and another appeared with the image of the face of Jesus on it. Then the Blessed Virgin Mary appeared at the corner of the piazza borne aloft and the crowd knelt. She was carried towards her Son and she wiped her eyes, which were red and swollen with weeping. As she wiped her tear-streamed eyes the bands played part of a Bach Passion. At the saddest and most wailing note she put her hands around the neck and across the breast of her fallen, fainting and bleeding Son. The mourning crowd, rising from their knees, were kept in order by the penitents in hoods and robes wielding their four-foot candles. The same procession that evening had Christ washing the feet of Peter, accompanied by solemn Passion music. The crowd saw Christ praying in the garden at Gethsemane and then bound with esparto grass to a pillar and beaten. Night fell and in the plaza the silent crowd held lighted candles. All was still and the wind could be heard in the mountains. At the crucifixion when Christ was raised up aloft thin streams of blood flowed from nail-pierced hands. 'I turned away sick and faint; it was all too frighteningly real.'[18]

Lady Herbert was similarly perturbed when in the Chapel of Calvary in Jerusalem she saw a Franciscan monk step forward and, leaving his brethren prostrate at the foot of the altar, he proceeded to detach the figure of Christ from the cross. As each nail was painfully and slowly drawn out he held it up, exclaiming, 'Ecce, dulces, clavo!', exposing it to the breathless congregation. A ladder was brought and the figure of Christ was lifted down into the arms of the monks at the foot of the Cross. 'As the last nail was detached, and the head fell forward as of a dead body, a low deep sob burst from the very souls of the kneeling crowd.'[19]

❦

Lord Lincoln, later Duke of Newcastle, was at Jerusalem at Easter in 1850 where he witnessed the 'miracle of fire' in the church of the Holy Sepulchre. Pilgrims had spent the night sleeping on its marble floors. At eleven o'clock the following morning Lord Lincoln sauntered towards the doors of the church to witness 'a scene perhaps the most painful and certainly the most degrading I ever beheld'. He viewed all this from a gallery in the dome and looked down on the thousands of quarrelling pilgrims, the fighting being held in check by sticks wielded by Turkish soldiers. After three hours of uproar the priests arrived, making a circuit of the Sepulchre three times. One of the priests made his way through the crowd and then thrust himself through a large round hole in the wall of the Sanctuary, where he remained for fifteen minutes. He emerged to face the agitated crowd with a large torch of fire encased in an iron grating. He forced his way out of the chapel with the help of the Turkish soldiers and the crowd made a rush at him, endeavouring to light their tapers. He made his escape and the crowd's attention was soon diverted by the lights which appeared throughout the chapel. In a few minutes the whole assembly was one blaze of torches. Lord Lincoln returned to his hotel 'humiliated as a Christian and disgusted with all the performers in the scene of blasphemous fanaticism ...'[20]

In Rome a different sort of igniting occurred in recognition of Easter when the façade of St. Peter's was lit up. At first the building was traced with lines of lamps, looking like brass nails on black velvet. In an instant the entire dome was lit up, transformed into what seemed like white marble glittering with diamonds, 'a play of light so bright and beauteous that it seemed the work of enchantment'.[21] Viewed from the Pincian hill the luminous dome became 'an aerial vision, floating between heaven and earth'. It was as if a shower of stars had fallen upon the building and were quivering and trembling with shock.[22] Beneath the dome, the Holy Father was celebrating Mass. At the moment of consecration the large congregation was absolutely silent.

How could the mystery of the Mass be explained? Countless times it could be glimpsed, viewed and observed, but unaccompanied by the gift of Faith it meant nothing. The kneeling, silent adoring crowds, anonymous priests, majestic music, vestments, chalices, gold and marble, all could appear as if part of a pantomime to those who knew nothing of its worth. Some English visitors watched the ceremonies with irreverent curiosity, thinking they were no more than 'dramatic entertainments performed by daylight.' The Mass that had once been celebrated in England for centuries was still being celebrated throughout Catholic Europe. It was viewed with disdain and disinterest by those who had been taught to believe it was superstition: pagan, heathen, un-godly, un-English. 'Oh those endless bowings and turnings – those genuflexions and salutations – the histrionic mummery which is constantly going forward; while the unlettered congregation, unacquainted with Latin are kneeling and simply looking on! ...'[23] Communicants receiving the Host on the tongue, kneeling at an altar rail that was covered with a linen cloth, who returned quickly to their seats were 'the most imperfect, lifeless, unimpressive act of Faith, perhaps, that a Protestant eye could witness'.[24] But at a Lady Chapel beyond a High Altar, the candles, flowers, incense, a priest in purple vestments, and a dense throng of worshippers, attracted the attention of one English traveller who recognised that

> a miracle was being performed; the Saviour of the world was coming into the consecrated bread and wine. He was giving Himself to His people ... The Sanctus bell rang sharply; the Host was being elevated. Every head bowed at once in silence; who was I, to know more than they and remain stiffly upright? I bowed with the others.[25]

Lady Herbert did not feel any inclination to bow with the others when in Cadiz she saw the canons in long black robes prostrate in a semi-circle before the High Altar, each covered with a black flag on which there was a red cross. That evening there was a procession with the Blessed Sacrament, followed by Benediction. Amidst the curling incense the evening sun caught the gold of the monstrance. The choir and people followed singing the *Lauda Sion* under the arcade shaded by orange trees, then disappeared into the sombre church. During the procession for the Feast of Corpus Christi in Rome the Pope bore the monstrance along the colonnade hung with tapestry and graced with garlands. At the beginning of the Octave of Corpus Christi flags and banners streamed in the wind and the blazing torches created a labyrinth of light. Benediction inside St. Peter's saw a moving forest of torches and tapers whose reflected light glittered on the gilded dome above. When the Pope held up the monstrance to bless the prostrate multitude there was a deafening roar of artillery from the Castle St. Angelo.[26]

At the elevation of the Host at the Mass for the promulgation of the doctrine of the Immaculate Conception, forty thousand worshippers became absolutely silent; the only sound was the momentary clank made by the soldiers presenting arms.[27] When Pope Leo XIII celebrated his Jubilee in 1902, at the elevation of the Host the Papal guards went down on one knee, their halberds striking the marble floor with one sharp thunderous rap before silver trumpets rang out in the dome.[28] As the chalice was elevated the silver trumpets continued to peal forth above the kneeling multitude, 'in tones soft and mellow as from another world'. Normally after the consecration wind instruments were heard from the entrance to St. Peter's. 'The air seemed stirred with the trembling of angelic wings; or as if the gates of heaven had been opened, and a 'wandering breath' from the songs of seraphs had been borne to the earth.'[29] Dame Mary Francis Roskell asked her readers to:

> Imagine a great church with a high throne at the altar end of cloth of silver, backed by a canopy and hangings of crimson damask and gold extending quite across the church. Imagine the Pope on this throne

and the altar for his Mass about two hundred feet down the church, and on either side, in five rows of stalls, seven hundred cardinals, patriarchs and bishops, all in white capes and mitres, except some of the Orientals, who wore gorgeous dresses of all colours and crowns of gold and silver. Then the various members of the court in robes of the middle ages, some in cloth of gold, others in black velvet and print lace; the noble guard in full armour; gentlemen of all nations in the uniform of their countries, some in the red of England, as Mr Monteith, Lord Denbigh, etc.[30]

The presence of the eighth Earl of Denbigh in St. Peter's for the Pope's High Mass came about after a long journey from the Church of England to the Church of Rome, a journey which had started some twenty years before. Lord Denbigh had visited Rome many times. Travel to a foreign land whose peaceful climate had drawn so many of his countrymen was accompanied for him by a spiritual quest which culminated eventually in his embrace of the true expression of Christianity. Many times he had made the journey to Rome, a journey that was, socially, perfectly acceptable. What was not acceptable among his fellow subjects was that he should fully embrace the doctrines of the Church of Rome. But therein he at last found peace.

Notes

[1]   H.J. Rose, *Untrodden Spain, and her Black Country; being sketches of the life and character of the Spaniard of the interior, Vol. I*, London, Samuel Tinsley, 1875, p. 265.

[2]   J.G. Cox, *Jubilee-Tide in Rome*, London, Burns & Oates, 1888, p. 2.

[3]   A.M. Brown, *Wintering at Menton on the Riviera. A Compagnon de voyage with hints to invalids*, London, J. & A. Churchill, 1872, p. 30.

[4]   Cox, op. cit. p. 41.

[5]   Ibid.

[6]   C. Kerr (ed.), *Cecil, Marchioness of Lothian*, London, Sands & Co., 1922, p. 157.

7   Mrs G. Gretton, *The Englishwoman in Italy. Impressions of life in the Roman States and Sardinia, during ten years' residence*, London, Hurst & Blackett, 1861, p. 76.

8   Greater London Record Office, Papers of Hon. Edward Legge, 4th March 1862, F/LEG/902.

9   F.W. Faber, *Sights and Thoughts in Foreign Churches and among Foreign Peoples*, London, J.G.F. & J. Rivington, 1842, p. 302.

10 T. U. Sadleir (ed.), *An Irish Peer on the Continent (1801–1803)*, London, Williams & Norgate, 1920, p. 184.

11 H. Morton, *Protestant Vigils; or, Evening Records of a journey in Italy in the years 1826 and 1827*, London, Seeley & Burnside, 1829, p. 152.

12 W. Ward, *Aubrey De Vere. A Memoir*, London, Longmans, Green & Co., 1904, p. 39. C.R. Weld, *Last Winter in Rome*, London, Longman Green, 1865, p. 479.

13 Mrs Winthrop Chanler, *Roman Spring. Memoirs*, London, Williams & Norgate, 1935, p. 62.

14 E. Dicey, *Rome in 1860*, London, Macmillan, 1861, p. 224.

15 A.M. Brown, *Wintering at Menton on the Riviera. A Compagnon de Voyage with hints to invalids*, London, J. & A. Churchill, 1872, pp. 34, 36.

16 H.J. Rose, *Untrodden Spain and her Black Country; being sketches of the life and character of the Spaniard of the interior, Vol. II*, London, Samuel Tinsley, 1875, p. 233.

17 Ibid., pp. 234–44.

18 Ibid., pp. 245–57.

19 Lady Herbert, *Cradle Lands*, London, Richard Bentley, 1867, p. 132.

20 University of Nottingham, Department of Manuscripts, Ne C 12, 983 'Lord Lincoln's journal of Mediterranean Cruise and tour, 1850', 4 May.

21 Marchioness of Londonderry & H.M. Hyde, *More Letters from Martha Wilmot. Impressions of Vienna 1819–1829*, London, Macmillan, 1935, p. 161.

22 J. Hillard, *Six Months in Italy, Vol. II*, London, John Murray, 1853, p. 151.

23 Ibid., p. 212. Rev. J.W. Burgon, *Letters from Rome to Friends in England*, London, John Murray, 1862, p. 113.

24 Rev. G.M. Musgrave, *A Pilgrimage into Dauphiné; comprising a visit to the Monastery of the Grande Chatreuse; with anecdotes, incidents and sketches from twenty departments of France*, London, Hurst and Blackett, 1857, p. 53.

25 W.F. Stead, *The Shadow of Mount Carmel. A Pilgrimage*, London, Richard Cobden-Sanderson, 1926, p. 53.

26 'Olinthus', *Reminiscences of Rome: or, a religious, moral and literary view of the Eternal City; in a series of letters addressed to a friend in England, by a member of the Arcadian Academy*, London, Paternoster Row, 1838, p. 93.

27 Kerr, op. cit., p. 141.

[28]   M. Baring, *The Puppet Show of Memory*, London, Heinemann, 1922, p. 253.

[29]   N. Hall, *The Land of the Forum and the Vatican; Or, Thoughts and Sketches during an Easter Pilgrimage to Rome*, London, James Nisbet, 1854, p. 316. Hillard, op. cit., p. 183.

[30]   Dame Mary Francis Roskell, O.S.B., *Memoirs of Francis Kerril Amherst, D.D. Lord Bishop of Northampton*, London, Art and Book Company, 1903, p. 286.

PART II – OVER TO ROME

Chapter Six

The most bitter moment

At St. David's Franciscan friary in Flintshire, the body of the eighth Earl of Denbigh lay on a high catafalque swamped with wreaths. It was the Eve of the Feast of St. Patrick, 1892. Divine providence had brought the devout Earl to his funeral on the eve of the national Feast Day of the Catholic country closest to his home. How did the Earl of Denbigh come to have a Requiem Mass in a Franciscan friary which he himself had founded, swept by winds from the Irish sea? Because once as an Anglican he had found himself deeply perturbed when crumbs left after Holy Communion had been carelessly swept away. Next, doubts about the validity of Anglican orders had been similarly swept aside by a Church of England clergyman. The Earl had sought counsel from a Roman Catholic Bishop, who, unaware that he was talking to a future peer of the realm, spent two hours of discussion with the doubting viscount. The result was that Viscount Feilding, later eighth Earl of Denbigh, became a convert to Roman Catholicism.[1]

It had been his wish to be buried in the humble habit of a Capuchin Franciscan friar. So it was that the Earl was carried to his last resting place by the Italian Capuchin friars whom he had brought to Wales. After a Requiem Mass which lasted many hours, the Earl of Denbigh was buried in the family vault while his family held lighted candles.

After Eton, Rudolph Feilding had been sent to Cambridge by his father precisely because of fears of the

High Church movement in Oxford. At Cambridge
Rudolph's inherited prejudices towards the Church of
Rome were reinforced. But it was his marriage to Louisa
Pennant, heiress of the Downing estate near Holywell in
Flintshire, which led to his review of the claims of Rome.
He had no suspicion then of the inclination of his wife
Louisa's mind towards the Catholic faith until he
happened to overhear her in conversation on the balcony
at Downing. She was expressing views which were to him
'Roman, papistical and idolatrous'.[2] Married in 1846, the
following year Lord and Lady Feilding wintered abroad. A
month before their departure for the Catholic continent
the Reverend Baylee, their chaplain at Downing, wrote to
Lady Feilding urging her not to forget the reformed
church, 'whose genuine doctrines are the Simplicity of
Scriptural truth'. He went on to remind her:

> Placed by God's providence at the head of so large a
> fortune and in so conspicuous a station, with your
> youth and many temptations, you have need of more
> than ordinary grace to be enabled to be the meek and
> lowly follower of a self-denying Saviour.... You will
> find many more to flatter & allure you to the world,
> than those who will venture to deal with you as an heir
> of the world that is to come, an heir of that other
> coronet which will shine in the brightness of the
> Divine Light.[3]

Lord and Lady Feilding arrived in Rome in January 1848
where they made the acquaintance of Henry Manning,
then Archdeacon of Chichester. They returned home in
the Spring and avoiding France, then in the turmoil of
revolution, they took a ship from Civita Vecchia to
Gibraltar. They journeyed through Spain and spent Holy
Week in Seville.[4] The Holy Week ceremonies could not
have failed to have left an impression on the young couple,
later described by Lady Herbert. She observed that any
English onlooker would have found the representations of
the Passion in the glare of a Seville sun 'simply intensely
painful'.[5] Lady Herbert found it 'touching and beautiful'

that 'men of the highest rank of royal blood, and of the
noblest orders, did not hesitate to walk for hours through
the dusty, crowded, burning streets for three successive
days, with the sole motive of doing honour to their Lord'.[6]
Inside the cathedral, where the great catafalque was
carried through the darkness of the long aisles, lit by a brilliant mass of light thrown by thousands of wax tapers,
'representations which looked gaudy in the sunshine were
mellowed and softened by the contrast with the night'. But
inside the cathedral English eyes could still be disturbed by
'the Blessed Virgin, decked out in gorgeous velvet robes,
embroidered in gold, and covered with jewels, with lace
pocket-handkerchiefs in the hand, and all the parapher-
nalia of a fine lady of the nineteenth century!'[7] The
Feildings would have seen the chapel hung with black on
Good Friday. Such was the darkness they would have stum-
bled across a kneeling congregation, all in deep mourning.
One light was thrown on a life-size picture of the crucifixion while a priest meditated on the seven utterances of
Christ on the cross, on His charity and His desolation.
There was music between each meditation, 'the lament of
the angels'.[8] The moon shone through the cloisters on to
the orange trees on the night of the Easter vigil, shining
with startling brightness on the Pietà, the silver light just
lighting up the tips of the cloister arches. Groups of black-
veiled figures knelt before the Tabernacle. 'Each heart was
pouring forth its sorrow of sin into the Sacred Heart which
had been so lately pierced to receive it.'[9] At two o'clock in
the morning the cathedral was transformed from darkness
to light when the organs played and the entire congregation sang with the choristers who in red cassocks, white
cottas and gold diadems processed down the aisle to the
High Altar followed by a line of priests. High Mass was celebrated, and Low Mass at the side altars. So much for the
hope expressed by the Reverend Baylee writing from
Birkenhead that the liturgical scenes witnessed by Lady
Feilding in Catholic Europe would endear her all the more
to the reformed church and the 'Simplicity of Scriptural
truth.'[10] Indeed, when the Feildings returned to Flintshire,
they persuaded the clergy at the church in Pantasaph to

process in surplices. Archdeacon Manning urged them both to take frequent Communion, to make prompt confession of serious faults and maintain a habitual recollection of God's presence. Louisa Feilding, carrying out the wishes of her mother, laid the foundation stone for an ornate Anglican church. She then read Newman's sermons on *Difficulties of Anglicans.* At about this time, after the Anglican communion service at Whitford, a village close to Pantasaph, Lord Feilding witnessed the crumbs after communion being swept away by the sacristan.

Such are the mysterious workings of Divine Grace. The Spanish liturgy, the sermons and the crumbs led Lord and Lady Feilding to re-consider Protestantism. It was not without painful conflict, expressed by Manning when he wrote to Lady Feilding in June 1850. 'My whole heart and soul are so bound up with the Church of England, that I must be torn from it and be parted, and until I see that necessity, I shall strive to work and pray.'[11] Soon afterwards Louisa fell ill and she and Lord Feilding travelled to Edinburgh to consult a specialist. During this time of torment Lord Feilding found solace in long and strenuous walks, sometimes accompanied by the clergyman whose church he attended in Edinburgh. During conversations about the differences between the two churches Lord Feilding found himself defending the Roman Catholic position. He bought books from a Catholic bookshop in Edinburgh to further his quest for the Truth. He enquired in the bookshop where a Catholic priest might be found; Louisa had expressed a wish to receive Communion and was having doubts about the validity of Anglican orders. The bookseller suggested Bishop Gillis, at St. Margaret's Convent. Lord Feilding set out for the convent walking all the way and praying for God's guidance. He explained to the Bishop all that was on his mind. After two hours his difficulties vanished. He saw 'the Church, his own life, everything, transfigured by a new vision.'[12]

Lord Feilding wrote to his father and his sister that he and Louisa had both decided to be received into the Roman Catholic Church. As the couple were setting out for St. Margaret's Convent from the Douglas Hotel, a letter from Lord Feilding's sister was thrust into his hand. Both she and her father had travelled immediately to Edinburgh and urgently needed to see them. The letter begged them to take no decisive step until they had all talked the matter over. Lord Feilding informed Bishop Gillis that his father and his sister and the Reverend Baylee, who had accompanied them, wished to discuss the matter. The agitated party arranged to meet the next morning in the Bishop's residence.

At the meeting held the following day, Bishop Gillis requested permission to ask Lord Feilding in his father's presence whether anything had been said or done by him to influence his decision to become a Catholic. The Earl replied that his son had already sent him a written statement of 'Reasons for Catholicity' but he wished to examine these reasons further and so had enlisted the help of the Reverend Baylee in order to do this. The statement was produced and the Earl asked for pens, ink and paper. Bishop Gillis later recalled that 'not deeming it courteous in my own house, to assume so very formal an attitude to those who had done me the honour to wait upon me, I sat with folded arms and listened to Mr Baylee ... as he proceeded to read Lord Feilding's reasons.'[13] The Reverend made the most of one or two oversights and inaccuracies in the statement and the discussion then moved on to the question of papal infallibility. As the Bishop began to grow somewhat restive at the discussion which then ensued, he suggested that if the present conversation were to be exclusively carried on between Mr Baylee, Lord Feilding and noble relatives, they were most welcome to the apartment which they now occupied for as long as they wished, but he had other duties to attend to. The argument continued for another two hours, at the end of which the Bishop was politely thanked for his hospitality by the feuding party.

The consequence of Lord Feilding's determination to join the Catholic Church was his disinheritance. He wrote to his father saying he 'must bow in silence and resignation to God's Will and endeavour to rejoice that He has thought me worthy so early in age to suffer shame and

persecution for His name's sake.' He went on: 'I begin now
to feel the force of Christ saying 'I come not to send Peace
on Earth but the Sword.'[14] Lord Feilding wrote to his sister
in a similar vein, saying he felt no sorrow but 'rather joy
that God has thought fit thus early in my Christian course
to manifest his solicitude for me by trying my faith and
trust in Him, and that He has thought me worthy of
bearing even so little of the Cross which my Saviour first
bore for me.'[15]

Disinheritance came after impassioned letters quoting
scriptural texts written by the Earl long into the night. The
first letter was written but never sent, expressing his 'first
emotion of broken heartedness in receiving the intelli-
gence of your fatal determination.'[16] But what he felt then
was 'painfully dispensed by the *utter* disregard you have
since shown to the most ordinary filial *love* or *duty*.'[17] He
had requested that his son wait a few weeks but his
response was to be received into the Church in a matter of
hours, prompting the Earl to speed hot-foot the hundreds
of miles to Edinburgh to urge him to re-consider. The Earl
accused his son of not having the moral courage to
suspend a decision 'of such vital consequence'. Lord
Feilding replied that he had read every Anglican book that
he could put his hands on to try and satisfy his scruples.
The Earl countered that these books must have been
written by Anglicans who were Roman Catholic at heart,
Tractarians who had led him and many others like him
step by step until he had fallen over 'the fatal precipice'.
The Earl assured his son of prayers and forgiveness, but
none of his children except the Viscount's sister would be
permitted to communicate with him. It was impossible for
the Earl to describe the most bitter moment of his life.
Dearly as he loved his son he would far rather have
followed him to his grave than see him renounce the true
faith, as he firmly believed it to be. He was thankful that
Lady Denbigh had been spared the greatest of all trials that
God had laid upon him. Although they may never meet
again in this world he would never cease to pray for his
son, whom he regarded as worse than dead. Any meeting
would cause him unspeakable anguish.

On the day of Viscount Feilding's reception into the Roman Church Lord Denbigh wrote that despite his son's protestations of loyalty the suddenness and obstinacy of his decision precluded all evidence of filial love or duty. 'You plead *conscience* but is that any expiation for an act of *sin?*' If his heir supposed that their future separation was intended as a threat he was mistaken. He realised that as far as Viscount Feilding was concerned, '*the greater the sacrifice the greater the merit*'. Lord Denbigh finally accused his son not of wilful hypocrisy but self-deception, believing him still honest enough to re-trace his steps 'however great the humiliation whenever it may please God to show you your errors and the fallacy of your present opinions.'[18]

The view of Viscount Feilding's sister was that her brother might be taking on a cross which was not meant to be his and was one of his own making. Lord Feilding replied that while he was able to carry the cross of disinheritance, his sister had no assurance of possessing the Truth. He wrote:

Your Faith – if Faith that can be called which is but opinion, is founded upon your own imperfect interpretation of Scripture ... You can only refer back 300 years at most for its beginning and it owed its origin solely to an incontinent monk, who in order to escape the trammels which the catholic religion imposed on him, threw off every yoke and carved out a religion for himself. I, on the other hand, have the uninterrupted faith of eighteen centuries to support me (for it has never yet been determined by Protestants when what they call 'Roman errors' began).[19]

The Hon. Mary Feilding replied that her brother should not talk such nonsense that her religion was only made three hundred years ago. All the truths she held were fundamental doctrines all found in Scripture. 'Rather it is for you to prove that yours are so, for *yours* is the *new* religion.' She thought her brother in the honeymoon of love for his new Church. He could neither distinguish truth from error nor see things in their true light had he not been so 'fascinated'. She could not bring herself to believe that her brother could hold 'all the gross errors of the Romish Church – the Treasury of Saints – prayers to the Virgin – purgatory etc ....'[20]

Meanwhile Lord Feilding was writing to Sir Piers Mostyn at Talacre not far from Downing that he and Lady Feilding both felt inexpressibly supported and comforted in their trials. A peace which none but God could give and which the world could not take away was theirs. Lord Feilding marvelled that he should have been 'such a blind fool all my life as never to have thought like this before.' Reasons for remaining in the Anglican communion seemed 'so much chaff which the first breath would blow away.'[21] His wife Louisa wrote in her note book that she and other converts could look back to the time when 'released from the trammels of a narrow and incomplete system of faith, they first received holy and awful mysteries'. She sympathised with those whose hearts sank at the thought of submitting every thought to the dominion of what then seemed 'so dry and harsh and graceless'.[22] In their daily walks at Downing Lord and Lady Feilding 'knew God and His angels ever to be with them; life became more deeply solemn but very glorious, for they knew that the Catholic Christian even on earth is made a citizen of heaven and the commonest and meanest has a fellowship in the communion of saints.'[23] Death was no destroyer now for there was a new tie with those they loved, as they shared the membership of a body whose unity was not broken in the grave. They could never now give up what had made life God-like and death glorious to them. 'Cost what it may, suffer as we may, we know *that* to be the Truth, and where the Truth is, there only will we be.'[24]

Lady Feilding's thoughts of death reached a painful conclusion when the following year she and her husband travelled to Italy in search of a suitable climate for the cure of her consumption. They sailed to Ischia – 'Paradise, alias the Island of Ischia' – and in the Spring of 1853 in a small villa above Naples young Lady Feilding died. Brought back to Wales, she was buried in the church at Pantasaph which her mother had wanted to be built and which had been later consecrated as a Catholic church. The newly-discovered relics of St. Primitus, given to the Feildings by Pope Pius IX, were placed under the altar in the Lady Chapel. While in Rome the Feildings had made the acquaintance of some Capuchin Franciscan friars and had suggested they set up a community near Downing. They had arrived unexpectedly in Flintshire, peering through the breakfast-room windows at Downing. Soon a chapel was set up in the house, one of the Capuchins walking from Pantasaph to say daily Mass. When the church was consecrated on 13th October 1852 Lord Feilding wrote to Catherine Berkeley at Spetchley Park in Worcestershire that the church was '*crowded* with Cats and Prots. The latter behaved on the whole most decorously and I should hope many a good seed was sown that day.'[25]

The Hon. Catherine Berkeley's cousin Mary later became Viscount Feilding's second wife. At Spetchley Park the Blessed Sacrament had always been reserved in the house, exuding 'a peculiar serenity and joy'.[26] Thus it was that the old Catholic family of Berkeley was united with the newly Catholic widower, Viscount Feilding. It was this marriage which caused the Earl of Denbigh to relent. He could not in conscience attend a nuptial Mass, so it was arranged to hold the wedding ceremony first, enabling the Earl to leave the church before Mass began.[27] The couple were married by Cardinal Wiseman and set off for their honeymoon in Newnham Paddox, the Feildings' ancestral home in Northamptonshire. Here they were met by a torchlit procession of tenant farmers on horseback, who accompanied the couple to the house, where they were greeted by singing schoolchildren in the hall. They then travelled to Downing, making a pilgrimage to St. Winefride's Well at Holywell on the way. The devout couple had each spent a week on retreat before their wedding, Lord Feilding with the Jesuits at Manresa House in Roehampton, the Hon. Mary Berkeley with the Dominican nuns at Stone in Staffordshire.

Work on the Capuchin friary at Pantasaph started in 1858. On 26 May 1859 a son and heir was born to the Feildings. Lord Denbigh asked if the bells should be rung at Newnham for the birth of his grandson. On being told that bells could not be rung for a Catholic heir Lord Denbigh remained silent. He then said 'Let the bells ring.' He destroyed the will that had disinherited his son, saying he had never been happy for the nine years since he had made it following the furious flight to Edinburgh. Lord Denbigh lived for another four years until 1863 when Newnham Paddox became the family home of his Catholic heir, whose three sisters had to leave their house. The chapel was re-arranged and re-consecrated. Lady Denbigh recalled her distress not only at having to displace the three sisters from their home, who had always shown their brother and sister-in-law such kindness, but knowing also that 'the very sound of the bell for Mass or prayers went through them like daggers. The mere sight of the priest going about the house was that of a vampire'.[28]

Newnham Paddox, since demolished, was an idyllic home with its rose garden, cherry-tree walk, walled kitchen garden, orchard, conservatories, farm buildings, stables and laundry. There was a croquet lawn, an Italian garden, lawns, shrub-beries, rhododendrons, ponds and a lime walk exquisitely scented in June which led to the chapel where the Blessed Sacrament was reserved. The priest's house was just outside the grounds in the park at the end of an avenue of elms.

Lady Denbigh rose at 6.30 every morning for half an hour's meditation. After their prayers the children – by now three sons and four daughters – sat on stools around their mother's dressing-table sewing or crocheting for the poor. The maid dressed Lady Denbigh's hair while she read to her children lives of the saints. Holy Mass was at 8.30 and on Sundays the Gospel was learnt by heart. Lady Denbigh taught her children some aspect of the history of the Church – its councils and the 'strange heresies on which they sat in judgement'.[29] Newnham became a haven for Catholic visitors – Lady Newburgh, Lady Londonderry, Lady Herbert of Lea and the Hon. Lister Drummond – all of them converts. For them 'it was a wonderful introduction to their life as Catholics – at least they always said so – to be in the midst of a family whose activities and life were centred round the presence of the Blessed Sacrament. The cheer, the peace of the house came from the chapel.'[30] This holy atmosphere nurtured two vocations. Of the seven Feilding children the Hon. Basil became a priest and Lady Edith a Sister of Charity.

From an early age Lady Edith Feilding was brought into contact with 'the most profound of all teachers, the sick, the suffering and the poor.'[31] A childhood spent at the heavenly home of Newnham, of prayer and daily Mass, riding, tennis, dancing and acting reached its conclusion when Lady Edith and Lady Clare were presented at court. But Edith decided to enrol herself at once among the humble daughters of St. Vincent, feeling drawn towards a vocation as a Sister of Charity. After making this decision she gazed in silence one evening around the dining room and said to Father Vaughan, 'This is the last time I shall ever dine here.' When the day of final parting came her courage never failed. She left in a carriage accompanied by her parents for the convent of the Sisters of Charity in London, never once looking back to the home she loved so much. At Carlisle Place she went to the front of the convent chapel to kneel before the Blessed Sacrament. When her family departed she did not turn round.

Later in her novitiate Lady Edith went to the House in Paris, where half a century before another Sister of Charity, St. Catherine Labouré, had had a vision of the Blessed Virgin Mary who had asked that a medal be forged, later known to millions of Catholics as the Miraculous Medal. At the Rue du Bac Edith found herself in the same community as her cousin, Sister Berkeley. Lord Denbigh visited his daughter in Paris, bringing with him Dom Bosco, who was seeking funds for churches. Founder of the Salesian Brothers in Turin, Dom Bosco gave the young novice his blessing.

Dom Bosco was regarded as a saint in his own time because of the innumerable miracles witnessed in his presence. One such had occurred in Turin when the Denbighs, accompanied by Lady Lothian, Lady Londonderry, the

Duchess of Buccleuch, Lady Herbert of Lea and George Lane-Fox, were in the basilica of Our Lady Help of Christians. The English party saw a woman with a dumb boy trying to get in to the sanctuary. Dom Bosco led the boy in to the sanctuary, turned to the congregation and asked them all to join with him in asking the Blessed Virgin through the joy of her motherhood that the boy be cured. Dom Bosco knelt down and seemed to pray with all his body. He turned to the boy and said: 'Say the Hail Mary with me'. The priest and the boy said the prayer together. The boy was handed back to his mother.[32]

Dom Bosco's work in Turin centred on the poor boys of the city. Having received the future saint's blessing Lady Edith Feilding, now known as Sister Clare, commenced her religious life helping the poor not in Turin, but in north London, Liverpool, York, Manchester and Dunfermline. In Scotland the famous white cornettes of the Sisters of Charity appeared to the Scots as 'the very livery of Satan'. When the sisters went out of the convent they were met with Protestants who wanted to annoy them or Catholics wanting to protect them. The first procession of the Blessed Sacrament in Dunfermline took place on the Feast of St. Margaret of Scotland amid much rejoicing. It must surely have passed through Sister Clare's mind that it was at St. Margaret's Convent in Edinburgh that her father had been received into the Roman Catholic Church. She wrote to her brother Basil, then considering a vocation, of 'the longing for the better part'. She went on: 'Do be a saint! The whole world is going to ruin because all forget God. If only God would send some saints to wake us up! Do try to be one. Read the lives of St. Aloysius and St. Stanislaus and then imitate them ...' On his decision to become a priest she sympathised with the mingled feeling of sorrow of separation from a loving and happy home and the joy of doing God's will. She reminded him that 'Our Lord fills up the void in one's heart in a wonderful manner, truly the hundredfold in this life that He promised in the gospel.'[33]

The Hon. Basil Feilding was ordained in 1898 and received a Doctorate of Divinity in Rome. He was given a poor parish in Wolverhampton, where he lived in the most

squalid part of the town in a small house by the canal. Not
long afterwards he and his brother took a boating trip on
the Rhine and both were drowned. He was a brilliant
speaker with a vivid personality, astonishing memory and
tireless energy. Sister Clare's reaction to her brother's
death was that God had taken him when his soul was ripe.

Having been sent to Dover to run an orphanage for small
boys, Sister Clare next received orders to proceed to China.
She helped run a hospital in Shanghai and a school in
Chentung fu. From here she wrote that the Chinese children
had been taught to sing the *Ave Maris Stella*, the *Ave Maria* in
Solesmes chant and the *Tantum Ergo*. Every day the Chinese
children prayed for peace, prayed for the Pope and sang
hymns. From a childhood of devotions and prayers in
country houses in Northamptonshire and Flintshire, Lady
Edith Feilding had brought her Faith to the children of
China. And after her death she was seen in an apparition.

A Chinese woman whose children had died one after
another had decided to leave the mission. She was then
visited by a nun whom she did not recognise, who told her
that she must become a Christian and must make this
promise in writing. The woman said she did not know how
to write and called her husband. The nun told them both
that she belonged to the mission at Chentung fu and her
earthly remains were in Petang cemetery. She was later
identified by a photograph as Sister Clare. The Chinese
woman and her husband were both later received into the
Church as well as a neighbour who had walked into the
house during the apparition.[34] Such was the nature of
Sister Clare's missionary work in China. Sister Clare's
younger sister Lady Winefride Feilding led a life which
took rather a different course. In 1889 she married the
celebrated tenor Gervase Elwes.

∞♦∞

One of the first cedars of Lebanon to be planted in England
was on the Billing estate in Northamptonshire. It was to
Billing that Valentine Cary-Elwes brought his young bride
Alice in 1866. A year after their marriage, the young couple

rented the Villa Visconti at Nice and on the way to the villa
they attended High Mass at the church of St. Roch. Brought
up in an Ulster parsonage the attitude of Alice Cary-Elwes
towards Catholicism was one of 'polite abhorrence'. Yet at
the High Mass at the church of St. Roch in Nice, Mozart's
'Gloria in Excelsis' was something 'too beautiful' for her.
Nevertheless in the afternoon the couple attended the 'quiet
and refreshing' service in the Protestant church frequented
by English sojourners on the French Riviera.

In 1874, seven years later, Valentine and Alice Cary-
Elwes were received into the Roman Catholic Church in
Nice. They were following in the footsteps of a Cary-Elwes
cousin, a Captain in the Scots Fusiliers. At the age of seven-
teen Windsor Cary-Elwes had been received into the
Church after spending some time with a German family in
Hanover. In true military fashion, he had made his deci-
sion on the basis of empty Lutheran churches and full
Roman Catholic ones. His grandmother, the Hon. Mrs
Arabella Heneage of Hainton Hall in Lincolnshire and a
daughter of the first Lord Yarborough, had become a
Catholic. He also had a convert uncle, the Reverend Henry
Pelham Heneage who later became the first resident priest
at Erdington near Birmingham. But the person who influ-
enced him most was the Hon. and Reverend William Law,
brother of the second Lord Ellenborough. When William
Law became a Catholic in 1851 he had been reduced to
poverty, a fact which had outraged his Protestant relatives.
Captain Windsor Cary-Elwes married William Law's
daughter. It was the company of Windsor and his attractive
wife with her beautiful contralto voice which led to many
musical evenings with Valentine and Alice Cary-Elwes in
Nice. They were joined on these occasions by the old
Catholic Bodenham and Clifford families, who all went to
Mass at the Ursuline convent close by.

A sermon preached at the Ursuline convent by Abbé
Vallet on one Fold and one Shepherd caused Alice Cary-
Elwes to be assailed by doubts for the first time.[35] She went
straight to the Protestant church where she sought solace
in Handel's 'Hallelujah' chorus. The Bodenhams then
steered her towards the church of Notre Dame de

Laghetto. Here Alice Cary-Elwes thought the devotion of
the congregation a form of madness. She was introduced
to the Mother Superior at the Ursuline convent and once
again was impressed by the nuns' chaplain, the Abbé
Vallet. The Cary-Elweses then started to attend a course of
instruction at the church of Notre Dame. One evening in
Spring the Abbé came to their villa and talked a great deal.
The couple had arranged to return to England but
changed their plans. They installed their children with
their nanny in the Hotel Provence in Cannes and returned
to Nice. For the whole of May they followed a devout
routine and gradually Catholic devotion to the Blessed
Virgin Mary became clear. Alice Cary-Elwes wrote: 'Every
hour of every day there becomes a little more light, a little
more faith and a great deal more happiness and peace.' A
few days later she wrote in her diary: 'More and more
astonished; more and more startled at my gross ignorance
for so long. Père told Val that talking to me was like talking
to a Turk – Merci!'[36] With continued searching, questioning and answering, reading, studying and praying,
Valentine and Alice Cary-Elwes spent May in Provence,
many miles from damp Northamptonshire. On Trinity
Sunday 1874 they were received into the Church at the
Ursuline convent.

Alice Cary-Elwes wrote that it seemed 'like a little
paradise up there in the early morning, and when we got
inside and the Mass started with the children singing it was
as if Heaven had opened.' Just before they received their
first Communion Père Vallet spoke on the words 'The
Master is come and calleth for thee'. Alice wrote:
'Everyone in the chapel cried, and no wonder, it was such
an inspired word. Mère Superieure gave us music all
through, Mozart, which very much crowned the effect of it
all.'[37] After Mass they went to the convent parlour for
biscuits and wine and were presented with bouquets, later
placed on the High Altar at Notre Dame in thanksgiving.
The Cary-Elwes family and their English Catholic friends
lingered under the orange trees until lunch. Vespers in the
afternoon was followed by tea with the Cliffords. They
heard a sermon at the convent on the conclusion of the

May devotions to the Blessed Virgin Mary and the couple consecrated themselves to her. 'We spoke of our happy day, and said how we had felt one day not long enough, the sky, the sun not bright enough to express our feelings of thankfulness and joy.'[38]

'I do indeed mourn as if two deaths had happened in one day in my family', wrote the Bishop of Lincoln when he heard the news. 'But God's will be done, and if we cannot pray with you nothing shall prevent our praying for you'. Valentine and Alice travelled back to England, calling on the Bodenhams in Paris and Windsor Cary-Elwes in Boulogne on the way. They completed their journey with a reunion with George Lane-Fox at the Jesuit church in Farm Street. It was not long before Billing gave the impression of a country house long inhabited by Catholics. 'It seemed impossible to imagine Billing without its beautiful little chapel containing always the Blessed Sacrament and its essentially Catholic atmosphere, scarcely sensed and yet all pervading and apparently immemorial.'[39] The Rector at Billing, outraged at the change, called the tenant farmers on the estate for a meeting of protest and arranged for a Scripture reader to be sent from Northampton to deliver sermons against Catholicism. But Valentine and Alice Cary-Elwes pressed ahead. They created a church out of a disused school-house in Billing village. At Brigg in Lincolnshire, where the family also had a foothold, they built a Catholic church with 'basilica-like proportions, with two chapels in the transepts'. In 1876 their son Gervase was received into the Church. Alice recalled: 'It was a sight to be long remembered, his sweet, earnest face buried in his hands. All the servants received Holy Communion with him and he knelt between his father and me only two years after *our* first Communion'.[40]

It was the convert Gervase Elwes who in 1889 married Lady Winefride Feilding. While Lady Winefride's parents-in-law had been received into the Church in the heavenly bloom of a provençal spring, her father had reached the same destination in a windswept convent in Edinburgh.

Lady Winefride Feilding first saw Billing 'covered with wistaria blossom and standing surrounded by its glorious trees, with rolling lawns running down to a line of ponds...

I have never known a house where the feeling of home prevailed so powerfully. The place was haunted with it.'[41] This was praise indeed from someone who had grown up at Downing and Newnham Paddox. Like her mother before her, Lady Winefride went on a retreat before her wedding and was encouraged by a Jesuit to say her morning and evening prayers with her husband. After the baptism of their eldest son, he was laid on the altar of the Lady Chapel at Billing, a prayer said over him and the new born baby was consecrated to the Blessed Virgin Mary. Thus it was with each of their children.

Gervase Elwes's talent for singing was nurtured at entertainments and festivities at Hainton in Lincolnshire, home of the Heneages. He became in demand more and more for public performances, singing the part of Gerontius in Elgar's oratorio of John Henry Newman's poem. Such a performance combined the talents of three English Roman Catholics: singer, poet and composer. A member of the audience wrote to Gervase that the fear of death had for long been a source of distress to him:

> The night I heard *The Dream of Gerontius* a new vision came to me and the whole point of view was changed; it was exactly as though a great burden of darkness and horror fell away and light and peace took their place. The joy was very wonderful and my impulse was to write at once to tell you. I decided, however, to wait a year in order to test the reality of the change. As no change has come except an added assurance and thankfulness of experience, I feel I should like you to know this. I cannot, of course, explain how the change came. ...[42]

Notes

1 'The late Earl of Denbigh', *The Times*, 17 March 1892, p. 11.
2 W. Elwes, *The Feilding Album*, London, Geoffrey Bles, 1950, p. 40.
3 Warwick Record Office, CR2017 To Louisa Pennant from J. Baylee.
4 Elwes, op. cit., p. 42.

5   Lady Herbert, *Impressions of Spain in 1866*, London, Richard Bentley, 1867, p. 111.
6   Ibid.
7   Ibid., p. 112.
8   Ibid., p. 115.
9   Ibid., p. 117.
10 Warwick Record Office, op. cit.
11 Elwes, op. cit., p. 46.
12 Ibid., p. 49.
13 Warwick Record Office, CR2017/F170. Facts and Correspondence relating to the admission in to the Catholic Church of Viscount and Viscountess Feilding by Right Reverend Bishop Gillis, Edinburgh, Charles Dolman, 1850, p. ii.
14 Elwes, op. cit., p. 52.
15 Ibid., p. 57.
16 Warwick Record Office, CR2017/C415/5.
17 Ibid.
18 Warwick Record Office CR2017/C415/3.
19 Elwes, op. cit., p. 57.
20 Warwick Record Office CR2017/C415/5.
21 Elwes, op. cit., p. 54.
22 Ibid., p. 55.
23 Ibid.
24 Ibid.
25 Ibid., pp. 68, 70, 71, 73.
26 Ibid., p. 80.
27 Lady C. Kerr, *Edith Feilding. Sister of Charity*, London, Sands & Company, 1933, p. 9.
28 Elwes, op. cit., p. 99.
29 Ibid., pp. 115–16.
30 Ibid., p. 126.
31 Kerr, op. cit., p. 11.
32 Elwes, op. cit., p. 165.
33 Kerr, op. cit., pp. 25, 26.
34 Ibid., p. 59.
35 W. Elwes and R. Elwes, *Gervase Elwes. The Story of his Life*, London, Grayson & Grayson, 1935, pp. 11, 17, 18, 19.
36 Ibid., p. 21.
37 Ibid.
38 Ibid., p. 24.
39 Ibid., pp. 22–26 *passim.*
40 Ibid., p. 29.
41 Ibid., p. 56.
42 Ibid., p. 214.

Chapter Seven

A place of refuge

When the Feildings witnessed Dom Bosco's cure of the
dumb boy in the basilica in Turin, one of their travelling
companions had been Cecil, Marchioness of Lothian. In
May 1877 the Marchioness lay dying in the Hotel Roma in
Rome. She had come to Rome with fellow English
Catholics to celebrate the Jubilee of Pope Pius IX. Staying
with her at the Hotel Roma was Lord Ralph Kerr, the Duke
of Norfolk and his two sisters. Four years before, this same
party had taken part in the first pilgrimage to leave
England since the Reformation. Their steamer from
Newhaven to Dieppe had flown the Standard of the Sacred
Heart and they had thence made their way to Paray-le-
Monial. 'There was a mixture of religious and national
patriotism in our minds which produced feelings of the
purest happiness.'[1] On the day the English party in Rome
was due to have their audience with the Holy Father, Lady
Lothian took to her bed. Not long afterwards, surrounded
by her prayerful friends she opened her eyes, looked about
her, looked up to heaven and closed her eyes for the last
time. She said: "Janua Coeli, ora pro me." At the moment
of her death the bells of San Carlo and other churches
happened to ring out their joyous peals. The blinds were
drawn open and the rays of the setting sun flooded the
room, illuminating the Marchioness's calm and beautiful
face.[2]

Cecil, Marchioness of Lothian had been born in 1808 at
Ingestre Hall in Staffordshire, the daughter of the second

Earl Talbot. Her childhood was centred on regular atten-
dance at church, quiet Sundays with no music or card
playing and daily family prayers. There was 'a deep sense of
morality and respectability, and a dread of enthusiasm or
exaggeration – such was the old-fashioned Church and
State orthodoxy which reigned supreme in Lord Talbot's
family'.[3] Lord Talbot displayed some sympathy with
Catholicism when he allowed the chapel attached to Tixall
Hall near Ingestre to be moved to Great Heywood, when
Tixall fell into Protestant hands. When in 1831 Cecil
Talbot married the seventh Marquess of Lothian Lord
Talbot gave his daughter spiritual direction, urging her
simply to trust God. 'Make Him the idol of your heart,
refer to Him in all your difficulties, and whatever may be
the storms of your life, He will bring you at last to a place
of refuge.'[4] She should obey her husband, be watchful of
his looks and fulfil his wishes, be open and unreserved with
him, but reserved and cautious with all other men. She
should be cautious with women friends, relying only upon
those who were good and religious. Married life being one
of either happiness or misery, much depended on the tact
and conduct of the wife. Cecil followed her father's advice
and was supremely happy. Her life was spent travelling
from house to house in Scotland, following the annual
whirl of landed entertainment of the time. She struck up a
particularly close friendship with the young Duchess of
Buccleuch, formerly Lady Charlotte Thynne, a daughter of
the Marquess of Bath. The Marchioness and the Duchess
had close connections with the Church of England. The
Marchioness's brother-in-law, Lord Henry Kerr was Vicar
of Dittisham in Devon and the Duchess's brother Lord
Charles Thynne, Vicar of Longbridge Deverill in Wiltshire.
Both the Reverend Lord Henry Kerr and the Reverend
Lord Charles Thynne later became Roman Catholics.

Ten years of supreme happiness were cut short by the
death of the Marquess of Lothian. Cecil was inconsolable
and wrote in her diary on the last day of 1841 that she was
parting with the last year of her happiness. She only hoped
that God would support and guide her during the sad
remainder of her days. On the first day of 1842 she wrote

that she was entering on the year with an aching heart and
that each day her misery increased. 'Oh, may He give me
strength to bear the burden laid upon me, and turn it into
good.'[5]

The Marchioness's bereavement coincided with the
search for Truth among a certain group of Anglican clergymen in Oxford. Far away in Scotland the young widow
found herself increasingly reluctant to attend the services
in the kirk and more inclined to go to the episcopal
church in Edinburgh. When she was in London she
attended services in Westminster Abbey. On Easter Day in
1844 she woke in the morning with a joyful heart for the
first time since her bereavement. In 1845 she travelled to
France and went to Vespers at St. Ouen. The procession of
priests in their rich vestments carrying candles and
chanting, an altar blazing with lights while the setting sun
shone through the brilliant stained glass, she never forgot.
Meanwhile in Scotland a Mr Robertson was appointed
chaplain to the new episcopal church which the Duke of
Buccleuch was building in Dalkeith. Among Mr
Robertson's congregation was a woman whose sister had
become a Catholic. She gave Mr Robertson a copy of an
old Venetian breviary, which he started to use. On her
return to Scotland the Marchioness of Lothian became a
regular attender at Mr Robertson's high church services at
Dalkeith, walking the mile and a half to early communion
every Sunday. After a couple of years Mr Robertson
resigned his post and became a Roman Catholic. The
Marchioness wrote to the Duchess of Buccleuch expressing
great sympathy with her, who had had 'her full share in all
the distress which Mr Robertson's secession has occasioned
to us.'[6]

In the material sense the Reverend Robertson suffered
greatly as a result of his conversion in 1847. He was
ordained to the priesthood and worked among the poor in
Greenwich, until his failing health prompted him to retire
as chaplain to the nuns of the Sacred Heart at
Roehampton. He was a 'scholar and saint combined; the
Catholic priest graft upon the Oxford don.'[7] Almost his last
act at Roehampton was to give Extreme Unction to a lay

sister of seventy-three whose death was imminent. She made a rapid recovery and lived for another twenty years. Father Robertson prophesied accurately the date of his own death and was buried in the cemetery at Roehampton.

The Marchioness of Lothian was finding herself drawn closer and closer to the Church which the Duchess of Buccleuch's chaplain had joined. Her son, Lord Ralph Kerr, noticed that prayer and inquiry were leading his mother to Rome but 'the prospect it offered for the future was sufficiently terrible to appal the strongest heart' – separation from friends and children, the misunderstanding and puzzlement of friends. The problem centred on the guardians of her children, who were her brother-in-law Lord Henry Kerr, not then a Catholic, Lord Home, Lord Clanwilliam and her brother John Talbot. When the children's governess became an ardent disciple of the recently departed Mr Robertson, the guardians insisted on her dismissal.

It was the Gorham Judgment in 1850 when Privy Councillors ruled that it was not necessary to believe that baptism was a Sacrament, which provided the final blow for Cecil Lothian. Several months earlier she had written to her brother saying she did not feel she could be a martyr for the Church of England. In December 1850 she declared: 'I am very unhappy. I feel as if I were trifling with the concerns of eternity out of sheer cowardice, catching at every straw as an excuse for waiting.'[8] On Passion Sunday 1851 Henry Manning and James Hope-Scott were received into the Roman Catholic Church. For a long time Cecil had said that Manning's course would settle hers. In Scotland she offered to drive one of Mr Robertson's converts to St. Margaret's Convent in Edinburgh in her pony carriage. They arrived at the convent and when the door was opened Cecil looked in curiously, saying she would look around the court and then in the chapel. The chapel door was open. She went in immediately to kneel in front of the Blessed Sacrament. In the presence of the consecrated Host exposed in the monstrance she had at last found her spiritual home. Her misgivings about Anglicanism had centred on the lack of authoritative teaching on Holy Communion. She was troubled that some believed that it was the Body and Blood of Christ and that others thought that it was merely bread and wine taken in remembrance of the crucifixion.[9] In the Catholic Church, the consecrated Host was God.

Cecil, Marchioness of Lothian, was received into the Church by the Jesuit Father Brownbill at Farm Street on 11th June 1851. She had been visiting the church of the Immaculate Conception in Farm Street since the beginning of June, finding the Latin Mass confusing and distressing. Four days later she was able to follow the Mass with less difficulty. Three days after that she announced that it was a glorious service. Father Brownbill spoke to her in a comforting way about the condition of those who 'in simple Faith remain in Protestant Churches'. She made her first Confession and after her first Communion spoke of the 'blessings unspeakable and inconceivable' which followed. Thereafter her last thought at night and the first on waking was the 'happy thankful consciousness' of being a Catholic. She wrote to Lord Henry Kerr that she wished all doubters could receive Holy Communion: 'One communion would dispel all doubts. They would disperse as mists before the sun.'[10] She acknowledged that the High Anglican church had nurtured her prayerful search for the Truth, and wanted to kneel and give thanks for reaching the end of her quest when she passed St. Mary's church in Edinburgh. She also knew that offering her Communion for her husband on the anniversary of his death helped him. It was the happiest remembrance of his death for ten years.[11]

In 1852 the late Marquess of Lothian's brother, Lord Henry Kerr, followed his sister-in-law into the Church of Rome. A month after that he was followed in turn by his wife Louisa, sister of James Hope-Scott, and their children. Then Lady Lothian's daughters, Lady Alice and Lady Cecil started to receive Instruction. The Marchioness's spiritual isolation was coming to an end but the guardians of her children were not pleased. Lady Alice Kerr wrote to Lord Feilding in January 1854 describing the drama of the thwarted attempt by the guardians to prevent her brothers from being received into the Church, – for the success of which she thanked her Guardian Angels. Afraid Lord Lothian would take his younger brother Lord John Kerr off to school by force, the Marchioness took Lord John to Edinburgh at dawn, having arranged for a carriage to meet them on the way. Lord Ralph, who had been hesitating, decided at the last minute to follow his mother and brother and go to Edinburgh with them, where the two boys were received into the Church. Lady Alice told Lord Feilding: 'The boys are very happy and so are we. The bishop has been most kind. John is going to Ushaw and Ralph I think to a place near Birmingham which I can't spell. It begins with an E, something to do with the Oratorians.'[12]

When Lord Ralph Kerr left the Oratory School at Edgbaston he joined the Army, married Lady Anne Fitzalan Howard, daughter of the 14th Duke of Norfolk and became a Major-General. His younger brother Lord John died while still in the seminary at Ushaw. Lord Lothian married his cousin Lady Constance Talbot and died at a young age. His brother Lord Schomberg inherited the title and married a daughter of the convert Duchess of Buccleuch, neither of whom became Catholics. Another brother, Lord Walter Kerr, an Admiral of the Fleet, married Lady Amabel Cowper, and both were converts. Of Lady Lothian's daughters, Lady Alice Kerr later married and Lady Cecil Kerr entered the religious life, becoming a nun of the Society of the Sacred Heart.

⚜

The Society of the Sacred Heart was founded in France in 1826 by St. Madeleine Sophie Barat, the daughter of a Burgundian craftsman. From a small beginning at Amiens in 1800 the number of the Society's schools for the education of girls in the wake of the Revolution grew and continued to grow after the death of Madeleine Sophie in 1864. A convent was opened in Roehampton which Lady Cecil Kerr entered in 1859, the same year in which her cousin Henrietta Kerr first met Mother Madeleine Barat in Paris.

The Hon. Henrietta Kerr was the daughter of Lord
Henry Kerr, formerly vicar of Dittisham in Devon. Her
mother, Lady Louisa Kerr had saintly qualities; on first
meeting her one Jesuit regretted that the times of persecution were over; 'I know of no one who would have walked
up to the scaffold so gallantly as she.'[13] The Kerrs had
visited Paris in 1845 and attended Mass on the Feast of the
Assumption at the school of the Christian Brothers. Lord
Henry wrote: 'All has the appearance of truest devotion.
Alas! I cannot join in it. The heat is so great, the smell of
the incense so powerful and the organ and other instruments so overpowering that my head, already aching,
cannot stand it'.[14] But while taking a cure for gout in
Clifton seven years later Lord Henry was visited by Father
William Vaughan and through the mysterious workings of
Divine Grace he was reconciled to the Church.

The family visited Monteviot where Lord Henry's
mother was distressed at their new found Faith. Henrietta
remembered entering the room during controversial
conversations and finding her grandmother in tears. Once,
on opening a letter from Lord Henry, 'she lost all self-
control and accused him of killing my mother and
disgracing the family'.[15] The young Henrietta then over-
heard a nursery maid discussing the news of Lord Henry's
conversion, saying he had been seen in the Popish chapel
'kneeling before the altar, receiving Confirmation from a
Popish Bishop'. Henrietta protested that it was all lies and
nothing would induce her to follow her father's example.
At that moment Lord and Lady Kerr sent for their
daughter to tell her of their decision to become Catholics
and that they would never return to Dittisham. 'This news,
and the thought of giving up my pony and boat, the
church, my little garden, and all the things of which I was
so fond, quite upset me, and I cried myself ill.'[16] For two
weeks Henrietta did not yield despite the kindness of
Bishop Grant and her mother's endeavours. But the reception of one of her brothers intrigued her. Like her aunt
Cecil, Marchioness of Lothian, Exposition of the Blessed
Sacrament at Benediction prompted her wish for
Instruction. Henrietta was received on the Feast of Mater

Admirabilis, 20th October 1852. From Dittisham the Kerrs moved to Huntlyburn near Melrose, where the Blessed Sacrament was reserved in the chapel in the house.

Henrietta Kerr's Scottish Catholic childhood reached a new turning point after her conversion when she read the lives of the Japanese Martyrs, St. Paul Miki and his companions, Jesuits and Franciscans crucified near Nagasaki in 1597 – Christianity having been brought to Japan by St. Francis Xavier in 1549. Reading their lives by the fire in Huntlyburn three hundred years later, Henrietta's brother recalled his sister 'springing forward with her hands clasped and her hair all tumbled back, every bit of shyness and reserve gone, and a perfectly brilliant light shining over her face. "Oh, mama" she exclaimed, "do you think there is any chance we might still be martyrs?" '[17] It was not long after this outburst that Henrietta met Madeleine Sophie Barat, foundress of the Sacred Heart nuns in Paris. Mother Barat put her hands on Henrietta's shoulders almost forcing her to kneel down for her blessing and said in a very marked way: ' "Mon enfant, je prierai pour vous." ' [18]

The following year found Henrietta in Rome, where she was 'growing by degrees to realise more and more the privilege of treading on the very ground made sacred by the martyrs, of breathing the air sanctified by the lives of so many servants of God ...' Back in Scotland she was happy but was conscious of something holier than the most perfect home-life, 'sanctified as hers was by the virtues of her parents, the Catholic atmosphere which, in the midst of a Protestant country was breathed with marvellous purity at Huntlyburn ...' While out riding on the Scottish moors she told her father of her decision to become a nun. She saw how bitterly he was grieving. He took out of his pocket Thomas à Kempis's *The Imitation of Christ* and tried to read a verse or two. She heard her father was not reading it well and saw that it was because of his tears.[19]

Amidst the austerity of the novitiate at Conflans, the Reverend Mother pronounced that God had never bestowed a greater gift on the Society of the Sacred Heart than Henrietta Kerr. Her father said farewell to his daughter and went to the Jesuits' church nearby, saying a prayer at Our Lady's altar where they had received Communion that morning, a *Suscipe* at the High Altar and an *O Deus meus* at the altar of St. Francis Xavier. He went back to the hotel, said a prayer by his daughter's bedside, paid the bill and went to the station. Henrietta was not the only one of his children to enter the religious life. Her brother the Hon. Schomberg Kerr later became a Jesuit.

Born on the Feast of the Assumption, 1838, Schomberg was educated at Winchester. Revisiting the college fifty years later it was with particular pleasure that he pointed to the statue of the Blessed Virgin Mary which still remained in its niche and which Wykehamists honoured by raising their caps when they passed beneath the archway.[20] His parents became Catholics while he was at Winchester and three years after he left he was himself received. His family had been surprised one morning to see Schomberg returning from an early Mass at Galashiels while they were on their way to High Mass. He was received into the Church the following morning – 'Lady Henry, weeping for joy, rang the bell to tell the butler the good news and the family and household went to the chapel at Huntlyburn to give thanks.'

Schomberg joined the Royal Navy and used to say the five sorrowful mysteries of the rosary during the first and middle watch at sea. After one very stormy transatlantic homeward crossing he sent a statue of Notre Dame De La Garde to the church at Halifax in Newfoundland in thanksgiving for his safe return, having a particular devotion to the seafarers' shrine in Marseilles. In 1867 he joined H.M.S. *Bellerophon* but on becoming ill returned to Scotland. He returned to his ship but was struck down again. During his sick leave he consulted a Jesuit and decided to leave the Navy and become a priest. He later wrote that he had always preferred the church to the ballroom and recalled that he and his sister Henrietta had made a promise as children to serve God in the religious life. His fellow officers in the Mess were not surprised at his chosen vocation. But he had nevertheless always put off going on a retreat to decide his future, 'accepting some accidental excuse as God's will, fearing it might end in my being called.'[21]

Captain the Hon. Schomberg Kerr R.N., with a brilliant future ahead of him at sea, entered the Jesuit novitiate to explore the depths of Ignatian spirituality. He had not pursued any further Latin studies after Winchester but forged ahead with a patchwork of 'elegant Ciceronian terms', wanting to know the Latin for 'to cut one's cable'and 'get things ship-shape'. As the scion of a landed family he had never spent more than four months in the same place. But he never flinched from the monotony of life in the novitiate, saying that the Navy had taught him obedience and fortitude, courage and loyalty to superiors. As a novice he later travelled by sea from Liverpool to Greenock. The Captain discovering that he was on board sought him out. The Captain remembered the glorious sunset, glimpses of the Irish coast and the humility of Brother Schomberg, formerly Captain Schomberg Kerr, who 'listened to our immature and inexperienced remarks as if we were a veritable Sorbonne.'[22]

In 1871 Brother Schomberg had gone to the Jesuits' college of Mount St. Mary's near Chesterfield and there introduced the custom of marching the boys to chapel. Two years later he was at St. Beuno's College in Wales. During a sojourn at Barmouth the Jesuits were joined by some Benedictines from Belmont and together they manned a flotilla of four-oared boats. Brother Schomberg, cruising about in a pair-oar and signalling with flags, gave his ecclesiastical crews lessons in rowing. When they hit a sandbank he took over, shortening some sail and spreading others, giving everyone on board a rope to pull and managing to swing the boat round into deeper water, when the local boatmen were ordered about in a way to which they were not accustomed.[23] Two years later Brother Schomberg was ordained as Father Henry Kerr and in 1879 he was sent as Army chaplain in Cyprus. His next post was as chaplain to the Roman Catholic Viceroy of India, the Marquess of Ripon. In preparation for this, Father Henry visited again the shrine of Notre Dame de la Garde in Marseilles. In Malta he lunched with former brother-officers on the troop ship *Tamar*. At Port Said he left the *Tamar* and said Mass in steerage for twenty Catholics on board H.M.S. *Torch*. When he set sail for India with the Marquess of Ripon, Father Henry said Mass daily in the Viceroy's cabin. They arrived in May 1878, and as soon as they were ashore Father Henry called on the Catholic Bishop of Bombay, also a Jesuit, before arriving in time to say grace at Government House. There was a reception with band and fireworks 'cloths of scarlet, many-coloured coats of dazzling splendour, diamonds, jewels, stars of India....'[24] The splendid library at Government House was used for Mass, attended by the Viceroy holding a rosary, thirteen troopers and a few servants.

From India Father Henry was sent to the Jesuits' Zambesi mission. General Gordon, then Private Secretary to Lord Ripon, had asked Father Henry to join him on the Khartoum Expedition to evangelise the Egyptians and Sudanese. Instead Father Kerr ended his days with the Jesuits' mission. Shortly before setting off he spent a day with his brother, who heard his Confession. 'Schomberg, in his humility, knelt down in a corner of the cold, dreary custom-house shed to make his confession and receive absolution from me before the midnight train arrived.' He died on the mission. The priest who was with him in his last moments said that half an hour before he died he raised his arm to his forehead to make the Sign of the Cross and Father Ryan finished it for him. He ceased to breathe so gently that the priest was praying with him for some minutes after his death. Another priest recalled taking his leave from the dying Father Kerr: 'I still remember the cheerful, encouraging farewell he gave me as I parted with him.'[25]

Notes

[1] E. Butler, *An Autobiography*, London, Constable, 1922, p. 99.
[2] C. Kerr (ed.), *Cecil, Marchioness of Lothian*, London, Sands and Company, 1922, pp. 229–230.
[3] Ibid., p. 2.
[4] Ibid., p. 11.
[5] Ibid., p. 36.
[6] Ibid., p. 75.

[7]   A. Pollen, *Mother Mabel Digby. A Biography of the Superior General of the Society of the Sacred Heart 1835–1911*, London, John Murray, 1914, p. 118.

[8]   Kerr, op. cit., p. 88.

[9]   Ibid., p. 91.

[10]   Ibid., pp. 96, 108.

[11]   Ibid., p. 112.

[12]   Warwick Record Office, Letter from Lady Alice Kerr to Lord Feilding, 22 Jan. 1854; CR2017/C448.

[13]   J. Morris, *The Life of Mother Henrietta Kerr, Religious of the Sacred Heart*, Roehampton, 1887, p. 6.

[14]   Ibid., p. 11.

[15]   Ibid., p. 20.

[16]   Ibid., p. 22.

[17]   Ibid., p. 29.

[18]   Ibid., p. 40.

[19]   Ibid., pp. 68, 78.

[20]   Hon. Mrs Maxwell-Scott, *Henry Schomberg Kerr. Sailor and Jesuit*, London, Longman, 1901, p. 6.

[21]   Ibid., p. 82.

[22]   Ibid., p. 118.

[23]   Ibid., p. 125.

[24]   Ibid., p. 171.

[25]   Ibid., p. 282.

Chapter Eight

No Romanists in the house

Mother Henrietta Kerr, sister of Father Henry Kerr S.J., was attended in her last days by a novice at the Sacred Heart convent in Roehampton who had entered in 1882. She was Janet Erskine Stuart, daughter of the Rector of Cottesmore in Rutland. Her father's parsonage in the 'blue-flowering county of Rutland', surrounded by 'innumerable tiny chimes rung by the heather and of the indomitable delicacy of harebells joining in that music, of swimming mists and a tingling air' was where Janet discovered Roman Catholicism.[1] The Reverend Andrew Stuart lived in a grey stone rectory with high gables and mullioned windows, its walls overgrown with lichen and ivy, in a county of rich meadow lands, hedgerows, oaks and woodlands, of hills which swept down to low fen lands. In springtime the woods were carpeted with bluebells; in summer the bright blue of the flax lit up the hillsides. Corn-growing, cattle-breeding, nightingales, wild duck and hunting; Anglo-Saxon kings bestowed Rutland as a dowry on their Queens.

The Stuarts of Castle Stuart were descendants of the Earl of Fife and Monteith, created Duke of Albany in 1398. The Reverend Andrew Stuart married in 1849 a niece of the first Earl of Gainsborough from Exton Park, two miles away. Mary Noel was the rector's second wife, and Janet was the youngest of their six children. Her mother died when she was two and Janet was brought up by her elder sister Theodosia who was close friends with her Noel cousins at

Exton. In 1866 Exton Park became a Catholic home when the convert second Earl and Countess of Gainsborough inherited the estate. Their daughters Lady Constance and Lady Edith Noel became friends with their Stuart cousins.

One evening when Janet Stuart was thirteen she and her brother Douglas were working in silence in the school room at Cottesmore. Douglas looked up from the book he was reading and said 'Aristotle says every rational being must have a last end. What is yours?' Janet said she did not know. 'I made up my mind that it must be found. The search lasted seven years and was one of the happiest times of my life. It began by my examining the grounds of my faith, and they all melted away.'[2] Lady Edith Noel, who later became a Sister of Charity, had lent Archbishop Ullathorne's *Ecclesiastical Discourses* to another of Janet's brothers, which Janet perused. Then, talking with Lady Edith she later recalled that 'It came upon me like a flash of lightning, that it might be in the Catholic Church that I should find the last end and the truth.' That night was spent reading the Penny Catechism. The first question and answer ('Who made me? God made me) impressed her with a conviction she never lost. She then read Manning's *Grounds for Faith.* She wrote to a friend that her devotion to the Blessed Virgin Mary began with a recitation of the *Memorare,* which 'took me off my feet at once, for it was so daring a statement that I thought it would not have lived if it had been a lie'. She said it constantly and clung to it as 'the first definite something that seemed to come automatically after my seven years of groping in the dark'.[3]

Frequent visits to Exton followed during which Janet little realised the influence of those first nights spent under the same roof as the Blessed Sacrament. Here she met Catholic priests for the first time and absorbed the atmosphere of a devout Catholic household. The second Earl of Gainsborough had become a Catholic in 1850 along with his wife. As Viscount and Viscountess Campden it was seventeen years before they inherited the title. Viscountess Campden was a daughter of the sixteenth Earl of Erroll and was known as Queen Ida because of her descent from King William IV. She died within a week of taking possession of Exton, 'after sighing and pining because her title was so long a-coming....' Five bishops and thirty priests were present at her funeral in 1867 and 'the poor Queen was laid in a vault made on purpose on the site of a little chapel of which the foundations have only just been traced out'.[4] The Archbishop of Westminster preached a short sermon and a bishop present remarked that such a funeral reached the heart of many for whom it was an introduction to Catholicism. Eleven years later Janet Erskine Stuart breathed in the atmosphere at Exton and 'thus was begun a new work of God in her soul'.[5]

An after-dinner conversation with one guest, a Mrs Ross, led to their arranging to meet in London, it not being possible to continue their conversation at the Hunt breakfast the following day. The two women met in Curzon Street and soon afterwards Janet Stuart was introduced to Father Gallwey from Farm Street. When he arrived it was not the Jesuit of fiction who walked into the room 'but simply Father Gallwey ... with the vision in his eyes, and his kind smile, and his quick shuffle and his reassuring abruptness of speech ...' He talked of the existence of God, the Church as the Divine Teacher and the only authentic witness of the Truth, the living authority on earth. In his turn he was impressed that Janet did not come back to the same point once it had been answered.[6]

Three months later, in March 1879, the daughter of the Rector of Cottesmore was received into the Church at the Sacred Heart chapel in the church of the Immaculate Conception in Mayfair. She knew that it would break her father's heart. He had urged her to be loyal to the church of her baptism, to hang on until better times, not to desire a philosophy as well as a religion, and not to commit the grave sin of moral suicide. Although her father never lost his love for her, as a clergyman he felt he could not have a Romanist in his house. His daughter's response was, 'Yesterday has gone, let it go utterly ... even the sweetness, even the light of yesterday. It did its work, it was a stepping stone, safe for a moment, then engulfed.'[7]

For the next three years the rector's daughter spent her days hunting and fishing, her evenings in prayer and study.

She went to Ireland for grouse-shooting at Dunlewy House in north-west Donegal and there she learned salmon fishing. She took long walks in the hills from where she gazed at the crashing Atlantic waves. Two miles from Dunlewy was a small chapel dedicated to the Sacred Heart, where she went to daily Mass. She then went to Huntingdonshire, where she learned to hunt; something she had never done despite her upbringing in Cottesmore. Fearless on horseback, she had many falls. 'Oh! The thrilling breathlessness of seeing the flash of four shining hoofs over one's head, as one extricates oneself from a muddy ditch.' Once in a ditch she stopped her terrified horse from bolting just by her voice. The horse stood still, trembling until she was able to creep back and reassure him. But Father Gallwey hinted that she was born for greater things than horses and fish. She herself observed that once thrown off a horse 'one goes home in a meditative mood'.[8]

She went to Paris, Dresden, Munich and Oberammergau. She returned to England, not to the blue-flowering hills of Rutland, but to London, where in Regent's Park her attention was caught by some blue late-flowering hyacinths. In that mysterious moment she saw it all. She had that day been praying about a calling to the religious life on her way to the convent of the Helpers of the Holy Souls. Entering the chapel, the Blessed Sacrament was exposed in a monstrance. The nun who was praying was replaced by another as she arrived. Janet asked God that if indeed a vocation to the religious life was hers, she would be at the prie dieu. At that moment the nun got up and asked the prayerful figure of Janet Erskine Stuart to take her place, saying she was too ill to stay.

A retreat at the Sacred Heart convent at Roehampton which followed found her in extreme desolation of spirit. After such an active life could she sacrifice the world for these thirty three acres? She braced herself to offer herself to God. At once the chapel and the rooms at Roehampton were 'flooded with light and echoed glory'. The last few months in the world were spent saying farewell to the fields and hills which had been the silent witnesses of her spiritual journey. For one last time she went to Ireland and visited Knock, where three years before in 1879 villagers had seen the Blessed Virgin Mary, St. Joseph and St. John in front of an altar surrounded by angels, upon which was a cross and a lamb. Fifteen people of all ages saw the vision and they watched in the pouring rain for two hours reciting the rosary. The parish priest at Knock blessed Janet Stuart. These were months of intense living and intense dying. She returned to Cottesmore for the first time as a Catholic and the wrench of departure was keenly felt. So too was her first encounter with religious life: '... one simply gives all and goes in for death or life or whatever God chooses and that is better than any high spirits or excitement'.[9] Her next few years were like 'a hillside of brown and broken bracken, through which the tenderest luminous green fonds irrepressibly project themselves, but curled and crumpled back'. At the Mother House in Paris the 'green fronds began to un-curl in the gentler airs of spring'.[10] On 12th February 1889 she made her final profession in Paris and returned to Roehampton.

The Reverend Mother at Roehampton was Mother Mabel Digby, who shared Mother Stuart's passion for hunting. As Mistress of Novices, Mother Stuart drew on hunting analogies to illustrate the battles of the soul. 'We are not riding out for exercise, Sisters, we are hunting for Sport's sake, hence these fences, bull-finches, five-barred gates and even occasional rolls in the mud are all part of the day's sport.' One novice was told to handle her rebellious nature 'as your father taught you to handle your Arab chestnut'. 'You must be thorough-breds, Sisters.' Mother Stuart recalled a moment in her own hunting history to illustrate a point. 'For two or three awful moments I was able to call the hounds off and hold them back till the huntsman came up. We do not always kill the stag, and this one we let go. Do you understand?'[11]

When Mother Digby died at Ixelles in 1911 Mother Stuart, Superior since 1895, kissed the hem of Mother Digby's habit. She genuflected in the chapel but did not know where to sit. 'Mais vous êtes Vicaire Générale' she was told. After the funeral, Mother Digby's coffin was slowly carried between the long line of nuns. The black plumes of the horses could be seen on the other side of the convent wall as it started its journey back to England. A sacred past had silently closed with Mother Digby's death. A new life of ceaseless travel and relentless responsibility had opened up for Mother Stuart, now Vicar General of the Society of the Sacred Heart. No longer confined to the thirty three acres in Roehampton she spent the rest of her days visiting Sacred Heart convents throughout Europe and in Egypt, Australia, North America, South America and Japan. One hundred days were spent at sea, one hundred convents visited. She was likened to the Society's foundress, 'une autre Mère Barat'. She died at Roehampton. Before the Requiem Mass began a robin sang and flew near the coffin covered with flowers. Birdsong united with the Office of the nuns. She who had spent her childhood searching for the Faith in the country, was in death accompanied by a small bird undaunted by the singing, candles or incense. 'Thus the poem of her life was finished, its last line written; the first among the woods and flower-strewn fields of childhood, the last on the threshold of a fairer life ... she was the happy huntswoman to the finish.'[12]

Saints are born of saints; St. Paul the child of the prayers of St. Stephen, the succession of holy Abbots of Cluny distinguished themselves by the zeal in which they prepared for their successor. Thus it was that Mother Stuart became the spiritual child of Mother Digby. Both were 'solitary within their own souls', Mother Stuart with 'the remoter solitude of the mountain peak, standing calm and immovable beneath the blows of time, inspiring awe and admiration as well as the deepest love'. Mother Digby bore the impress of 'that strange solitude of nature lying even at our feet, so near yet never fathomed; full of sunshine and joy, thrilling to every human interest, a home for the human heart'.[13]

Mabel Digby was born in 1835, the daughter of the heiress

of the last Baron Haversham. It was a long journey which led her to become Superior General of the Sacred Heart. At the moment of her birth it was thought she was dead and her mother dying. Driven to distraction by his grief her father ordered his horse and galloped aimlessly across country for hours. He returned to discover the mother and child were alive and well. Mabel was baptised with rose-water, for fear of a chill but her sister Gertrude was struck down with scarlatina at the age of five. She looked forward to heaven 'with considerable interest' and divided up her toys, giving a large portion to the poor and bequeathing the rest to her brothers and sisters. Illness struck the Digby family again in 1849 when the Hon. Mrs Digby was recommended a sojourn in France for her health. The family moved to Montpellier.

The Hon. Mrs Digby was well-travelled and spoke fluent French, entering into any conversation into which religion was frequently interwoven. After two years in France the Digby daughters noticed that more and more their mother would send them out into society with a chaperone while she stayed at home to study. She was reading Bossuet's *Exposition de la Doctrine de l'Eglise Catholique*. Three years after their arrival in France the Hon. Mrs Digby and her daughter Geraldine were both received into the Church in September 1852. Her husband was furious and summoned the family into the dining room, where each child had to choose between each parent. Geraldine and Eva went to their mother, Mabel and her brothers joined their father who took them back to England to be educated. In England Mabel fell ill and returned to Montpellier where she was followed by her father. Here he tried to persuade his daughter Eva to relinquish Catholicism. 'No, papa, I've found out by myself that the Catholic religion is the best one.'[14]

Meanwhile Mabel's French friends were anxious for her conversion, one journeying to see the Curé d'Ars. She was told by him that God would soon have complete mastery over Mabel's heart. After much prayer and penance the friends decided somehow to persuade Mabel to enter a Catholic church. Telling her that there was some beautiful singing in a church nearby she reluctantly agreed to accompany them. Amid the kneeling congregation for Benediction, Mabel defiantly sat in one of the pews. The singing over, the priest slowly removed the monstrance from the throne and the congregation bowed low. Mabel threw back her head haughtily as if in protest. The bell rang as the Blessed Sacrament was raised in Benediction.

> In an instant Mabel Digby had slipped from her seat on to her knees and flung her arms across her breast with a clutch that gripped both shoulders. Her face seemed to be illumined; her tearful eyes were fixed upon the Host until the triple blessing was complete, and it was replaced in the tabernacle. Then she sank crouching to the ground, whilst the last short psalm was intoned; she remained bent low and immovable...[15]

After a quarter of an hour she rose to her feet and took her sister's arm in the church porch. 'Geraldine, I am a Catholic. Jesus Christ has looked at me. I shall change no more.'

Mabel Digby was received into the Church on the Feast of St. Joseph, 1853. In May the Digbys left Montpellier for Tours and moved into a chateau at Luynes, where one of the round towers was converted into a domestic chapel. Here the Blessed Sacrament was reserved. Mabel's godmother told her: 'You can never love Him enough; He is the only One to be loved without danger.'[16] Watching the procession of Corpus Christi slowly advancing through the streets of old Tours Mrs Digby spontaneously turned to her daughter and asked her if she was still considering becoming a nun, a subject which had never been discussed between them. Four years later this is what she did. The servants thought that she was to make a rather longer journey than usual, for the sake of her health. The last thing she did was go to the stables to see her horse. At the Sacred Heart house in Paris Mabel met Mother Madeleine Sophie Barat, then aged 77. A perfect confidence and mutual understanding was established between the aged

French foundress and the young English novice. At the novitiate at Conflans she found herself a contemporary of Marcella Digby, the daughter of the writer Kenelm, whose works had been read to Mabel as a child. Also at Conflans was Mother Henrietta Kerr, then Mistress of Discipline. She was followed by Charlotte Leslie, whose mother had been instrumental in the conversion of many well-to-do English women, including the Duchess of Buccleuch. And when they moved to the convent at Marmoutier, Cecil, Marchioness of Lothian whose daughter was also in the community, gave a croquet set to the English nuns there.

Marmoutier near Tours had been acquired in 1847 by Madeleine Barat. The Abbey buildings were enclosed by high buttressed and battlemented walls, with towers and gates. The abbey was like a cathedral and the cloisters were surrounded by trees, vineyards and gardens. Smaller chapels nestled among farm buildings, workshops and stables. It was all built over the grotto of St. Martin, '... the pride of all France till the revolutionary furies seized the revenues, drove out the monks, tore down the roof and broke up the stained glass and stone work'. There the nuns spent idyllic summers, studying and gardening and planting fruit trees. They went for walks across the vast property and visited a small chateau on a hill called Rougemont, from where they looked across the lovely country. Sometimes the nuns would sit and work while some old book was read, borrowed from the great library at Tours. Mother Barat told her nuns: 'You are honoured, my dear children, in being allowed to tread the soil of the saints.' In 1872 Mother Mabel Digby returned from France to England, to Roehampton.[17]

At Roehampton, she found herself in a classical building with domed ceilings, fine brass-work, carved mantelpieces and large mirrors; George IV had danced in the ball room. The house was originally owned by Lord Ellenborough, whose wife was a sister of the ninth Baron Digby and a distant cousin of Mabel's. In this country house on the edge of London the thirty three acres contained a farm and a park with lawns, a lake, shrubberies, winding paths and trees 'in varied species rare and common, with copper, shaded green and silvered foliage artistically juxtaposed', revealing a prospect of partial vistas 'with narrow glimpses of blue distance, so that the grounds appeared constantly varied and larger than they were'. Over the next twenty years it was the task of Mother Digby to adapt this home to a convent. The first thing that was added was a beautiful chapel and the alterations went ahead without a wasted sovereign. Mother Digby headed a gang of novices when partitions needed to be removed or wood or bricks carried. Stone monuments to favourite pets were removed and a Calvary was reconstructed. Classical statues were replaced with images of saints and a shrine to the Blessed Virgin Mary was constructed by the lake.

This was the setting for retreats for many converts to Rome, among them the Duchess of Buccleuch, whose chaplain Father Robertson later ended his days as chaplain to the nuns. Cecil, Marchioness of Lothian made her annual retreat at Roehampton for twenty years as did Lady Victoria Kirwan, Lady Georgiana Fullerton, Lady Denbigh and Lady Clare Feilding; 'they served two worlds, but never two masters'.[18]

When Mother Stuart had stood on the terrace at Ixelles, watching the coffin of Mabel Digby depart, she had returned to the chapel to pray. When Mother Digby's coffin arrived at Charing Cross thirty mourners waited at the station with wreaths. It was so early in the morning that few Londoners were about but those that were, bared their heads as the coffin, covered with flowers, surmounted with a large brass crucifix and accompanied by a procession of friends, whose whole demeanour spoke of love and grief, was borne towards the hearse. In the convent at Roehampton a sunbeam fell upon the brass crucifix and made a dazzling light as the coffin was carried in. It was laid upon the trestles in the chapel of the Sacred Heart and covered with a pall. With a low and broken voice Father William Kerr began to say Mass. It was Ascension Day, the Feast Day on which the foundress of the Society of the Sacred Heart, Madeleine Sophie Barat, had died.[19]

Lord Braye at Eton. Later as a Catholic he founded the chapel dedicated to Our Lady of Sorrows, close to the College, in 1915

*The Marquess of Bute, aged 17. Becoming a Catholic in 1868
soon after leaving Oxford, he devoted his fortune to the founding
and re-building of churches and monasteries.*

The Marchioness of Lothian on her marriage in 1831. Widowed in 1841, she became a Catholic ten years later. A patroness of churches and charities, she later took part in the first pilgrimage to leave England since the Reformation, in 1873.

Father Frederick Faber. Formerly Rector of Elton, in Huntingdonshire, he became a Catholic in 1845 and an Oratorian priest in 1848. Founder of the Oratory in Brompton Road; the Duke of Norfolk and the Duchess of Argyll were among its benefactors.

The Hon. Henry Schomberg Kerr, R.N. The son of Lord Henry Kerr, who as Vicar of Dittisham near Dartmouth became a Catholic in 1855, he followed his father into the Church three years later.

Father Henry Kerr, S.J. Leaving the Royal Navy to become a Jesuit in 1878, he became Chaplain to the first Catholic Viceroy of India, the Marquess of Ripon.

Viscountess Feilding. Heiress to the Downing estate near the shrine of Holywell in Flintshire, she became a Catholic in 1850, dying three years later in a villa overlooking Naples.

The Earl and Countess of Denbigh. Formerly Viscount Feilding, he married the Hon. Mary Berkeley, from an old Catholic family, as his second wife. He founded the Capuchin Franciscan friary in Pantasaph in 1858.

Sister Clare Feilding, daughter of the Earl and Countess of Denbigh. As a Sister of Charity she died as a missionary in China.

Mother Janet Erskine Stuart, daughter of the Rector of Cottesmore, became a Catholic in 1879. After three years of hunting, fishing and praying, she joined the Society of the Sacred Heart, later becoming Vicar General.

The Venerable Ignatius Spencer. Son of the second Earl Spencer, he became a Catholic in 1830, when Vicar of Brington near Althorp. As a Passionist priest he travelled all over England, Ireland and the Continent, preaching and seeking prayers for England.

Father Paul Pakenham. Son of the second Earl of Longford and a Captain in the Grenadier Guards, he became a Passionist priest in 1855. Thirty years after his death his body was discovered incorrupt.

Father Luigi Gentili. A priest of the Institute of Charity, founded in Italy by his contemporary Antonio Rosmini, he came to England as a missionary in 1835. Against much opposition Gentili introduced into England public devotions of the Stations of the Cross, Exposition and processions of the Blessed Sacrament, processions in honour of the Blessed Virgin Mary, public recitation of the rosary and wearing of scapulars and religious medals.

Blessed Dominic Barberi. Arriving in England from Italy in 1841, he received Newman into the Church in 1845. In a chapel in a church in Lombardy he had had a vision of the conversion of England, as had the founder of the Passionists, St Paul of the Cross, in 1720.

The Marquess of Ripon. A former Grand Master of the English Freemasons, he became a Catholic in 1874.

The ninth Duke of Marlborough outside Blenheim. Wanting to end his days in a Carmelite monastery in Spain, he became a Catholic in 1927, following the lengthy deliberations over the annulment of his marriage to Consuelo Vanderbilt.

Notes

1   C.C. Martindale, S.J., *Mother Stuart*, London, Catholic Truth Society, 1933, p. 1.
2   M. Monahan, *Life & Letters of Janet Erskine Stuart, Superior-General of the Society of the Sacred Heart, 1857–1914*, London, Longmans, 1934, p. 15.
3   Ibid., p. 24. The *Memorare* prayer is: 'Remember O most Blessed Virgin Mary, that never was it known that anyone who fled to thy protection, implored thy help or sought thy intercession, was left unaided. Inspired by this confidence I fly unto thee, O virgin of virgins, my mother. To thee I come, before thee I stand, sinful and sorrowful. O mother of the Word Incarnate, despise not my petitions but in thy mercy hear and answer me. Amen.'
4   S. Leslie (ed.), *Letters of Herbert Cardinal Vaughan to Lady Herbert of Lea 1867 to 1903*, London, Burns Oates, 1942, pp. 36–8.
5   P. Smith-Steinmetz, *Life of Mother Janet Stuart*, Dublin, Clonmore and Reynolds, 1948, p. 8.
6   Monahan, op. cit., pp. 25–26.
7   Martindale, op. cit., pp. 4–5.
8   Monahan, op. cit., p. 34.
9   Ibid., p. 48.
10 Martindale, op. cit., p. 10.
11 Monahan, op. cit., p. 75.
12 Ibid., p. 472. Martindale, op. cit., p. 25.
13 Monahan, op. cit., p. 49.
14 A. Pollen, *Mother Mabel Digby. A Biography of the Superior-General of the Society of the Sacred Heart 1835–1911*, London, John Murray, 1914, p. 16.
15 Ibid., p. 20.
16 Ibid.
17 Ibid., pp. 28, 78, 91.
18 Ibid., p. 126.
19 Ibid., p. 384.

Chapter Nine

A Trinity from Trinity

When Mabel Digby was a child her mother used to read her the works of her cousin, Kenelm Digby. From an Anglo-Irish background and a descendant of the Barons Digby of Sherborne, Kenelm had inherited a fortune from his brother and landed property from his wife. He was the son of William Digby, Dean of Clonfert and Rector of Geashill in King's County, who in his youth had been a skater, runner and jumper. This athlete had a passion for painting, carpentry, mechanics and landscape-gardening. He was a Hebrew scholar and European traveller. By his third wife he had two sons, the youngest of whom, Kenelm, was born 'in the last year or two of the eighteenth century'.[1] Kenelm spent a happy childhood at his father's rectory at Geashill, 'with its distant prospect of the purple, heathy, hill-range of Slieve-bloom, in the very centre of Ireland'.[2] He was sent to school in England, to Petersham near Richmond where he rowed on the Thames, continuing this art when he went up to Trinity Cambridge. He found 'the tubs that then did serve for boats, on which the drowsy Fen-man floats' inferior to the craft on the Thames. He and some friends persuaded the boat-keeper at the locks on the Cam to construct eight-oared shells and they rowed down the Cam and the Ouse to the sea. Kenelm took his B.A. in 1819 and in the following year he won a prize for an essay on 'Evidences of the Christian Religion'.

As a child Kenelm had read the poems of Walter Scott and his mind now turned to medieval history. He was fascinated by chivalry. He and another medieval-minded friend held a solemn tournament in Sussex, riding ponies for steeds and using hop-poles as lances. He was majestic in appearance, six foot tall, with dark hair and dark eyes, a 'grand, swarthy fellow, who might have stept out of the canvas of some knightly portrait in his Father's house – perhaps the living image of one sleeping under some cross-legg'd Effigies in the Church'.[3]

When Kenelm Digby was not living out his medieval pageants in England – once charging at night to Hurstmonceux Castle to touch its walls with a lance – he was travelling to Belgium, France, Italy, Germany, Austria and Switzerland, 'avoiding the Puritan North, the Scandinavian lands, Prussia and 'cold' Berlin'.[4] In Switzerland:

> There one might walk through delightful meadows interspersed with groves like a continual garden, watered with a number of clear rivulets, sparkling amidst violet beds, studded with beautiful convents, chapels and crosses, with villas and pavilions adjoining. There one heard ascend through the clear air the sweet liquid symphony of the bells of the different monasteries, which are tolled at every elevation of the sacred mysteries and these too seem to answer one another from hill to hill.[5]

As a schoolboy at Petersham, Kenelm had come across two elderly Catholic gentlemen, Charles Butler and Sir Henry Englefield. He was impressed by 'a certain tone and reserve and mysterious stamp about them'. Charles Butler was a barrister and nephew of Alban Butler, who wrote the multi-volume *Lives of the Saints*. Kenelm never forgot entering a Catholic church for the first time. He was not yet twenty when he first witnessed what he then called Popish superstition. Women in black knelt before the altars and one man 'knelt by himself in a corner praying very earnestly to some thin wax candles on which his eyes were rivetted'. Impressed by the devotion of Catholic congregations he thought the priests conjurors, the way they turned themselves about at Mass. Yet he was puzzled as to why English congregations should be inattentive while Catholic ones, in the midst of such apparently ridiculous actions on the altar, were rapt with reverence. At Trinity he loved the singing in the chapel. Could he ever resolve to cease to hear at evening prayer the soft 'Lighten our darkness' or on chill Advent mornings 'Now in the time of this mortal life'? He would have to sacrifice the singing at King's, Eton and St. George's Windsor, but his heart was turning towards Rome. He was in Paris when he first approached a priest to receive instruction. The priest looked amazed, told him he was far too young and besides, he had a great deal of proof-reading to do. Back in England Kenelm eventually tracked down a Jesuit in London 'who, at last, guided him through the narrow door where one must bend one's head into the internal space and freedom of the eternal and universal Catholic Church'.[6]

Digby returned to Cambridge for further study in its magnificent library, where the Fellows looked upon the young convert with a certain easy tolerance, regarding him as somewhat eccentric. As liberals they were supporters of Catholic Emancipation and Kenelm observed that the 'Liberal Cambridge Protestant sailing cheerfully on the unfathomed deep, was safer than the Oxford Tractarian, driven by the Catholic wind on to the rocks of the Roman shore.' He always displayed a coolness towards the Oxford movement (Newman's conversion occurring twenty five years after his) and regarded Anglo-Catholics as the type who 'procured copies of pinnacles and crosses, and even the iron hinges of the old doors of churches; while the spiritual hinge, on which the whole system turns, they were content to suppress for ever ...'[7]

Digby's contribution to the revival of Catholicism was to write with warmth and affection about the Middle Ages. For three centuries they had been viewed as a barbarous age, centred on a Church whose visible centre was Rome. His first book, published in 1822 was *The Broad Stone of Honour*, a study of the ethical principles which lay behind medieval chivalry. *Mores Catholici*, later read to his cousin

Mabel Digby by her mother and which planted the seed of her conversion, was an eleven-volume study published between 1831 and 1842, which explored the extent to which pre-Reformation men and women were influenced by Christ's teaching in the Sermon on the Mount. There followed the seven volume *Compitum*, which appeared between 1849 and 1854, which examined the way men and women's lives had been enriched by the teaching of the Church.

The historian T. E. Bridgett, who was first drawn to Roman Catholicism as an undergraduate at St. John's when he requested a copy of St. John Fisher's sermon preached at the funeral of the foundress of the college, Lady Margaret Beaufort, had read both Newman's sermons and Manning's sermons. But 'the day of grace for me was when I picked up in my bookseller's shop a volume, just come out, by Kenelm Digby'. This was the first volume of *Compitum*. 'The name, the title, even the little black cross on the title page, seemed so strange that I bought it and had not read many pages when I felt myself in a new world.'[8] He made inquiries about Digby's conversion and bought *The Broad Stone of Honour*. 'From that day my heart was with the Church of the Saints.' The scholar, having had no connections with Catholics, claimed never to have met a Catholic even accidentally in Society, until he was received into the church and was later ordained. He wrote to Digby:

> ... I have always looked on it as the most happy day in my life when in a bookseller's shop in Cambridge I took up the first volume of *Compitum*. The few pages I read caused such a strange joy that I carried the book home, and soon made acquaintance with your precious writings. From you, my dear Sir, I learnt to know and love the Church; and now after five and twenty years of very intimate acquaintance with the modern workings of that church whose ancient works you had taught me to admire, I feel that joy as fresh as ever though far more deep. I remember well how in 1850 I walked down the Strand wet with the water of

my conditional baptism in the oratory of King William
Street. Pushing my way through that busy crowd I
could almost have laughed in their faces that I was
now in communion with those great and brave and
holy men whom I had first learnt to love in the pages
of *Compitum* and *The Broad Stone of Honour*.[9]

Such was one instance of Digby's influence on a generation
only just beginning to wake up to the glories of medieval
Roman Catholic culture – its manuscripts, architecture,
monasticism, and tender spirituality. Indeed, by 'perme-
ating every aspect of life, the medieval Church made sense
of it by verifying and integrating it: it was the universally
adhered-to matrix and template of life'.[10] In contrast, there
seemed to be no universally accepted orthodoxy in
England. Protestantism was seen to be the very author of
and monument to disintegration and alienation. The
Romantics of the nineteenth century found that they could
not idealize Protestantism because it was the phenomenon
of the modern age, without a long glorious past. But
Catholic sacramentalism, founded on the mingling of the
physical and the spiritual, appealed to some Romantics in
their search for the transcendent. At the same time the
Church of England was coming under increasing criticism
for the splendid way its Bishops lived in their palaces. An
increasingly secular and wealthy nation was accusing the
medieval church of worldliness. Anglicans, whose church
was coming under increasing attack, accused the Church of
Rome of gross corruption and immorality.[11] History itself
was written with an overriding sense of past corruption, brilliantly illuminated by Newman in his analysis of historians
who amplified the prejudices of their predecessors. An
imperial nation regarded Gibbons' *Decline and Fall of the
Roman Empire* as a standard text, Gibbons being opposed to
any sort of religious enthusiasm, despising any reverence
towards saints and relics, crusades and monasticism.
Contrary to what his readers thought, Walter Scott
regarded Catholicism as 'a mean and depriving superstition' hoping that it would 'sink into dust with all its absurd
ritual and solemnities.' For Macaulay, twelfth century

society was utterly 'miserable, wherein the most debasing and cruel superstition exercised boundless dominion over the most elevated and cruel minds'.[12] Kingsley believed that since the Anglo-Saxons were a female race complemented by the great male race of the Norse, the English had the correct proportions of male and female and could not therefore tolerate the intrusion of an effeminate Latin Church. What such writers did not understand, they ridiculed. Newman saw that the beginnings of the Oxford Movement, 'struck an original note, ... a new music, the music of a school *long unknown* in England'.[13]

☙❦❧

'Thou art', wrote Ambrose Phillipps De Lisle, addressing England, 'still a noble instrument, though now mute or discordant ... let but the master arise who can revive the Catholic chord, and thou wilt again send forth the sweetest music.'[14] Before the Oxford Movement began, three Cambridge converts contributed to the revival of this music long un-heard. Kenelm Digby was one of three converts each with an equally fervent yet distinct approach towards the re-conversion of their native land to Rome. He was joined by the Hon. George Spencer and Ambrose Phillipps De Lisle.

In 1857 Newman wrote to Ambrose Phillipps De Lisle: 'If England is converted to Christ, it will be as much due, under God, to you as anyone.'[15] Ambrose Phillipps De Lisle was born at Garendon Park in Leicestershire in 1809 and at the age of eleven he went to a school at Maisemore Court near Gloucester, where one of the teachers was a French emigré priest called Abbé Giraud. Ambrose became interested in Catholicism and during the holidays joined his father in Paris where he visited churches, observing the ceremonial. He arranged for a cross to be placed on the altar of the church at Shepshed near Garendon Park, said to be 'the first cross planted on an Anglican altar since the introduction of Protestantism into the country'.[16] He was confirmed by his uncle, the Bishop of Lichfield, but shortly afterwards he had a dream in which he saw Mahomet as the Anti-Christ, because of his denial of the Father and the

Son. He wrote to the priest of St. Peter's church in Birmingham, whom he had met briefly and asked to meet him again. The priest was impressed by Ambrose's knowledge of the points of Roman Catholic doctrine and soon afterwards the devout fifteen year-old was received into the Church. The nearest Catholic chapel to Garendon at that time being Leicester, Ambrose Phillipps De Lisle received Holy Communion for the first time from a Fr Macdonell in an Irish labourer's cottage near Loughborough.

In 1826 Ambrose Phillipps De Lisle went up to Trinity, riding every Sunday twenty five miles to St. Edmund's College in Hertfordshire for Mass. In 1830 Lady Arundell wrote to him: 'You will be the first founder or rather restorer of monastic institutions in this wretched country, such is my prophecy, mark my words.'[17] In 1833 Ambrose married a granddaughter of the recusant fourth Lord Clifford of Chudleigh and in 1835 the young couple went to live in Grace Dieu manor, not far from Garendon Park, and to which a small chapel was attached. Grace Dieu had once been an Augustinian convent. Here Ambrose decided to build a monastery, the first since the Reformation.

'This Trappist monastery on the Charnwood Hills, according to the idea and purpose of its Founder, was a silent preacher to England; and by its contemplative spirit was an offering of a perpetual sacrifice of prayer to God.'[18] A later convert to the Roman Catholic Church recalled his first impression of the Abbey of Mount St. Bernard:

> The great doors to the East were wide open and the sun, ... was rising over the distant farmland; at each of the dozen or so side-altars a monk, finely vested but wearing heavy farmers boots ... was saying his private Mass. Voices were low, almost whispers, but each Mass was at a different stage of development, so that the Sanctus would ring from one altar to be followed half a minute later by other rings from far away. For perhaps five minutes little bells sounded from all over and the sun grew whiter as it steadily rose. There was an awe-inspiring sense of God expanding, as if to fill every corner of the church and the whole world.[19]

The revival of Gregorian chant in the Leicestershire countryside, sung by Trappist monks in a Gothic abbey, was immensely significant. So too was Ambrose De Lisle's meeting with the Italian priest Rosmini at the palace belonging to Count Mellerio in Milan. From this friendship the Italian order of Rosminians came to Leicestershire to preach and convert and teach in a new school, Ratcliffe College. Of equal importance in terms of spiritual reverberations was Ambrose Phillipps De Lisle's meeting with the Hon. George Spencer in Cambridge.

The Hon. George Spencer, seventh son of the second Earl Spencer of Althorp, was born at Admiralty House within the last week of the eighteenth century. His father was then First Lord of the Admiralty, his mother a well-known society beauty whose portrait was painted by Reynolds. The family had three houses – one a beautiful colonnaded house overlooking Green Park, another at Wimbledon Park and the ancestral home at Althorp in Northamptonshire. In the nursery at Althorp, George Spencer's Swiss governess began to tell him of the Kingdom of God. From an early age he showed a particular attachment to things religious and in 1808 he went to Eton, where he came under the influence of an evangelical tutor and became 'fascinated by long prayers and ascetical practice'.[20] His parents were concerned about such developments, he was taken away from Eton and given a tutor at home. In 1817 he went up to Trinity, by which time early evidences of piety had been cast aside. He recalled that whatever he thought desirable in the world 'abundance of money, high titles, amusements of all sorts, fine dress and the like – as soon and as far as I understood anything about them, I loved and longed for; ...' Nevertheless at Trinity he found himself 'mysteriously protected from joining in the profane contempt of God's worship which prevails generally in the college chapels at Cambridge'. So too was he protected from consenting to 'the practice of open immoralities, or even pretending to approve them'.[21]

In the late summer of 1819 the Hon. George Spencer

travelled to France, arriving at Calais on 15th September,
'a day most interesting to me as I then considered, because
the first of my setting foot in a foreign land, but much
more, I now must reckon, as being the first on which I trod
Catholic ground and entered a Catholic church'.[22] At
Amiens Cathedral he saw Mass being celebrated and
described the distinct difference between Protestant and
Roman Catholic worship.

> This is a mystery to Protestants who see Catholic rites
> for the first time. They are taught to look upon true
> worship as consisting in the meaning of some well-
> written sentences, pronounced with emphatic
> unction, and responded to some degree with fervour.
> The service, the fine old psalms, anthems and collects
> of the Prayer Book, issuing forth in melodious accents
> from the lips of a God-fearing man, is about the
> highest kind of public worship they can have any
> notion of... But service and sermon must be heard,
> and listened to, and understood. With this idea in
> their minds, and accustomed to see the minister
> assume a manner and mien calculated to produce
> prayerful thoughts in his congregation, they are
> surprised, if not shocked, at the Catholic Mass. They
> find the Priest hurrying off through Latin prayers,
> and producing breathless attention by his own
> silence; they see him arrayed in unintelligible attire,
> moving one way and another, bowing, genuflecting,
> standing still or blessing ... It is not our object to
> explain Catholic mysteries, but it may be as well to
> hint that if a stranger to Jerusalem happened to
> wander to Calvary on the great day of the Crucifixion,
> and believed in the divinity of the Victim who hung
> upon the Cross, he would find more devotion in
> kneeling in silence at His feet than in listening to the
> most eloquent declamation he could hear about it.
> Such is the case with the Catholic now as then; he
> knows the same Victim is offered up still, and when
> the great moment arrives in the middle of the Mass,
> he would have everything to be hushed and silent,

except the little bell that gives him notice of the awful moment.[23]

In Paris, the Hon. George Spencer went to the opera. It was at the end of *Don Giovanni*, when Don Giovanni is engulfed in flames in the midst of his licentious career that George Spencer knew 'that God, who knew what was within me, must look on me as one in the same class with such as Don Giovanni, and for once this holy fear of God's judgment saved me: and this holy warning I was to find in an opera-house at Paris'.[24] He returned home, collected his first class degree from Trinity and stayed on in Cambridge to prepare himself for the Anglican ministry. He attended Theology lectures and regular chapel where he received the sacrament. Writing to the diocesan examiner of Peterborough to ask which books he should read to prepare himself for ordination he was told that for someone who was so well-known to the examiner, and who possessed such talents and qualities, he should only be required to translate a verse from the Greek Testament and an article of the Church of England into Latin. The doctrinal part of the examination would be given by the bishop himself, but since this was restricted to previously prepared questions, it would be more a test of opinions than scholarship. He was ordained in 1824 and became Vicar of St. Mary the Virgin in Brington, near Althorp.

A good and holy pastor of his flock, the Hon. & Rev. George Spencer found his immediate concern was unity among the so-called Dissenters – Wesleyan Methodists, Baptists and Independents – and the Anglicans. He did all he could to draw the Dissenters back, unburdening himself to a fellow scholarly clergyman – the Rev. Peter Elmsden, Professor of Ancient History at Oxford, who was visiting Spencer for a month. The Reverend Professor did not sympathise, saying High Church leanings were in effect Catholic leanings, and therefore had no room in the Church of England. Spencer recalled:

I did not answer him, but as a soldier who has received what he feels to be a mortal wound will suddenly stand still, and then quietly retire out of the *melee*, and seek a quiet spot to die in, so I went away with my High Churchism mortally wounded in the very prime of its vigour and youth, to die for ever to the character of an Anglican High Churchman.[25]

Further discussions with Dissenters made him doubt this position and he became more evangelical in his approach, while drawing closer to God. He declared in 1825 that he would solemnly devote the next year and every day and hour and minute of his future life to coming nearer to Him, 'to learning His ways and word, and leading others to the same knowledge, in which He has caused me to exult with a joy formerly unknown'.[26] But two years later exclusive concentration on the Bible was causing the graduate of Trinity to question how the doctrine of the Holy Trinity could be derived exclusively from its pages. Reading the early Church Fathers had also set him thinking in another direction. About to set off for the Isle of Wight he looked for a book to take with him in the library at Althorp.

I hit upon a copy, in Greek, of St. John Chrysostom on the Priesthood ... I read, and read it again. Is it possible? I thought to myself. Why, this is manifest popery. He certainly must have believed in the Real Presence. I had no idea that popish errors had commenced so soon; yes, and gained deep root, too; for I saw that he wrote as of a doctrine about which he expected no contradiction.[27]

He entered into long discussion with Catholic priests and teachers. Soon afterwards he received an anonymous letter from Lille. The writer had heard of his difficulties and from then on a succession of clear expositions of Roman Catholicism landed on the floor through his letter box in the rectory at Brington. They were written by an English woman who was herself a convert and who later entered Madeleine Sophie Barat's Sacred Heart convent in Paris – she died before making her final profession. The first letter arrived in 1827 and they continued to arrive in the following year, by which time Spencer had met two Catholic priests.

In the barrack yard of the soldiers' quarters in Northampton Spencer met Father William Foley. A few days later they met again and the priest thanked the aristocratic rector for his charity towards him, adding that it was 'Providence that had sent Mr Spencer there at such a time'. Spencer wrote in his diary: 'Really these Papists believe in Providence.'[28] His next encounter with a Catholic priest was in the Dowager Lady Throckmorton's drawing room, when he met Father John Fletcher, Lady Throckmorton's chaplain, formerly professor in Paris to the incarcerated seminarians of St. Omer during the French Revolution. Pius VII had conferred a doctorate of theology on the priest, who was a prolific and controversial author. Spencer then visited a local Catholic school and dined with the priests there. 'I came away with this thought on my mind. They are gentlemen and they are scholars and yet so determined Catholics! How is this?'[29]

It was the scholarly and gentlemanly Ambrose Phillipps who invited Spencer for a week's visit to Garendon Park, who nudged 'the last vibration of the needle to the pole of Catholic truth'.[30] The twenty year-old Phillipps had invited other Anglican and Catholic guests. In the discussions that followed, in which the young Ambrose displayed such manifest authority in the face of eminent opponents, Spencer had to submit to Rome. After years of torment and searching he was received into the Church the following week, by a Belgian priest called Father Caestryck at the Holy Cross church in Leicester.

Earl Spencer had always been favourable towards the Catholic minority in England and had supported Catholic Emancipation. This was however more in a spirit of generosity to a fallen and injured people than from conviction of the truth of their cause. He little imagined that his son would be one of the first to benefit from the liberalising measures he had advocated in the House of Lords. The night before his reception into the Roman Catholic Church, George wrote to his father an exhaustive letter explaining his reasons, which was at the same time a simple announcement written with emotion. Lord Spencer, in the family's Liberal Whig tradition, adopted an understanding attitude, giving his son a generous allowance to make good the loss of the benefice at Brington. But George's favourite sister Sarah, governess to Queen Victoria's children, wrote:

> My other dear and poor, poor brother! What shall I say of him? I mean George, who is become a Catholic – we fear a Catholic priest. His motives have been pure, and such has been his state of uncertainty and doubt and unfixedness upon all but practical piety in religious matters for years, that we have no reason to be surprised at this last fatal change. But it is so deep an affliction to my dear Father and Mother, so great a breaking up of our family, so painful a loss at Althorp, where his presence and ministry, though but imperfect pleasures, were yet invaluable pleasures to us, that it weighs us all down. He took this step suddenly, and with very insufficient forethought and knowledge. Altogether a bad business.[31]

Two months later in March 1830 Spencer set off to Paris with Ambrose Phillipps, to the city which had first nurtured the beginnings of his conversion in the magnificent surroundings of the Opera House. There they met up with Kenelm Digby, and the three Trinity graduates, now all Catholics, became firm friends. Each had a distinct mission, and each supported the other with correspondence and prayers during the strenuous years that lay ahead. Spencer then went on to the English College at Rome; Lord Spencer was anxious for his son not to be an embarrassment to the people on the estate in Northamptonshire. For Spencer it required a real effort to attend all the Theology classes. After a few days he met Dominic Barberi, then lector in Philosophy at the monastery of SS. John and Paul on the Coelian Hill.

In Rome at that time was the seventy year-old Sir Harry Trelawney from Cornwall, a recent convert who was training for the priesthood. He needed a priest to teach him how to say the Mass in Latin. Knowing Dominic

Barberi's zeal for the conversion of England – a zeal which was the spiritual inheritance of the Passionist Order of which he was a member, Cardinal Odescalchi asked Father Dominic to undertake this task. But Sir Harry needed an interpreter. Hearing of the arrival of George Spencer in Rome, Sir Harry's daughter Laetitia asked the former Rector of Brington to step in. So it was that George Spencer was introduced to Dominic Barberi for the first time. And a daily visitor to the Passionist monastery in Rome at the time was Ambrose Phillipps.

'All over Italy revolution was in the air but within the quiet walls of the Venerabile the vocation of George Spencer matured in perfect peace.'[32] After two years in the English College, George was ordained on the Feast of St. Augustine, May 26th, 1832. The ordination took place in St. Gregory's church on the Coelian Hill, the spot from which the Apostle of England had first set out in 597. From the hills above Rome, he returned to England to start his priestly vocation in a poor parish in West Bromwich. Visiting the poor and the sick, he was taunted, spat on, jeered and attacked. Two years later Lord Spencer died and Father Spencer went to Althorp where he was welcomed by his brother, the third Earl, in a kindly way. But at the same time he was forbidden to speak to any of the people working on the estate. Mortified, he responded with a humble 'Thank God' and returned to West Bromwich thankful to mix freely with his beloved poor. Nevertheless through his sister Lady Lyttleton, he made the most of her connections as Lady-in-Waiting to the young Princess Victoria and her mother the Duchess of Kent. He visited Kensington Palace where he gave an account of his conversion and concluded with a defence of the truth of Roman Catholicism, to which the Princess listened politely.

In 1838 Father Spencer went to France to visit Ambrose Phillipps and his family to recover his health after the rigours of his priestly labours in the West Midlands. Together they visited Paris where they met the Archbishop. They were on a mission, which was to start a crusade of prayer for the conversion of England. They were assured by numerous priests that they would offer Mass every Thursday for the conversion of England. This idea was derived from the Benedictine convent of Colwich in Staffordshire where Spencer had discovered that every Thursday High Mass was offered for this purpose, followed by Exposition of the Blessed Sacrament. Spencer wrote that this was a solemn act of reparation for 'the outrages committed against the Divine Eucharist'.

> It seems to me that this was a devotion peculiarly suited to the object of obtaining from Almighty God graces for England, one of whose most crying sins is the blasphemy of the Blessed Sacrament authorized by law for three centuries.[33]

Reparation and redemptive prayer struck a chord in the French devotional heart, the land of Margaret Mary Alacoque's vision of Christ and His Sacred Heart at Paray-le-Monial in 1673. Father Spencer explained himself to the English in 1839 in a sermon entitled 'The Great Importance of A Reunion Between the Catholics and the Protestants of England and the Method of Effecting It.' He spoke of the destructiveness of prejudice, which sapped the energy of both groups, who should be working together in charitable causes. There was a need for mutual prayer, acceptance, understanding and co-operation – revolutionary sentiments for the time. Thus began the Crusade of Prayer for Christian Unity, prefaced by Spencer's declaration to Protestants: 'I plainly declare to you that I believe you to be in error and that I most ardently desire to lead you to believe as I do.' He asked that one 'Hail Mary' be said daily for the conversion of England.[34]

In the same year in which his Crusade of Prayer was launched, Father Spencer was appointed spiritual director to the seminarians at Oscott College. Not long afterwards the oriental scholar Nicholas Wiseman, Rector of the English College when Spencer was in Rome, arrived at Oscott to lecture in Theology. While in Rome he had been persuaded by Ambrose Phillipps to spend less time on

Syrian manuscripts and turn to the need for the conversion of England. As it turned out he fortuitously combined both. An article Wiseman had written in August 1839 in the *Dublin Review*, likening the Donatist controversy in the Early Church in Africa to the Anglican schism, caught Newman's attention and permanently disrupted Newman's concept of Anglicanism as a *via media*. Already Spencer's Crusade of Prayer seemed to be having an effect. Wiseman was at last in England, the number of Roman Catholic Vicars Apostolic had doubled and Newman was packing up to go to Littlemore.

At Oscott Father Spencer combined his teaching duties with the encouragement of cricket and shooting among the seminarians. He was visited by his brother-in-law Lord Lyttleton, by Gladstone and by Peel. When his brother Frederick became fourth Earl Spencer after the death of their eldest brother in 1845, he entertained him as well. He wrote that it was 'an afflicting thing for me to see my nearest relatives departing one by one and as yet no one received into the Church. I have only to say 'God's Will be done.' I begin again praying for those who remain...' By 1846 Father Spencer wanted to pursue his vocation further and made a thirty day retreat near Stonyhurst. Under the spiritual direction of the Jesuit Father Clarke he followed the Spiritual Exercises of St. Ignatius. The result of this long meditation was that he decided to join Father Dominic Barberi's Italian Order of Passionists. 'As the great moment of a life's decision came, Father Clarke entered the room, heard the choice, and confirmed it unhesitatingly'.[35]

In 1847 Father Spencer began the rigorous Passionist novitiate of mental prayer and fasting, of rising to say the Office at 2 a.m. at Aston Hall in Staffordshire, where Dominic Barberi had set up the first house of the Order of Passionists in England. As a Passionist Father, Spencer took the name of Father Ignatius of St. Paul. The brother of the 4th Earl Spencer now made the most of his aristocratic and political connections. Dressed in the distinctive habit of a Passionist priest, with its large badge depicting a cross and the words JESU XPI PASSIO encircled by the outline of a heart, which appeared in duplicate on the habit and on the long cloak, Father Ignatius trod the wide streets of Whitehall, Pall Mall and St. James's, all in close proximity to the magnificent London residence of Spencer House, overlooking Green Park. His sister, Lady Lyttleton, wrote that now her brother was dressed in a habit and cloak and large brimmed hat like a Spanish friar, she was relieved that he did not visit her at Buckingham Palace, where she was governess to Queen Victoria's children. Yet she said that he looked better and happier than for years, his manner more strikingly gentlemanlike and calm than ever. On hearing that he was asking everyone to pray for unity in the truth, she replied that her interpretation of those two words was different from his. 'He said it did not matter. I was to pray as he asked, and the prayer will be heard as it pleases God.' Then he went to Downing Street. His appearance immediately precluding entry into Number Ten, he asked: 'Will you be so good as to say to him that, ... Lord Spencer's brother would wish to speak with him.' Within moments he was talking to the Prime Minister, Lord John Russell.[36]

In Dublin he went to see the Viceroy, Lord Clarendon. Once at Cambridge together, Father Ignatius mused on 'George Villiers, of St. John's, and me as George Spencer of Trinity, walking together in our college gowns at Cambridge, and now I should see him in his Viceregal Palace, and me before him in my poor Passionist habit.' Telling the Viceroy that he was in Ireland to preach to the Irish people a crusade for the conquest of England, Clarendon fixed on the priest a searching look and said deliberately, 'Taking the view of things which you do, I think you are right.' But when he spoke to Palmerston, the Foreign Secretary continued turning the pages on his desk. Visiting Earl Spencer's son at Harrow, Father Ignatius was refused permission to see his nephew and was mobbed by the boys.[37]

When in 1849 Dominic Barberi died after nine years in England, Father Ignatius found himself Superior of the Passionists in England, much against his will, being an apostle rather than an administrator. He died in 1864, after years of preaching and mission work, eating little, sleeping little and attacked by mobs. Mother Mary Mackillop, at one time a novice of the Sisters of the Cross and Passion, recalled Father Ignatius.

No one doubts now that he was a saint of God, and he looked it then. He was a man of singular presence. A tall, gaunt, somewhat awkward figure, with awkward movements... his accents slow almost to hesitation. But he had the face of a saint, and with all its peace and blessed resignation. Moreover, his manner was cheerful and affable, with an expression of simplicity and piety about what he said and did... There was nothing light or frivolous in his words, but without any pretensions, he spoke of God and holy things as naturally as he breathed.[38]

Kenelm Digby in his poem *By Friendship* wrote of Father Ignatius:

'Spencer – my hand too coarse should fear to paint
The English noble, and the Christian saint –
There was not one whose presence did not bring
For dulness Fairyland, for Heav'n a wing.'[39]

Notes

[1]   B. Holland, *Memoir of Kenelm Digby*, Sevenoaks, Fisher Press, 1992, p. 9.
[2]   Ibid., p. 10.
[3]   Edward Fitzgerald, *Euphranor.* Ibid., p. 14.
[4]   Ibid., p. 22.
[5]   *Mores Catholici*, vol. iii, p. 47.
[6]   Ibid., pp. 38, 40, 42, 44, 45.
[7]   Ibid., p. 47. K.L. Morris, 'The Cambridge converts and the Oxford movement', *Recusant History*, vol. 17, no. 4, Oct. 1985, pp. 388–9.
[8]   C. Ryder, *Life of Thomas Edward Bridgett. Priest of the Congregation of the Most Holy Redeemer, with Characteristics from his Writings*, London, Burns & Oates, 1906, p. 14.
[9]   Holland, op. cit., p. 225.

10   K.L. Morris, *The Image of the Middle Ages in Romantic and Victorian Literature*, London, Croom Helm, 1984, p. 13.
11   See J.H. Newman, *Lectures on the Present Position of Catholics in England*, London, Burns Oates & Company, 1851.
12   Morris, op. cit., p. 76.
13   Ibid., p. 208.
14   Morris, 'Cambridge converts', op. cit., p. 386.
15   E.S. Purcell, *Life and Letters of Ambrose Phillipps de Lisle*, London, Macmillan, 1900.
16   W. Gillow, *Bibliographical Dictionary of the English Catholics*, Vol. II, p. 39.
17   Purcell, op. cit., p. 53.
18   Purcell, op. cit., p. 72.
19   A. Guinness, *Blessings in Disguise*, London, Hamish Hamilton, 1985, p. 40.
20   J. Vereb, C.P., *Ignatius Spencer Apostle of Christian Unity*, London, CTS, 1992, p. 3.
21   Rev. Father Pius, *Life of Father Ignatius of St. Paul, Passionist. (The Hon. & Rev. George Spencer.) Compiled chiefly from his Autobiography, Journal and Letters.*, Dublin, James Duffy, 1866, pp. 4, 24.
22   Ibid., p. 58.
23   Ibid., p. 58.
24   Ibid., p. 90.
25   J. Vanden Bussche, C.P., *Ignatius (George) Spencer Passionist (1799–1864)*, Leuven, Leuven University Press, 1991, p. 22.
26   Ibid.
27   Pius, op. cit., p. 119.
28   U. Young, C.P. *Life of Father Ignatius Spencer, C.P.*, London, Burns, Oates and Washbourne, 1935, p. 33.
29   Vanden Bussche, op. cit., p. 24.
30   Young, op. cit., p. 37.
31   *Correspondence of Sarah Spencer*, quoted in Busshe, op. cit., p. 29.
32   Young, op. cit., p. 53.
33   Bussche, op. cit., p. 41.
34   Vereb, op. cit., pp. 11, 12.
35   Young, op. cit., pp. 129, 136.
36   Ibid., pp. 173, 4.
37   Ibid., pp. 175, 200.
38   Ibid., p. 201.
39   Bussche, p. 241.

Chapter Ten

The Islands are waiting

He had everything in his favour ... his manner and address were singularly graceful and winning. He was tall and slight, very fair and of a fair complexion. Large, clear and most expressive blue eyes, with light brown curly hair, gave his face a most youthful and innocent appearance, while there was something of such dignity and sweetness in his regular features that one could not help respecting him at the first glance.[1]

The Hon. Charles Pakenham, who had everything in his favour, was the fourth son of the second Earl of Longford and nephew of Lady Katherine Pakenham, wife of the Duke of Wellington. His mother was Lady Georgiana Lygon, daughter of the first Earl Beauchamp of Madresfield Court in Worcestershire. He was born in 1821 at Pakenham Hall in County Westmeath, went to Winchester and Sandhurst and became a Captain in the Grenadier Guards. He resigned his commission to become a Passionist priest. He was

a beau-ideal of the true Christian soldier, a *chevalier sans peur et sans reproche*; haunted, like another Sir Galahad, amid the activities and the pleasures of his military calling, by visions and presentiments of higher things ...[2]

When the Hon. Charles Pakenham was twenty, a coachman

gave him a holy book, Lady Katherine Freke gave him a religious medal and he decided to read Newman's *Parochial and Plain Sermons*. He started to fast. He was later amused to remember 'with what a self-satisfied feeling I would step into my cab or stalk along the streets in the fashionable hours, knowing that I had not tasted food that day'.[3] He was received into the Church by Bishop Wiseman on the Feast of the Assumption, 1850. He recalled that 'the spirit of irreligion had sunk so very deeply into society in England that I stood quite alone. I met no sympathy anywhere.' His uncle, Major-General Lygon, advised him to travel. His brother, Lord Longford, looked upon him with contempt and amazement. He was reminded of what St. Jerome had said to Demetrius. 'If thou canst not brook the look of relatives, how could thou face the tribunal of persecutors?' But Major-General Lygon relented and 'after the first words of brusque, soldier-like remonstrance were out, he made up his mind to accept the inevitable'. The Hon. Charles Pakenham then went to live with his uncle the Major-General at Spring Hill in Worcestershire, where he was regarded as the heir to the estate. The nearest Catholic church belonged to the Passionist priests at Broadway, three miles away. The presence of the tall handsome young guardsman at Mass every Sunday caused something of a sensation and even more so when he was admitted into the monastery as a novice, exchanging the uniform of a Guardsman for the rough black habit of the Passionists. The Duke of Wellington was more sanguine. 'Well, you have been a good soldier, Charles; strive to be a good monk.' The Major-General remonstrated with his beloved nephew, deeply distressed that he should lose his heir. Then, one Saturday afternoon, early in May, Captain Pakenham rode out of the park gates, accompanied only by a groom. They headed their horses for Broadway. 'At the monastery gates Pakenham dismounted and sent back his horse in care of the groom, with an affectionate note bidding farewell to his uncle. That was their parting.'[4] One of his relatives wrote:

I wish he were dead, but the worst of it is we shall be like the Spencers, who have not only the sorrow of losing their new relative, but the shame of seeing him go about barefoot, like a dirty, mad, mendicant, begging prayers for the conversion of England.[5]

Inside the Passionist monastery, Captain Pakenham suffered. The liturgy was monotonous and meant nothing. The sound of the bells tormented him. He experienced indescribable anguish. But after three long days his heart suddenly overflowed with sweetness and consolation, which, once gained remained with him always. Every day his happiness increased. In this holy state he was visited by Lord Northwick and Viscount Emly, Lord Campden and the Marquess of Exeter, his brother-in-law. His uncle sent him presents, which he then gave to the Community. Long summer days were filled with work and prayer,

> flitting by lightly and pleasantly as some heaven-sent dream: and, as the novice entered his cell after the evening prayer and glanced out on the quiet land-scape still glimmering under the soft and mystic light of departing day ... the quietude and beauty of his surroundings mirrored the peace of his beautiful soul. 'How little have I given up for so much!' was his thought each evening as he knelt for a last word of thanksgiving to God before composing himself to rest.[6]

Taking the name of Brother Paul Mary of St. Michael the Archangel, he took his solemn vows as a Passionist on 23rd May 1852. On this day, absorbed in prayer before the Tabernacle in the chapel, 'his almost transfigured look, the pale ascetic features lighted with a joy and peace not of this earth, gave token of the extraordinary graces with which his soul had been favoured.' His tall figure lying prostrate before the altar, the bell tolling mournfully, the purple-stoled priest reading aloud the passion of Jesus Christ, 'surely never was symbolism with more moving appeal, and never did it verge so closely on reality.'[7] He was

ordained a priest on the Feast of St. Michael at Oscott in
1855. The following year he went to Mount Argus in
Dublin to be Superior of the Passionist House there. He
was renowned as a preacher and evangeliser; even to see
him was enough, without hearing him speak a word. When
he later fell ill, it was with a painful effort that the dying
Superior of Mount Argus addressed a few parting words to
his religious, kneeling grief-stricken by his bed. No longer
able to eat or drink, the doctors directed that from time to
time he should be given a spoonful of champagne. He died
on 1st March 1867. Among the friends from the aristocratic military world he had left, two brother officers came
to his funeral. The poor were there in great numbers, as
were tenants from the Pakenham estates in the Midlands.
When thirty years later his coffin was moved, the body was
found perfectly intact and incorrupt.[8]

When Father Paul Mary had first entered Broadway as a
novice, the Superior had doubted whether the austerities
would have been tolerable to him – the cutting discipline,
the broken sleep, the severe fast, the stern vow of life-long
poverty. Would not the 'subtle and chivalrous Order of
Loyola for a noble and a soldier – or the simple and genial
rule of Saint Vincent – or the gentle, liberal air, half
ascetic, half poetic, of dear old Saint Philip's Oratory, have
been more appropriate?' It seemed only to be the Duke of
Wellington who comprehended the step that he took, and
who visited him in his cell, finding him not the fiery
fanatic, 'but more gentle, and genial, and graceful in all
his ways than he used to be in the drawing rooms of St.
James's.[9] As Superior at Mount Argus in Dublin, Father
Paul Mary had been determined not only that the spirit of
the founder of the Passionists, St. Paul of the Cross, should
live and flourish, but that the fervour and austerity of the
early days when St. Paul of the Cross and his holy brother
lived as hermits on the island of Monte Argentario in Italy,
should live on in England and Ireland.

❦

Monte Argentario was a beautiful island off the Tuscan
coast, seen from a ship for the first time by Paul Danei on

his journey from Genoa to Civita Vecchia in September 1721.[10] He was on his way to Rome to gain approval from Pope Innocent III for a community he had founded in his home town of Castellazzo, four miles from Alessandria on the Lombardy plain. Due to his meekness and humility rather than to any papal hostility, he had been unsuccessful and had immediately set off to return to northern Italy. From Civita Vecchia he decided to walk to Portecole, the town closest to Monte Argentario. Not knowing his way, his only guide being deep cart-ruts which diverted him across hayfields and corn fields, he eventually reached Portecole, where a priest told him that on the heavenly island of Monte Argentario there was an abandoned hermitage and church. Paul went over to the island at once and walked through its groves of myrtle and bay. He looked over the cliffs and wandered through its sloping meadows. The hermitage was among the ruins of an old monastery, where there was still a picture of the Annunciation. The picture reminded him at once of the vision he had had a year before, a vision which had been the true beginning of the Order of Passionists.

In the summer of 1720, St Paul of the Cross, then Paul Danei, the son of poor and saintly parents who would rather have seen their children free from sin than raised to honours and riches, was returning home to Castellazzo when he was suddenly rapt in ecstasy and saw himself attired in a long black tunic, with a white cross on the breast and JESU written in white letters under the cross. He heard a voice from inside him say: 'This is to signify how pure and spotless ought to be the heart which bears engraven upon it the Sacred Name of Jesus.' Shortly afterwards he had another vision. This time the Blessed Virgin Mary showed him the same habit, but to the word JESU were added XPI PASSIO: The Passion of Jesus Christ. Then the Blessed Virgin Mary appeared to him again, this time wearing the habit, and asking him to found a congregation of religious who would be dressed in this way.

Paul Danei related these visions to the Bishop, and a few months later on 22nd November 1720 he left his father's house at dawn, wearing a coarse sack-cloth dyed black, and went to live in a dark miserable cell close to the church of San Carlo in Castellazzo. There and then he adopted the rigorous routine of what would later become the Passionist Order. Rising at midnight and shivering he went to the Blessed Sacrament to recite Lauds and Matins and meditate for two hours. He said Mass at dawn, spending the day fasting and in penance. While he was in the chapel he had another vision. On 28th November he saw the founders of other Orders interceding for him. Without any book or rule or earthly guide he finished writing his Rule on 7th December. He recalled that he wrote as if there had been someone sitting in a professor's chair dictating to him; he felt the words come from his heart.

On 26th December 1720 Brother Paul of the Cross was praying before the Blessed Sacrament. He began to reflect 'upon those misguided men who deny the Real Presence of Our Lord in this mystery.' He saw England. From that day until his death he never knelt in prayer without petitioning for the conversion of a country he had never known, whose language he had never spoken. At the very end of his life, fifty-five years later, he suddenly exclaimed:

'Ah, England! England! ... Let us pray – let us pray for England. I cannot help praying myself, for whenever I begin to pray this kingdom presents itself to my mind, and it is now fifty years since I began to pray unceasingly for the conversion of England to the faith of its fathers.'[11]

He fell into an ecstatic state and when he returned to normality he said to the brother who was with him: 'Oh, where have I been now? I have been in spirit in England, thinking on its heroic martyrs; and oh, how I have prayed to God for that kingdom!'[12]

The prayers began in November 1721 from the moment Paul returned to Monte Argentario with his brother, when together they began the Passionist life of fasting and prayer. Meditation on the Passion accompanied him through his life; such a life lived under the shadow of the cross had fortified those called to suffer for their new-found Faith in St. Paul's beloved England. When friends deserted or betrayed him, he thought of Christ in the Garden. When he was slandered, he remembered the hall of Pilate. When he was oppressed with pains of body and desolation of mind, he repeated the words heard on Calvary. On Monte Argentario the two brothers rose at midnight and sang Matins. They fasted for nine days in preparation for Feast Days and occasionally spent time in silent reparation living off only roots, herbs and fruit from the island.

The Congregation of the Passion was formally recognised in May 1725 and in 1727 the two brothers were ordained. When celebrating Mass Father Paul was 'seen to glow with heavenly beauty'. Sometimes he 'was raised aloft in the air whilst contemplating his Incarnate God as He lay upon the corporal, and often again was he enveloped in a strange but lucid cloud.'[13] When the brothers decided that they should go back to Castellazzo they were given a firm sign that they should stay. Three ships were about to set sail from the island but the one in which the brothers were did not move. All attempts to get the ship out to sea failed. Paul was praying in the Captain's cabin and decided to go up on deck. He stepped ashore with his brother and the ship set sail.

The two brothers set about putting in order another hermitage on the island and walked to a part of the island where a gently rising hill led to a green and open plain which looked across to Orbetello on the mainland. Back at the church Paul knelt in front of the Blessed Sacrament and after a while returned to the plain. Using a stick he made an outline of a church and a monastery. On the Feast of the Exaltation of the Cross in 1737 the church was consecrated. Boats in the bay transported the inhabitants of Orbetello to the Retreat, the civic authorities were there in long and gorgeous robes, officers in uniform, a band, the local clergy in gorgeous vestments, all gathered to see Paul and his companions, dressed in their austere garb, emerge from the Retreat. The church was blessed, High Mass followed and the founder, wearing a rope around his neck, preached.

After a life of preaching, prayer and privation, 1770

found Paul of the Cross in Rome. For many months he was incurably ill. Hearing of his worsening condition, Pope Clement XIV declared: 'We do not choose that he should die now. Tell him we grant him an adjournment, that he must stay with us a little longer, and that I command him to do so under holy obedience.' Paul wept, turned to the Crucifix and said: 'My crucified Lord, I will obey your Vicar.' He rallied, was restored to health and survived the Pope who had commanded him to live.[14]

In 1773 the basilica of the early Roman saints John and Paul on the Coelian Hill near the ruins of the Coliseum was handed over to the Passionists. Two years later, on 18th October 1775, Paul of the Cross, founder of the Order of Passionists, died, while the Passion was read to him.

All was still, all was quiet, and everyone was waiting for the last agony. Suddenly a glow of celestial brightness lit up the countenance of the dying Saint; he beckoned with his hand as if motioning to somebody to approach, and then closed his eyes, never to open them again.[15]

ॐ

Thirty years after the death of the founder of the Passionists, a young Italian priest, Fra Domenico Barberi, was saying Mass at the altar of the Blessed Virgin Mary in the church of San Carlo in Castellazzo, where once St. Paul of the Cross had had his vision of England. The young priest saw himself in a vision as a victim, part of a holocaust immolated for the conversion of souls, in particular for the conversion of England. As a Passionist novice Dominic Barberi had met several fellow monks of St. Paul of the Cross at the Retreat at Monte Argentario. For Dominic, the island was a heaven on earth. To the north stretched the rugged Tuscan coastline and the Mare Nostrum, upon which the sun projected an endlessly varying medley of light and colour. Looking east to the shimmering causeway, the sea reflected the woods of the mountainside. From the distant peaks of the Apennines the hills rolled towards the island like waves, 'stilled by magic, quilted by a harlequinade maze of colour'.[16]

Dominic Barberi was from a poor family. Like St. Paul he developed a deep attachment to England, and composed the following prayer:

> 'Lord, if You wish me to go mad, or to be unfrocked or hung, or ostracized from human society; if You wish to annul me; if You wish to condemn me to Purgatory until the day of Judgment, if You wish that I should never enjoy any satisfaction in prayer or that I should be tormented by scruples; if You wish to condemn me to suffer all the pains that the English would have to suffer if they were damned I am content, provided only that they all return to You. My God, I protest that I will never allow my heart any consolation until I witness their conversion. If You desire to give me a proof of Your love, open the way to their conversion in whatever way pleases You.'[17]

Fra Domenico developed a miraculous and unexpected fluency in English. One Palm Sunday during the procession outside the church, he was so overcome by feelings of compassion for his beloved English that he almost collapsed. 'I seem to see them', he wrote later, 'crying to be let in.' In 1825 he promised the Blessed Trinity that for England's sake he would never again eat fruit during the forty days preceding the Assumption and that he would say Mass in thanksgiving for all the graces given to the Blessed Virgin Mary. The result of these devotions was his declaration: 'The Islands are waiting, yes, they are waiting to share these delightful fruits' – meaning the fruits of mystical union with God.[18]

In 1831 he wrote *The Lament of England*, a series of profoundly emotional prayers imploring the conversion of that Anglo-Saxon land. By this time his only contact with England and the English had been a fleeting glimpse of Bishop Milner in Rome. But then the introduction came to Father George Spencer via Sir Harry Trelawney's daughter Laetitia, whose father needed to be taught how to say Mass

and who needed an interpreter. So it was that Father
Spencer introduced the Passionist Italian priest to
Ambrose Phillipps. The three took every opportunity they
could to discuss their future plans, in the gardens of Rome.

Six years later Dominic Barberi was still pining to see
England. He wrote to Ambrose Phillipps in 1836: 'Is there
any hope that I shall see you on this earth? Is there any
hope that I shall cross the sea and convey my body to that
island whither, twenty-two years ago, I sent my heart?'[19]
Four years later his prayers were answered. In 1840 Father
Dominic Barberi set out for northern Europe on the Feast
of Our Lady of Help Christians, arriving at the Passionist
Retreat at Ere in Belgium on the Feast of Our Lady of
Mount Carmel. Here he spent some months, tantalisingly
close to his beloved England. Finally he stepped ashore at
Folkestone on 5th October 1841, twenty-seven years after
his vision of England in the tiny chapel of the Blessed
Virgin Mary in the church of San Carlo in Castellazzo in
Lombardy. The passengers who jostled him as he left the
ship 'had no idea of the violent emotions, tumultuous as
the waves of a stormy sea, that surged in his heart.'[20] He
went straight to Oscott, where Father George Spencer and
Bishop Wiseman received him with great joy.

In England at last, Dominic Barberi was bitterly disap-
pointed. At Oscott he was distressed by the lack of zeal on
the part of the recusant Catholics, conscious of there being
'too much egoism, too much politics and too little charity'.
'Everything is calculated, but calculations serve to make
good mathematicians, but not good Christians.'[21] In 1842
he went to Aston Hall near Birmingham, to start a
Passionist Retreat there. This Italian priest who spoke
fluent if somewhat stilted English, overlaid with a Latin
and Italian vocabulary, became the object of ridicule.
Kneeling down at the altar rails at Aston in the choir dress
of the Passionists, the resident priest ordered him to vest
correctly. Dominic retired to the sacristy, returning in a
crumpled surplice. His meekness impressed some of the
parishioners. But when he started to speak there was an
outburst of laughter. Dominic wept.

In his Passionist habit and cloak Dominic tramped the

roads of Staffordshire, receiving abuse and laughter from villagers and clergy. But gradually the attitude of the people changed. Those who had been the most opposed to him became the most affectionate. He wrote:

> 'Oh, if I could find many persons able to labour in the vinard [sic.] of God. I can do nothing, nothing, nothing. Italian fire is not enough to inkindle the hearts of English men. For that purpose is necessary the heavenly fire, which come from God only.'[22]

At Aston he felt trapped, and yearned to spread the truth of Catholicism throughout England. He started to preach in towns and villages, giving missions. Some were converted just by watching him ascend the platform. Passionist Retreats were founded at St. Helens in Lancashire and at St. Joseph's, Highgate Hill. As Superior General of the Order in England, he was always on the move, preaching, hearing confessions and travelling, always taking the most uncomfortable seat. In October 1845, Newman asked to see him in Littlemore. Father Dominic was then in Aston. He travelled on the long journey to rural Oxfordshire on the outside seat of the stage coach in pouring rain. He arrived at Littlemore an hour before midnight. His cloak was wet and he took it off to dry in front of a blazing fire. The door opened quickly, he turned round and there stood Newman. In a moment Newman was kneeling at Dominic Barberi's feet, praying to be admitted to the Catholic Church.

Notes

[1] Rev. Joseph Smith, C.P., *Paul Mary Pakenham, Passionist*, Dublin, M.H. Gill & Son, Ltd., 1930, p. 12.
[2] Ibid., p. 13.
[3] Ibid., p. 20.
[4] Ibid., pp. 24, 25, 32, 35.
[5] Ibid., p. 32.
[6] Ibid., p. 47.
[7] Ibid., p. 60.

8   Ibid., pp. 101, 104, 108.
9   Ibid., p. 113.
10   Rev. Father Pius, *The Life of St. Paul of the Cross: Founder of the Congregation of Discalced Clerks of the Holy Cross and Passion of Our Lord*, London, P. J. Kennedy & Sons, N.Y., 1922, p. 60.
11   Ibid., p. 411.
12   Ibid.
13   Ibid., p. 94.
14   Ibid., p. 327.
15   Ibid., p. 383.
16   A. Wilson, *Blessed Dominic Barberi. Supernaturalised Briton*, London, Sands & Co., 1967, p. 50.
17   Ibid., p. 67.
18   Ibid., p. 87.
19   Ibid., p. 162.
20   Ibid., p. 232.
21   Ibid., p. 238.
22   Ibid., p. 246.

Chapter Eleven

The Angelus shall ring again

As soon as Ambrose Phillipps heard that Newman had been received into the Church he immediately wrote to him:

'You are now a Catholick! you entered the blessed communion on the day of the glorious Saint Denis the Areopagite! I said the Te Deum to thank our good God for His great mercy yesterday evening. Words are wanting to express the feelings of the soul on such an occasion. It is a wonderful thought to me that the humble instrument chosen from all Eternity to make you a partaker of this great blessing should have been that good Monk Father Dominick the Passionist, who in 1831 told me in confidence how Our Lord had assured him in a vision that he should come to preach the Catholick Faith in England and to found there the Passionist Order, and that he should be an instrument for the approaching conversion of our Dear England ...

You also know doubtless how it was the Founder of their Order the Ven. Fr. Paul of the Cross, who, without any connection with England or knowledge of Englishmen personally, was moved by God the first to pray fervently for the reconciliation of our poor country, and of the remarkable extasy he had about England 3 years before his Death. Ah! my dear Mr Newman, perhaps what took place in your little holy oratory at Littlemore on St. Denis's Day was at that moment, more than 60 years ago, foreseen in a poor cell on a mountain in Italy!'[1]

Ambrose Phillipps De Lisle's dedication to the conversion of England, nurtured since his undergraduate days at Trinity, culminated in his founding the Cistercian monastery of Mount St. Bernard in Leicestershire. Phillipps had written to Newman describing how the founding of the first monastery in England since the Reformation came to be.

In 1833 Ambrose Phillipps had gone to Mass at Moorfields Chapel in East London with Lady Constantia Clifford and her daughter Laura, who later became Ambrose's wife. They were seated not far from the High Altar. When the Deacon walked across the Sanctuary to the lectern to sing the Gospel, Phillipps was convinced that he was a Cistercian monk. Phillipps's instincts were confirmed in conversation in the sacristy after Mass. The monk was invited back to Lady Constantia's house where the three discussed the possibility of an English Cistercian foundation. The monk was Father Norbert Woolfrey, who had been sent from his abbey in County Waterford to England to collect alms. For twenty-three years between 1794 and 1817, there had been a Cistercian community at Lulworth made up of French monks who had come from La Trappe. They had returned to France to Melleray in Brittany, but a few had sailed to Cork. In this roundabout way and through a chance encounter in a small chapel in East London, the Cistercians came to their nineteenth century English home in the Midlands. Phillipps was advised by the Vicar Apostolic of the Eastern District not to talk of a Trappist monastery but rather of an agricultural and philanthropic community.

In 1837 a temporary monastery was completed at which Father George Spencer preached. Two years later the Earl and Countess of Shrewsbury visited Grace Dieu Manor and heard the monks singing Sunday Vespers. After Vespers Ambrose Phillipps and the Earl walked across the land near the monastery and came to a rock where the Earl thought the permanent monastery should be. Phillipps agreed, nothing more was said until after dinner when the two went for another walk, during which the Earl of Shrewsbury announced that he was so delighted by what he had seen that he would give £2,000 there and then towards the building of a permanent monastery – on condition that it was built on the spot on which they had both decided. The architect chosen was Pugin.[2]

Augustus Welby Northmore Pugin, three years younger than Ambrose Phillipps, was brought up a reluctant but constant worshipper at the Caledonian church in Hatton Garden, whose congregation followed the teaching of Edward Irving. Pugin's father was an architect who had arrived in London from Switzerland and became much sought after by patrons of the Gothic ecclesiastical style of architecture, increasingly popular for its distinctiveness from the stern classicism of the eighteenth century. Pugin inherited his father's talent for brilliant draughtsmanship, developing a keen interest in the intricate details of medieval architecture and artefacts. In the summer of 1832 the Earl of Shrewsbury, who was restoring Alton Towers in Staffordshire, called in at the dealers in London where Pugin then worked. He was looking for furniture and noticed Pugin's drawings lying on a table. From their mutual interest in the medieval revival a friendship was established between the Earl and the architect.

Pugin left London soon afterwards for Salisbury, where in the shadow of the cathedral spire he designed a Gothic manor house with its own chapel. While Salisbury provided continued inspiration in his quest for Gothic perfection, Pugin found the cathedral services beneath its vaulted roof cold and meaningless.

> Then did I discover that the service I had been accustomed to attend and admire was but a cold and heartless remnant of past glories, and that these prayers which in my ignorance I had ascribed to reforming piety, were in reality only scraps plucked from the solemn and perfect offices of the ancient Church.[3]

Pugin's dedication to the Gothic revival was now injected
with the quest for the revival of Roman Catholicism. The
result of his prolific output, which continued unabated
until his early death, was the appearance of medieval style
Roman Catholic churches throughout the towns and
villages of England.

Pugin's Roman Catholic patron the Earl of Shrewsbury
lived in great austerity amidst the splendours of Alton
Towers. His life and fortune were dedicated to the re-estab-
lishment of Catholic churches and religious houses.
Appropriately it was the Earl's ancestor Bertram de Verdun
who had first brought the Cistercians to Staffordshire. And
across the valley from Alton Towers Shrewsbury built the
church where his body now lies. Clustered around it were
'buildings in warm and mellowing stone, convent, school,
priest's house and guild-hall ... the peace and quiet of a
country church and the loveliness of cloistered stone'. It
was the chief concern of this Catholic nobleman that
schools and almshouses 'would demonstrate what Catholic
art and Catholic charity had meant to the English villages
before the Reformation'.[4] To make this truth manifest, he
and Pugin worked together closely. But their view of
Gothic architecture as the supreme expression of English
Catholicism received vigorous opposition from another
quarter, namely Newman and his Italian Congregation of
Oratorians. Pugin visited Rome in 1847 and wrote:

> I have now seen Rome and what Italian architecture
> can do, and I do not hesitate to say that it is an imper-
> ative duty on every Catholic to defend true and
> Christian architecture with his whole energy. The
> modern churches here are frightful, St. Peter's is far
> more ugly than I expected, and vilely constructed – a
> mass of imposition – bad taste of every kind seems to
> run riot in this place ... I feel doubly grateful for
> living in a country where the real glories of Catholic
> art are being revived and appreciated. In Rome it is
> hopeless, unless by a miracle. I assure you I have felt
> quite depressed and miserable here; I shall be quite
> glad to get away. Were it not for the old Basilicas and

the associations connected with early Christian antiq-
uities, it would be unbearable – the Sistine Chapel is a
melancholy room, the Last Judgment is a painful
muscular delineation of a glorious subject. The Scala
Regia a humbug, the Vatican a hideous mass and St.
Peter's is the greatest failure of all.[5]

In the same year in which Pugin visited Rome Newman was
considering plans for an Oratory. He wrote to Wiseman:

> As to the Oratory itself, its structure must be different
> from anything ecclesiastical hitherto built in
> England... It must be built for preaching and music;
> not an open roof certainly, no skreen. I am afraid I
> shall shock Pugin. As it will be used only in the
> Evening, it need not have many windows, and I should
> be much against spending money on outside decora-
> tion, nay inside, I don't mind its being almost a barn,
> as it is a place for *work*.[6]

Meanwhile Pugin was praising the Vicar Apostolic of the
Eastern District, whose jurisdiction stretched from Wales to
East Anglia, whose support 'really advanced the dignity of
religion. Dr Walsh found the churches in his district mere
barns worse than barns; he will leave them sumptuous.'[7]

In May of 1848 the conflict between Newman's followers,
many of whom had had their fill of Gothic Oxford, and
Pugin's followers, who wanted to drink deep of England's
glorious medieval past, was sparked off by an argument at
Pugin's church at Cotton, near Alton Towers. The argument was between Ambrose Phillipps, Pugin and the future
Oratorian priest Frederick Faber. It centred on Pugin's
belief that the gestures of the priest at Mass were invested
with a particular mystery when he was separated from the
congregation by a rood screen. When Southwark
Cathedral was opened, this controversy was brought into
the public domain and filled the pages of *The Rambler* and
The Tablet throughout 1848. Six years later the *Sacristan's
Manual or handbook of Church furniture ornaments*, derived
from the liturgical decree of the first Provincial Synod of

Westminster, set out rules that were entirely Roman: the altar should be of correct dimensions, with a free-standing tabernacle; there should be a Benediction throne, six candlesticks with reliquaries, 'statuettes'. Natural or artificial flowers and altar cards were now *de rigueur*. Confessionals should be fixtures. Statues of the Blessed Virgin Mary, pictures of the Blessed Virgin Mary fitted with branch candlesticks, and the Stations of the Cross should all be incorporated into Roman Catholic churches, making them as distinct as possible from Protestant ones. Benediction was encouraged, the opening of churches for private devotion was encouraged, the Forty Hours' devotion of the Blessed Sacrament in a magnificent monstrance surrounded by candles and flowers was encouraged. The result was that 'Pugin imposed a Gothic gloss on the liturgy and Wiseman an Italianate gloss on the Gothic revival.'[8]

A startling figure who brought an Italianate flourish to the revival of Roman Catholicism in London was Frederick Faber. The magnificence of the Oratory church in London came about as a result of his meeting the future patron of the Oratory, the Earl of Arundel, later 14th Duke of Norfolk, through having nobody else to talk to on a wet afternoon at Alton Towers. After the death of the 14th Duke his Duchess became a generous benefactress, having been received into the Church by Faber in 1850. The 13th Duke of Norfolk had been a traditional recusant Catholic who had revelled in the underground persecuted church in England; the simple neo-classical chapels, Low Mass, eighteenth century French prayer books, gentlemanly priests and

> the four episcopal Vicars-General with their Marian blue, not purple, cassocks symbolic of the old tradition that England was the 'Dowry of Mary' and their wonderful romantic titles *in partibus infidelium*: Anazorba, Cambysopolis, Helenopolis, Hierocaesaria, Trebizond. Who would want to sweep all that away and replace it with Bishops of Salford and Birmingham, cheap Gothic churches in mean towns ...?[9]

Indeed, at the restoration of the Roman Catholic hierarchy the 13th Duke joined the Church of England in protest, later being reconciled on his deathbed.

How different from his heir the fourteenth Duke, who as Earl of Arundel became a Member of Parliament in order to defend the Irish peasantry, and plead for Catholics who were in workhouses, in hospitals and in the army, none of whom had chaplains at the time. As fourteenth Duke he sought to turn Arundel into a Catholic paradise where the Angelus would ring again and estate workers would be given time for choir practice.[10] These sort of aspirations were mirrored by the sixteenth Earl of Shrewsbury at Alton Towers. It was therefore appropriate that the Duke of Norfolk should have encountered Frederick Faber at Alton Towers, with its 'figures in armour, the trophies of arms, emblazoned banners, gold-embroidered armigerous crimson curtains.'[11]

Such was the friendship that developed between the Duke and the priest that when in 1860 the Duke lay dying at Arundel, Faber administered the Last Rites. He died 'after an evening of quiet agony. He tried to kiss his crucifix, whispered "Jesus! Mary!" and placed his head on his wife's shoulder.' All the fathers from the Oratory came for the obsequies, singing the Office for the Dead in the library and then the Requiem in the old Catholic chapel in the castle. It was another thirteen years before Arundel Cathedral, built by the fifteenth Duke, rising from the hill on which the town was built, and a replica of a fourteenth-century French cathedral, would stand as a symbol of triumphant Gothic revivalism. Meanwhile Father Faber looked out from the windows of the castle. 'This gloomy north-aspected quadrangle with its quite unutterable gothic takes my very wits out of me, as well as my spirits. It is a singularly odious and mournful house.'[12]

Father Faber's influence in the Church was like 'fireworks over water – a pyrotechnic display, whose effects linger and remain in the mind's eye.'[13] The same Oratorian priest observed that Newman's influence was more like that of 'a very powerful depth-charge going down and exploding every so often with ever greater force, the outward movement of the shock waves getting larger and larger until it meets the shore'.[14]

Faber first left the shores of the Lake District to go to Harrow, and then on to Balliol where he attended services at the University Church where Newman was Vicar. In 1837 he became a Fellow of University College, returning to the Lake District during vacations and taking long rambles with Wordsworth. In 1839, on the Feast of St. Philip Neri, Faber was ordained in the Anglican ministry. Soon afterwards he travelled to Belgium and Germany, returning with a contemptuous attitude towards the doctrine and liturgy of Catholicism. Two years later he travelled to the Continent again, visiting France, Italy, Turkey, Bulgaria, Hungary and Austria, returning to England to become Rector of Elton in Huntingdonshire. Before commencing these pastoral duties he had decided to make a thorough study of pastoral methods in Catholic countries, particularly in Rome, where Wiseman gave him letters of introduction. The original connection between the Huntingdon rector and the Roman prelate had been a scholarly one. In *Sights and Thoughts in Foreign Churches* Faber had disagreed with Wiseman that the services of Holy Week were dramatic. Owing to a printer's error the citation was not acknowledged and Faber wrote to apologise. This initiated a friendly correspondence between two of the leading exponents of Roman Catholicism in nineteenth century England.[15]

On his 1843 European tour Faber was now overcome by the glories of the cathedral at St. Ouen. At Pisa he found the cloisters 'glorious though inferior to Gloucester'. On arrival in Rome in May, he was now deeply conscious of the Eternal City's link with the living past.

> You walk through the streets – there stood the centurion's house, and beneath that church St. Luke wrote the Acts of the Apostles – there St. Ignatius shed his blood – from that pulpit St. Thomas preached – in that room St. Francis slept – in that house St. Dominic first began his order.[16]

Visiting the Chiesa Nuova in Rome Faber developed a particular devotion to St. Philip Neri, little dreaming that he would one day become an Oratorian and that the priest who guided him around the Oratorian house in Rome would later become novice-master in Birmingham. At an audience with Pope Gregory XVI the Holy Father said simply: 'You must not mislead yourself in wishing for unity, yet waiting for your church to move. Think of the salvation of your own soul.' Faber knelt, the Pope laid his hands on his shoulders and said: 'May the grace of God correspond to your good wishes and deliver you from the nets of Anglicanism, and bring you to the true Holy Church.'[17]

Back in Huntingdonshire Faber set out to reclaim souls from sinful ways. During these years of prayer, fasting and pastoral activity his own soul was tormented with doubts about the Church of England. There was

> many and many an hour of bitter and earnest prayer … as to whether I should become a Catholic, many a kissing of the feet of the Crucifix and imploring Jesus to let me stay in the English Church if it could be His will, and many a heartfelt prayer that I might not draw back when His will should be made known.[18]

His will seemed to become clearer when Newman was received into the Church in 1845. And clearer still when Faber was sent a cheque from an acquaintance to pay off a lingering debt for an improvement to the Elton rectory. This financial dilemma solved, he was now free to leave Elton and follow his conscience to Rome. Six weeks after Newman became a Catholic, Faber informed his parishioners that the doctrines that he had taught them were true, but not true of the Church of England. 'That done, he came down from the pulpit, dramatically threw his surplice on the ground and hastily betook himself through the vestry to the rectory.'[19] Early next morning he left the parish, the villagers waving farewell from their windows. A family of orphan children to whom Faber had shown great kindness cried out 'Goodbye, God bless you, Mr Faber'. The next day Faber was received into the Church, writing at the end of a letter he wrote that day 'Peace – peace – peace!'[20]

This peace was at last found among a small band of converts living in a house with little furniture and no beds, depending on alms for their food, close to Pugin's St. Chad's Cathedral in Birmingham. A proper endowment was needed, and in 1846 Faber set out with a companion in search of a benefactor in Italy. In Lyons they came across a pastoral letter from the Archbishop giving directions for ceremonies of thanksgiving for the conversion of Newman and Faber. Arriving in Rome Faber's financial problems were solved again in an unexpected way; his companion, Dr Hutchison, would finance his new venture. When Faber had an audience with Gregory XVI the Holy Father congratulated him on giving up so much, urging him to convert his friends in England.

Back in Birmingham the community were known as the Brothers of the Will of God and that summer the Earl of Shrewsbury offered the community Cotton Hall and land near Cheadle. The large hall stood high up on the side of a valley above woodland – 'a wild and beautiful solitude among the hills of Staffordshire.'[21] There was a garden, a sloping lawn, with a picturesque Anglican church in Regency Gothic in the grounds. Deep in the country Faber and his community set to work, building a terrace, setting up walks, creating gardens and building a church designed by Pugin, which the architect claimed to be the only perfect church in England. Once again, it was Newman who prompted a radical change of plan. On hearing that Newman was to be Superior of the Oratorians, Faber felt instinctively that he wanted to become an Oratorian himself. In 1848 the entire community of the Brothers of the Will of God became Oratorians. With sadness they had to leave their beloved Cotton Hall. Such seemed to be the Will of God.

The Oratorians arrived in London in 1849. Led by Father Faber, they were given financial help by three laymen: David Lewis, Mr Alexander Fullerton and the Earl of Arundel. They found a home on King William Street near the Strand, where they preached triumphal Roman

Catholicism – considered too Roman by some Catholics. Until 1849 no religious body had been allowed to open a church in London and popular services on weekdays were unknown. The chapel was left open all day for confessions and prayer. The decoration of the Lady Altar with flowers and the lighting of candles in front of her Statue was then unheard of. In 1850 Faber was elected Superior of the London Oratory and in 1854 they moved to Brompton, where one of the most generous benefactresses was the Duchess of Argyll, who had become a Catholic in 1847.[22]

At Brompton the Duchess gave large sums for the temporary Oratory and £4,000 alone for the Sanctuary, the precious wooden inlaid floor having belonged to the 7th Duke. She later left the Oratorians the proceeds of the sale of her home in Ardencaple, which amounted to £20,000. In the summer of 1857 Faber wrote to the Duchess from Ardencaple, where he was on retreat.

> I am writing to you in the middle windows of the white room ... with the evening sun on the water and the hills, making all most beautiful. I do not think one of the old hermits in the Egyptian deserts could have a more profound stillness round him than I have. The smell of the jasmine is coming in at the windows ... I cannot tell you how happy and at *home* I feel. Rest from work, yet nothing to distract me from God – this is what I am always longing for, and have now got. How grateful I am to you for it![23]

Such were days of great solace for the weary Father Faber who after a life of pastoral ministry, poetic creativity and administrative burdens and toil, died after a long illness in 1863. Throughout his life he experienced miracles and consolations. One such he described to Lady Arundel.

A parishioner said that it had been revealed to her that the sixteenth-century Italian saint St. Mary Magdalena of Pazzi would cure him of his headaches, and suggested applying a relic of the saint to his forehead. After a night spent in great pain Faber applied a piece of sheet belonging to the saint to his forehead and 'a sort of fire went in to my head, through every limb down to my feet, causing me to tremble... I was filled with a kind of sacred fear, and an intense desire to consecrate myself utterly to God.' He had forgotten that two years before an old friend had written to him from Florence saying that his children had prayed at the tomb of St. Mary Magdalena of Pazzi whom they had asked to cure Father Faber's headaches. He wrote: 'After all this I am sure I will lose my soul if I do not serve God less lukewarmly: so please pray for me....'[24]

Notes

[1] L. Allen, 'Ambrose Phillipps De Lisle, 1809–1878', *The Catholic Historical Review*, April 1954, Vol. XL, p. 8.

[2] B. Elliott, 'The Return of the Cistercians to the Midlands', *Recusant History*, vol. 16 (1982–83), pp. 99–100.

[3] D. Gwynn, *Lord Shrewsbury, Pugin and the Catholic Revival*, London, Hollis & Carter, 1946, pp. 8, 17.

[4] Ibid., pp. xxxcii, 33.

[5] M. Trappes-Lomax, *Pugin. A Medieval Vision*, London, Sheed & Ward, 1932, p. 112–3.

[6] J. Patrick, 'Newman, Pugin & Gothic', *Victorian Studies*, Winter 1981, p. 198.

[7] R. O'Donnell, 'Roman Catholic Architecture in Great Britain and Ireland 1829–1878', University of Cambridge Ph.D., 1983, p. 29.

[8] *The Rambler*, 1855, p. 369, quoted in op. cit., p. 88.

[9] J.M. Robinson, *The Dukes of Norfolk. A Quincentennial History*, Oxford, O.U.P., 1982, p. 202.

[10] M. Napier and A. Laing, *The London Oratory Centenary, 1884–1984*, London, Trefoil, 1984, p. 51.

[11] Trappes-Lomax, op. cit., p. 100.

[12] Napier, op. cit., p. 58.

[13] R. Addington (ed.), *Faber. Poet and Priest. Selected Letters by Frederick William Faber*, D. Brown & Sons, Ltd., 1974, p. 20.

[14] Ibid.

[15] Rev. James Cassidy, *The Life of Father Faber, Priest of the Oratory of St. Philip Neri*, London, Sands & Co., 1946, p. 40.

[16] Ibid., p. 40.

[17] Ibid., p. 43.

[18] Ibid.

[19] Ibid., p. 54.

[20] R. Chapman, *Father Faber*, London, Burns & Oates, 1961, pp. 115, 6.

[21] Ibid., p. 153.

[22] R. Addington (ed.), *Faber, Poet and Priest. Selected Letters by Frederick William Faber*, London, D. Brown & Sons, Ltd., 1974, p. 280.

[23] Ibid., p. 280.

[24] Ibid., p. 219.

Chapter Twelve

This whirl of worldliness

Days of peace spent by Faber towards the end of his life at Ardencaple in Scotland were a source of inspiration for his strenuous apostolate in the metropolis. As young men he and Wordsworth had walked the hills of the Lake District, when the future priest's poetic imagination had pictured the country around Kirkby Stephen as it once was.

> The forests were re-planted; the chases were filled again with deer, the ancestors of the red deer of the Duke of Norfolk, which still drank at the brink of Ullswater by Lyulph's tower... The abbeys and chantries were haunted by church-music, while the lesser cells in the secluded pastoral vales heard once more the nightly aspirations of wakeful prayer, and Cistercian shepherds could scarcely be distinguished in their white habits from the sheep they tended ... From earliest times it was to me the land of knightly days, and the spell has never been broken.[1]

Thirty years later Faber used to take what he called his Vesper walk towards the loch by Ardencaple Castle. In his mind's eye the castle was Lyulph's Tower, Loch Fyne was Ullswater. It was not the red deer of the Duke of Norfolk but the red roe of the Duke of Argyll which munched the oats while Faber said his Office. 'Then this grand harvest moon has come', he wrote to the Duchess of Argyll, 'and won't let me go to bed, the scene is so beautiful: and amidst all this I must go ...'[2]

The Duchess of Argyll was the third wife of the seventh Duke whom she married in 1831, becoming a Catholic in 1847 a few months after her husband's death. The Duke's son by his first marriage became the eighth Duke and displayed considerable spiritual leanings but which did not stretch as far as Rome. He expressed dis-satisfaction with the Church of England, saying that Gladstone's book on Church and State he had picked up with eagerness but then dropped with disgust. He was put off by its narrow Anglicanism and 'high-sounding general principles tied down to purely provincial applications.'[3] The Duke carried out his own spiritual quest in Scotland, having a particular affection for the country near Loch Fyne. At the ducal residence of Rosneath near Helensburgh the early winter's sun streamed across the lawns and gardens towards the high range at the head of the loch, seeming, quoting the Book of Joel 'like morning spread upon the mountains'. The Duke took much to solitary meditations on the mountains that were his.

> I recollect looking up into the sky palpitating with light, when, as it seemed, a voice arose within one saying: 'What can people mean when they speak of death? There is no such thing as death. Death is an impossibility' ... it was the imminence and universality of life which was thus borne in upon me – life so filling and so full that it was, and must be, a fountain inexhausted and for ever inexhaustible.[4]

The Duke dimly remembered his mother urging her children to read the scriptures morning and evening, and at her funeral going in a steamer to the old church of Kilmun, the remains of a monastic establishment founded by the Argyll family in the fifteenth century 'and which has ever since been our burying place'. The Duke first met his future wife, Lady Elizabeth Leveson-Gower, daughter of the Duke of Sutherland, when she accompanied Queen Victoria to Taymouth in 1842. 'That view of Perth and of

the richly-wooded plain in which it stands with the winding
Tay is said to have so struck the Roman Legions that they
exclaimed in ecstasy, "Ecce Tiber!" The Duke did not find
eventual solace in the city on the Tiber, preferring the
maritime climate of Mull, with its 'masses and depths of
shadow, and such richness of contrasted lights as were
impossible in the brilliant but somewhat garish monotony
of the Mediterranean and of the Italian lakes'.[5]

The Duke died an Anglican in 1900. Three of his compatriots, the Marquess of Bute, Sir David Hunter-Blair and
James Hope-Scott each made the spiritual journey which
reached its conclusion in the Universal Church. Each
contributed towards the restoration of Roman Catholicism
in Scotland with the foundation of monasteries and
churches. An English convert with a Scottish title, Cecil,
Marchioness of Lothian founded the church of St. David
on the outskirts of Dalkeith. At its consecration in 1859
black-faced colliers stood at the door trying to look in.
Facing them was Bishop Gillis in full pontificals saying: 'My
dear brethren, you are surprised to see me in this dress.
This dress is one thousand eight hundred years old.' The
discourse that followed was listened to in breathless
silence. The pelting of stones against the wooden church
from the Protestant demonstrators outside soon subsided.[6]

The Marquess of Bute died in the same year as the Duke
of Argyll, his heart being taken to Palestine, to be interred
in the sacred soil of Olivet. It was reverently laid in the tiny
garden of the Franciscans, 'the traditional spot, half-way up
the holy mountain, where the Saviour shed tears over the
approaching fate of the beloved city'.[7] The Marquess's
funeral was on the Isle of Bute, the coffin having crossed
the Firth of Clyde where it was met by waiting mourners
who followed the cortège for five miles on foot.

> Through the russet and gold of the October woods it
> passed, preceded by the cross and a long array of
> bishops and clergy, ... Night was falling as our cortège
> reached the little chapel on the shore where the
> remains were to rest; and the pine torches threw a
> sombre glare on the coffin, on which were laid a black

and gold pall, and the dead peer's coronet and the chain and green velvet mantle of the Thistle. Vespers of the dead were sung; black-robed sisters watched by the bier all night; and next morning the dirge was chanted, the requiem mass celebrated, the five absolutions reserved for prelates and great nobles solemnly pronounced. The single bell tolled from the little turret as the mourners silently dispersed, leaving Lord John Bute to rest in peace within the ivy-covered walls washed by the waves which encircled his island home.[8]

As a schoolboy, Lord John Bute's headmaster's report at prep school had read 'RELIGION ... Unhappily not to the taste of the British public.' With a mother whose Protestant sympathies extended as far as seeking to convert the Irish labourers at work on the Bute docks in Cardiff, the young Marquess felt unaccountably drawn to a liking for 'Romish priesthood and ceremonial.' After Harrow and Christ Church, where his contemporaries were the Duke of Hamilton, Lord Rosebery, the Duke of Northumberland, Lord Cawdor, Lord Doune and Lord Willoughby de Broke, as soon as he could he went to Palestine, and from then on used his yacht *Ladybird* (purchased from Lord Herries, who had fallen on hard times) to cruise in the Mediterranean. At Oxford the young Marquess was unaware of the existence of any Catholic chapel, but on a visit to East Hendred, home of the recusant Oxfordshire Eyston family, he was moved to discover that the sanctuary lamp in the chapel had never been extinguished. He knelt so long before the altar that twice he was reminded of the long journey back. This was in the autumn of 1866. He soon came to the conclusion that the religion of the greater part of Christianity was right and that the British were wrong. Once his intentions were known, family and acquaintances, family solicitors, dons and guardians urged him to wait until he was 21 – it being thought better to lead a wasteful life than submit to Popery. After Oxford he met Monsignor Capel, then chaplain at Danesfield in Buckinghamshire, home of the convert Charles Scott-Murray. Bute later wrote that it was Monsignor Capel who 'made *many* think and say "Now is the time to arise from sleep". Only they are so chained by the habits of their lives and by the fear of what the wordly consequences may be if they follow their consciences.'[9]

After his reception into the Church the Marquess of Bute set sail for Nice in his yacht where the Scott-Murrays were staying. Thence to Rome, to give thanks for his new found Faith, where he donated a magnificent reliquary. He continued on to Jerusalem, taking Monsignor Capel with him as his Chaplain. He recalled: 'I am perfectly at peace in the Church ... in a condition that renders restlessness impossible and controversy absolutely superfluous.'[10]

At a magnificent ceremony at the Oratory in London in 1872 the Marquess of Bute married the Hon. Gwendoline Fitzalan-Howard, eldest daughter of Lord Howard of Glossop. This alliance opened up new avenues in society for the young Marquess, who found himself in the old Catholic world which was by its nature unostentatious and austere. He meanwhile used his wealth unashamedly to purchase abbeys that had been lost, starting with the abbey and castle of St. Andrew's and the site of Whithorn abbey, which became a Premonstratensian priory. Pluscarden Abbey he purchased from the Earl of Fife, and he bought Crichton Tower at Sanquhar, Falkland Palace and Old Place at Mochrum. When Mountstuart House was burnt down in 1877 he replaced it with a sandstone Italian Gothic mansion.[11] It was said of the Marquess that he preferred to restore an old chapel than to build a new one. Some of his happiest hours were spent 'wrapped in his long cloak and smoking innumerable cigarettes, while a band of workmen, directed by one of his many architects, dug out the foundations of a medieval lady chapel or broke through a nineteenth century wall in search of a thirteenth century doorway'.[12]

In Oban the Marquess wanted to found a cathedral in a town whose congregation lived in appalling conditions. He made the offer to the bishop on condition that the full liturgy of the Divine Office and daily High Mass was celebrated. The hard-pressed clergy being unavailable to carry out this request, the Bishop had to turn down the offer.

The following year a compromise was reached when the Marquess relented and provided the town with a beautiful pro-Cathedral prefabricated in iron, with the intention that if needed, it could be dismantled and used as small chapels.[13] The Marquess's architectural contributions comprised the 'feudal massiveness of Cardiff and Castell Coch, of Rothesay Castle and Mochrum, the graceful Gothic of Pluscarden, the Franciscan austerity of Elgin, the rich Renaissance and Jacobean details of Falkland, the Byzantine perfection of Sancta Sophia (copied by him in miniature at Gabton)...'[14] 'It is pleasant', wrote Lady Knightley, who dined with the Marquess in 1873, 'to feel one is with people who are deeply religious and really do *care* for God. It does one good in this whirl of wordliness.'[15] And at Raby Castle the following year one guest walked each day with Lord Bute listening to him talk incessantly of ritual and liturgy. He talked too of fasting, which he did sometimes for twenty four hours. He found cigars allayed hunger and with plenty of exercise he 'ate the air'. While lack of food did not make him ill-tempered, the Marquess agreed that some people were better fasting alone.[16]

Another boy at the prep school where the headmaster had written in such scathing terms of the young Marquess's religious propensities was Sir David Hunter-Blair. The only days on which boys were allowed to talk at meals were the Headmaster's birthday and Guy Fawkes Day. Hunter-Blair went on to Eton. He later asked if there was something in the spirit of the great school which prepared Etonians 'to act on our convictions with courage, sincerity and decision when the critical moment came?' This was after meeting eight Etonians who had become Oratorian priests. Had they been 'unconsciously inhaling ... the *aura* of Catholicism which still hung faintly about her venerable halls and cloisters?'[17]

❧

Religious education at Eton was for some uninspired. 'Sunday Questions' gave the merest dry bones of divinity. On Monday mornings there was a Greek Testament lesson and in the evening compulsory prayers in the tutor's dining room. For Hunter-Blair, it was reading Sir Walter Scott's novels with their gallant knights and gracious ladies which suddenly made him realise that it was Catholicism that had made them what they were. Scott's writings 'first helped me throw off the incubus of acquired and inherited prejudice which had weighed upon me from childhood'. Newman's novel *Loss and Gain* and the conversion of the Marquess of Bute (which was featured in Newman's novel) both played their part. Then a favourite uncle of Hunter-Blair's, a soldier, sportsman, artist, musician and linguist who had gone to the South of France and Italy in search of a cure for his health, became a Catholic and died shortly afterwards. Hunter-Blair felt his gallant uncle 'would never have taken such a step without the fullest conviction that he was doing right.'[18]

From Eton Hunter-Blair went on to Magdalene and at the age of 22 was received into the Roman Catholic Church on Maundy Thursday, 1875. He went to Rome, where he was entertained by Cardinal Howard with the 'stately *bonhomie* of a great prelate who still retained something of the military dash of an ex-officer of the Life Guards.' Three years later Hunter-Blair began his novitiate as a Benedictine.

In 1876 the site for a monastery at Fort Augustus had been given to the Benedictines by the fifteenth Lord Lovat. A Gothic design was thought most fitting, for which the Prior and Hunter-Blair made a detailed examination of the great Benedictine cloisters of Westminster Abbey. They took measurements by clambering on to the window ledges; while doing this they were taken by surprise by a small procession of deans and canons who emerged from a door opposite the chapter-house.

The Benedictine foundation of Belmont in Herefordshire was established thanks to the generosity of a convert, Wegg-Prosser, and it was here that Hunter-Blair spent the rest of his novitiate. The recusant Bodenham family at Rotherwas entertained the novices in the summer when 'a bountiful tea was spread for us under the immemorial oaks before we took our way back to our monastery by river or road.' If they went

by the river then Hunter-Blair led the novices in the Eton
boating song which they sang as they 'rowed down the last
reach under the Belmont woods'.[19]

While Sir Walter Scott's novels had initially brought Sir
David Hunter-Blair into the Roman fold, the novelist's
granddaughter had married James Hope, later a well-
known   convert.   Born   in   1812   at   Marlow   in
Buckinghamshire, the third son of General the Hon. Sir
Alexander Hope, he went to Eton and Christ Church,
becoming a Fellow of Merton in 1833 where he formed a
friendship with Manning. At Oxford Hope was very aware
of the monastic inheritance of college life.

> To be every moment subject to a sudden command
> for some common object, to be forced every now and
> then into the practical business of life; to be obliged
> to attend to dress, and punctuality in hours; to have
> no choice but associate with men of equal or superior
> ability every day; and, above all, to be brought contin-
> ually under the influence of a choral service and thus,
> when the heart is narrowed to some trifling object, to
> have it roused and expanded, whether it will or not,
> into a sense of God's presence, of the communion of
> saints and of the nothingness of all knowledge which
> does not point towards Heaven, are surely not expe-
> dient things alone, but where they may be had,
> necessary, and in all things most desirable.[20]

James Hope married Charlotte Lockhart-Scott in 1847, his
sister's husband, Lord Henry Kerr, then Vicar of Dittisham,
officiating. They spent their honeymoon at one of the
Duke of Buccleuch's houses in Richmond and then rented
Abbotsford from Charlotte's brother Walter Lockhart-
Scott. In London Hope attended the High Anglican
services at Margaret Street. In 1851 he and Manning were
received into the Church at Farm Street. Hope later wrote
to Manning: 'You do not need that I should say how
sensibly I remember all your sympathy, which was the only
human help in the time when we two went through the
trial, which to be known must be endured.'[21] It was not the

state of the Church of England which had prompted him to leave, but a review of the chain of events which led up to the Reformation. 'I can safely say that I left her because I was convinced that she never from the Reformation downwards, had been a true Church.'[22] A fellow parishioner at All Saints Margaret Street said of him that the 'frankness of his nature, his well-known good sense, the sound clearness of his judgment precluded the possibility of attributing his adoption of the Catholic faith to weakness of mind, duplicity, sentiment, eccentricity or excitability.'[23]

Six weeks after James Hope became a Catholic he was followed into the Church by his wife Charlotte. Two years after that his sister Louisa and Lord Henry Kerr became Catholics. In 1854 Walter Lockhart-Scott died and Abbotsford passed to Charlotte, when James adopted the name Hope-Scott. At Abbotsford he immediately set to work and a religious atmosphere soon pervaded the whole house. Newman came to stay. He then purchased another property, Lochshiel on the west coast of Inverness-shire opposite Skye. He wrote to Newman: 'We are here on the sea-shore, with wild rocks, lakes and rivers near us, an aboriginal Catholic population, a priest in the house, and a chapel within 100 yards.'[24] He built a chapel dedicated to Our Lady of the Angels at Mingarry and another dedicated to St. Agnes at Glenuig. A son was born in 1857 but a year later Charlotte died, his daughter died two weeks after that and his son a week afterwards. All three were buried in the vault of St. Margaret's Convent in Edinburgh. Hope-Scott wrote to Newman that it may be that further sacrifices would be asked from him, and that he might need more strength; 'but what I chiefly fear is that I may not profit as I ought by that wonderful union of trial and consolation which God has of late vouchsafed me.'[25]

Hope-Scott travelled abroad with his sister and her husband, Lord and Lady Henry Kerr, and made the acquaintance of the Earl of Arundel. In 1861 he married Lady Victoria Fitzalan Howard, the eldest sister of the fourteenth Duke of Norfolk, having knelt at the bedside of the dying Duke to receive his blessing. The one surviving daughter of his first marriage needed to spend winters in a warm climate. So it was that James Hope-Scott added a French property to his Scottish acquisitions, buying the Villa Madona near the Boulevard d'Orient at Hyères in the South of France. Having thinned the fir trees at windswept Abbotsford, he established in the South of France a vineyard and an olive grove, taking interest in all the culture that makes up a provençal farm; wine, oil, almonds, figs and fowls. He adorned the bank of his boulevard with aloes and yuccas and eucalyptus. He attended Mass regularly and made pilgrimages to l'Ermitage. 'Few who have seen him in prayer before the Tabernacle could forget his look of intense reverence and recollection, the consequence of his strong faith in the Real Presence.'[26]

In London he demonstrated his piety to one or two close friends, who were aware that he was saying the Angelus in the time he took to mount the stairs to the committee-rooms at Westminster. In London cabs he said the rosary or while walking the busy streets, and in walking the corridors of the House of Commons. But his life as a Queen's Counsel was secondary to his passion for church building. He built the church of Our Lady and St. Andrew at Galashiels, the church of Our Lady and St. Joseph at Selkirk, the church of the Immaculate Conception at Kelso, and churches at Durlie near Lochshiel, Oban and St. Andrews. In 1856 the church at Kelso was attacked by a Protestant mob and burned to the ground as was the adjacent schoolhouse and house containing vestments, furniture, and books all belonging to Hope-Scott.

The purchase of Lochshiel had been extremely providential. Its Catholic owners had had the Blessed Sacrament reserved in the house and a resident chaplain. When put on the market it was sold to Protestants from London. Two Catholic converts from this family asked the lawyer to postpone the signing of the deeds for nine or ten days. They commenced a novena and on the ninth day the property was purchased by Hope-Scott, whose attention to the property had been drawn by a lady in Edinburgh 'known among Scotch Catholics for her shrewd good sense and innumerable good works.'[27]

James Hope-Scott's good sense and good works were

mourned on his death in 1873. Indeed the opening of the cathedral of St. Philip Neri at Arundel was delayed so that the Fitzalan Howards could watch by his bed. The moment after he died a sudden change came over his face and 'in one minute he had become like what he used to be in very early years'.[28] Newman came to his Requiem Mass in Farm Street where the church was draped in black. Newman preached.

> That straightforward, clear, good sense he showed in secular matters did not fail him in religious inquiry. There are those who are practical and sensible in all things save in religion; but he was consistent; he instinctively turned from bye-ways and cross-paths, into which the inquiry might be diverted, and took a broad, intelligible view of its issues. And, after he had been brought within the Fold, I do not think I can exaggerate the solicitude which he all along showed, the reasonable and prudent solicitude, to conform himself in all things to the enunciations and the decisions of Holy Church; nor, again, the undoubted conviction he had of her superhuman authority, the comfort he has found in her sacraments, and the satisfaction and trust with which he betook himself to the intercession of the Blessed Virgin, to the glorious St. Michael, St. Margaret and all saints.[29]

Notes

1 J.E. Bowden, *The Life and Letters of Frederick William Faber, D.D.*, London, Thomas Richardson & Son, 1969, pp. 4–5.
2 R. Addington (ed.), *Faber. Poet and Priest. Selected Letters by Frederick William Faber*, D. Brown & Sons, Ltd., 1974, p. 285.
3 Dowager Duchess of Argyll (ed.), *George Douglas Eighth Duke of Argyll, K.G., K.T. (1823–1900). Autobiography and Memoirs*, London, John Murray, 1906, p. 309.
4 Ibid., p. 92.
5 Ibid., pp. 185, 232.
6 C. Kerr, *Cecil, Marchioness of Lothian*, London, Sands & Co., 1922, p. 116.

7   Right Rev. Sir David Hunter-Blair, *John Patrick Third Marquess of Bute, K.T. (1847–1900)*, London, John Murray, 1921, p. 228.
8   Ibid., p. 227.
9   Ibid., pp. 15, 27, 67.
10 Ibid., p. 78.
11 J. Davies, *Cardiff and the Marquesses of Bute*, Cardiff, University of Wales Press, 1981, p. 29.
12 Right Rev. Sir David Hunter-Blair, *A Medley of Memories. Fifty Years' Recollections of a Benedictine Monk*, London, Edward Arnold, 1919, p. 131.
13 R. Macdonald, 'The Catholic Gaidhealtachd' in D. McRoberts (ed.), *Modern Scottish Catholicism 1878–1978*, Glasgow, Burns, 1979, pp. 69–9.
14 Hunter-Blair, *John Patrick*, p. 222.
15 J. Cartwright, *Journals of Lady Knightley of Fawsley, 1856–1884*, London, John Murray, 1915, p. 24.
16 A.J.C. Hare, *The Story of My Life Vol. III*, London, George Allen, 1896, p. 271.
17 Hunter-Blair, *Medley of Memories*, op. cit., pp. 37–8.
18 Ibid., p. 46.
19 Ibid., p. 136.
20 R. Ornsby, *Memoirs of James Robert Hope-Scott of Abbotsford, D.C.L., Q.C.*, Vol. I, London, John Murray, 1884, p. 188.
21 J. Gillow, *A Literary and Biographical History, or Biographical Dictionary of the English Catholics from the Breach with Rome, in 1534, to the present time*, Vol. III, p. 382.
22 R. Ornsby, *Memoirs of James Robert Hope-Scott of Abbotsford, D.C.L., Q.C.*, Vol. II, London, John Murray, 1884, p. 84.
23 Ibid., p. 86.
24 Ibid., p. 150.
25 Ibid., p. 153.
26 Ibid., p. 192.
27 Ibid., p. 222.
28 Ibid., p. 247.
29 Ibid., p. 262.

Chapter Thirteen

The First Sunday after Ascot

James Hope-Scott was received into the Church with Henry Manning, later Cardinal Archbishop of Westminster. Manning was later to become known as the Apostle of the Genteels who made converts by conversation or as Ruskin put it 'by fascination'.[1] The Cardinal's funeral in 1892 was attended by more Londoners than that of the Duke of Clarence, eldest son of Queen Victoria. Both Hope-Scott and Manning were moved to join the Catholic Church in the wake of the Gorham Judgment. Gladstone described their departure from the Church of England as 'the rending and sapping of the Church, the loss of its gems'.[2]

The Gorham Judgment of 1851 prompted many Anglican clergy and laity to look for the first time with seriousness towards the Church of Rome. An elderly clergyman called Gorham, vicar of a small Devon parish, was suspected by Bishop Phillpotts of Exeter of not holding the Anglican doctrine of baptismal regeneration; the Calvinist clergyman did not believe that baptism was a sacrament. He was indicted for heresy and found guilty before the ecclesiastical court, the Court of Arches. On appeal he was acquitted by the Privy Council, with the concurrence of the Archbishops of Canterbury and York. Privy Councillors, politicians with no theological training, had ruled on a fundamental aspect of Christian doctrine. They had approved Gorham's belief that the language used at the baptismal service should be interpreted as a statement of devout hope rather than certain fact. Bishop

Phillpotts and the Reverend Gorham spent hours in dispute, lasting until one or other of the elderly clergymen neared physical collapse. The traditional Bishop's cause was lost. But the lawyer who represented him at the Privy Council started to receive Instruction as a Catholic, prompted by the theological and legalistic deliberations.[3] So too did many others, Manning being the shooting star among them.

He was born in 1808, the tenth child of William Manning, a Member of Parliament, a West Indian Merchant and later Governor of the Bank of England. In 1815 the family moved to Combe Bank near Sundridge in Kent, formerly the home of Lord Walter Campbell, son of the eighth Duke of Argyll. In 1831 William Manning was made bankrupt and Combe Bank had to be sold. Henry Manning spent his days in the early summer of that year 'mooning about the still unsold Combe Bank, where he fished and poeticized and dabbled to an infinitesimal shallow degree ... The beauty of the place, now it was to be taken away from him, seemed overwhelming.'[4]

The beauty of the Church of England was later to be taken away from him not as a result of financial bankruptcy, but of the bankruptcy of its doctrines – or so they were later perceived by the brilliant Manning. He went into the church after Harrow and Balliol, once having dreamed of the House of Commons when he had possessed 'the strongest worldly ambition for public life a man could have.' But on becoming a Catholic, 'I could not have become more exiled from the public and political life, from the private and social life, from the English homes, from the Parliament, from the court.'[5]

Exiled from the House of Lords, he was not however exiled from Lord's cricket ground where every year until 1888 Manning was present at the dinner which followed the Eton–Harrow match. His fellow Harrovian Charles Wordsworth had started the Eton–Harrow match in 1825. Manning himself played at the first match between Harrow and Winchester at Lord's that same summer. He later said 'When you take up the chalice you drop the cricket ball'.[6] Friendships were dropped as well, that with Charles

Wordsworth remaining dormant for thirty-one years. It was revived only when Wordsworth, as Bishop of St. Andrews, wrote some cricketing reminiscences in a Scottish news-paper which prompted Manning to write to him. As a young curate at Graffham in Sussex, Manning used to play cricket on the village green. Forty-five years later when Manning was considered a possible future successor to the Holy See on the death of Pope Pius IX, a villager said, 'I should dearly like to say as'ow I'd played a game of cricket with the Pope-o'-Rome'.[7]

Manning reminisced about the part of Sussex where he once played cricket, long after he had left to take up his metropolitan ecclesiastical duties.

> I loved the little church under the green hill-side, where the morning and evening prayers and the music of the English bible for seventeen years became a part of my soul.... If there was no eternal world I could have made it my home.[8]

It was here he married Caroline Sargent, who died four years after their marriage. He became Archdeacon of Chichester in 1840 and began to soak in the Tractarian influence emanating from Oxford. Then, in the year after Newman became a Catholic, Manning's sister-in-law Sophia and her husband George Ryder took the same step. Manning travelled. At Malines he attended Exposition and Benediction in the cathedral where 'the procession gave me a strong feeling of the reality of the Incarnation and of their way of witnessing it.'[9] He felt at home in Aix-la-Chapelle, the country being a mixture of 'North Wales, the South Downs, Stroud and Dove Dale'. Inside the churches that had never been anything but Roman Catholic, he was impressed by the number of well-dressed young men 'who used their rosaries with as much piety as the poor'. At Basle he announced that 'the effect of Protestant worship is dreary; want of object, aim, intelligibleness; cold, dark, abstract'.[10] In Nice he went inside more churches.

There was something very beautiful and awful in the

lighted altar, with the incense seen from without the open door. A sad contrast to our [Anglican] Evensong, where everyone so far as I know, sat through their prayers.[11]

In Rome in 1847, the first Englishman he came across was Newman.

On his way back from Rome Manning inspected the body of St. Charles Borromeo in the cathedral in Milan. He felt a direct calling from the saint. Seven years after his conversion he established in Bayswater a community of Oblates of St. Charles, based on the society established by the saint in Milan in 1578. But this was long after Manning, having resigned his Chichester archdeaconry in the City on 25 March 1851, walked across Blackfriars Bridge to Southwark. Entering the Catholic cathedral, he knelt before the Blessed Sacrament and said his first Hail Mary.

In the same year of his conversion Manning was already himself receiving converts into the Church. Before he left for France in 1851 he received Sir Vere and Lady de Vere and Lady Newry. At Avignon he received Aubrey de Vere. A year later he had received another seventeen converts; by 1865, 343. His brother-in-law Robert Wilberforce was finally landed 'after a titanic struggle against the combined forces of Keble, Gladstone and Samuel Wilberforce'.[12] The duel with Pusey over the soul of the Duchess of Argyll was fierce and persistent. No sooner had she reached Scotland than Pusey was in pursuit, there following eight days of constant argument. She never wavered. Nor did the Duchess of Buccleuch, to whom Manning wrote that 'it would be time enough to thank Dr Pusey for his past kindnesses when she had done her duty to God first'.[13] 'Do you see the Dss of Buccleuch is gone over to Rome thro' the hands of Manning – *how* much that man has to answer for', wrote Maria Josepha, Lady Stanley, to her daughter-in-law in 1855.[14]

The Community of the Oblates of St. Charles Borromeo of which Manning was Superior before his elevation to the Cardinalate had at one time Sir Francis Burnand, later Editor of *Punch*, among its novices. He recalled his first introduction to Manning, whom he first saw beneath a gaslight descending the steps in Bayswater, wearing a cloak and a broad-rimmed, low-crowned hat.

> 'Ah!' said Dr Manning, removing his hat and inclining his head towards me as I bowed, 'I have a few minutes to spare. Will you' – this to me most persuasively – 'come this way?'
> And turning, he ascended the steps, leading the way up another short flight into a wide corridor – I noticed nothing, except that the architecture was Gothic – at the end of which was a door; this he pushed open, and after the briefest possible pause, as if to ascertain whether there was anybody there, he beckoned to me, and made his way up towards the large fireplace of the plain Gothic hall which, as I found out afterwards, was the refectory. He motioned me to a chair on the right of the fireplace as he seated himself on a bench on the opposite side. Then, with his right hand, long and thin, screening himself from the fire, he looked me full in the face. What a wonderful look! The thin sharp outlines of the features, the massive forehead, the broad bald head, of which the crown was covered with a skull cap, called, as I afterwards ascertained, a *soli-deo*, because never raised except when in the presence of the Blessed Sacrament, in fact the whole appearance of the man who had given up everything 'for conscience sake' so strongly impressed me that for a few seconds I was utterly overcome; not with visible emotion, but I had no words.
> At once Dr Manning put me at my ease. His summary of his own difficulties years ago, an expression of the deepest sympathy with mine now, and, not only with mine, but with those of all whom I was leaving at the 'parting of the ways', at once won me. My doubts had been his doubts, my difficulties his difficulties, his course of action was to be my course of action.[15]

The Marchioness of Lothian expressed precisely these

sentiments when she received news of Manning's reception into the church in 1851. She wrote that for a long time it had been all but settled that Manning's course would decide hers. As a child she had lived close to Tixall Hall, long the home of the old Catholic Clifford Constable family. When Tixall later passed into Protestant hands Cecil Lothian's father had arranged for the Catholic chapel to be transferred to Great Heywood, where there were a number of Catholics in the village. But before this happened, another convert like her, of Father Brownbill's at Farm Street, was born at Tixall.

The Hon. Georgiana Leveson-Gower whose father Lord Granville had rented Tixall Hall from the Clifford Constables wrote: 'I must have been the first child born in that house outside the visible pale of the church. May not the Guardian Angels of the place have asked for me the grace of conversion to the true faith?' Georgiana's nurse at Tixall happened to be a Catholic. 'Who knows that she didn't say "Hail Maries" for the infant at her breast? and perhaps she may have taken me into the chapel which was enshrined amidst the ivied ruins, close to the house.'[16]

Georgiana was the granddaughter of the Duke and Duchess of Devonshire and the Marquess and Marchioness of Stafford. Her father, Lord Granville, was Ambassador in Paris. Her youth was spent in France, but she had come across some Catholicism in the English halls of recusancy. Although she never went into the chapel at Tixall, she remembered seeing the long files of men, women and children going to Mass there on Sundays, when she was told 'They are the Roman Catholics going to their church.' She heard Mass for the first time at Slindon House in Sussex, home of the Newburghs, where 'there was something in the sight of a Catholic rural congregation which made a strange impression on me.'[17] She had the sensation of having been in the chapel before. Brought up in a pious household, she was taught never to hold a Bible in a careless manner, or speak of a clergyman with disrespect. Pondering the power of prayer, she had thought that if friends were asked to pray for others, then why should the Mother of Christ and the Saints not be asked as well? She went into a room next to the school-room, knelt down and said several times 'Blessed Virgin Mary, pray for me.' The next time she was to utter this prayer was many years later, as a Catholic. One evening Lord Harrowby said to her: 'It is quite wrong to call the Roman Catholics idolaters, because they worship the Host. They only worship it because they believe that our Lord Jesus Christ is present in It.'[18]

In 1830 Georgiana met Alexander Fullerton, a Guards officer and heir to property in England and Ireland. They married in Paris three years later and stayed at the Embassy, where he was an attaché. Their only child Granville was born in 1834. Soon afterwards the Fullertons travelled to Nice, Genoa and Turin for Alexander's health. In Turin they visited Madame de Bombelles, formerly a Miss Fraser. While waiting in her drawing room, Georgiana picked up a book. It was Francis de Sales's *Introduction to the Devout Life.* 'She read it attentively, and as she went on, the troublesome thoughts in her mind were dissipated, and light seemed to come back to her soul.'[19]

In Paris, Lady Georgiana turned her mind to the poor, envying her sister Lady Rivers the ease with which she was able to distribute charity to her estate tenants in England; a Protestant woman living in Paris found it difficult to find effective avenues for her largesse. She was restricted to individual cases of need and in order to finance this small venture, she decided to write novels. Later becoming a renowned author, her works paid for her vast array of charitable endeavours.

The Fullertons left Paris when Earl Granville left the Embassy and went to Nice and on to Rome, again for Alexander's health. Here Alexander renewed his acquaintance with a Theodore de Bussière, an old friend of Alphonse de Ratisbonne. In January 1842 the Jewish Alphonse de Ratisbonne had seen the Virgin Mary in the church of Saint Andrea della Fratte. This was the talk of Rome by the time the Fullertons arrived. While Georgiana accompanied her parents around Rome, Alexander went about on his own. On 23rd April 1843, without telling anyone, he was received into the Church, re-joining the family in Florence, who were shocked to hear the news. But the family's attention was soon diverted by the huge success of Georgiana's novel *Ellen Middleton.* Back in London, Lady Georgiana herself began a course of Instruction with Father Brownbill, knowing how much her conversion would pain her parents. She attended the High Anglican church in Margaret Street, where she was impressed by the profound devotion of James Hope-Scott. Three years later she was torn by the illness of her father and her yearning to join her husband's Faith.[20] It was a time of great anguish. She expressed this to Father Brownbill, telling him that she did not want to join the Catholic Church.

> Father Brownbill was sitting near a table in the little parlour in which he received visitors. He listened to this declaration without moving a muscle. He sat silent, looking at the tips of his nails (as he often did). At last he said quietly, 'And what is the Church, then, that you intend to enter?'[21]

She was received into the Church on Passion Sunday, 1846.

The Fullertons returned to France five years later and saw the Mediterranean once more: 'I love its blue, which never seemed to me so deep, the sky so pure, and the sun so brilliant'.[22] Lady Georgiana was a Catholic in a Catholic country. She had once said that she would rather see a single hawthorn bush in bloom than all the fruits and flowers of the south, that she preferred the tossing seas of the north to the calm and tideless Mediterranean. Now she happily exchanged hawthorns and grey seas for the colours and climes of the Catholic south. This yearning reached its fruition in Rome. This new-found happiness was quickly followed by the death of her only son at the age of twenty.

Her bereavement moved her to dedicate the rest of her life to charitable works, feeling a particular affinity with the poor Irish in London, whose religion she shared. She was joined by other pious converts: Lady Londonderry, the Duchess of Buccleuch, Lady Newburgh, the Duchess of Norfolk, Lady Denbigh and Lady Herbert of Lea, as well as old Catholics – the Stourtons, the Langdales, the Maxwells, the Cliffords, the Petres. Wherever there was a need for schools or orphanages she did all she could to relieve distress among the poor, drawing on the income from her successful novels to pay for her labours. She travelled to France, where her eyes were cured by the holy oil at the convent at Marmoutier near Tours and where there was a particular devotion to the Holy Face of Christ. This devotion she incorporated into the church of the Sacred Heart in Bournemouth where she spent the last ten years of her life setting up a school for poor Catholics and a Guild of St. Walburga.[23] She died in 1885. During her illness Dom Bosco gave her a picture of Our Lady Help of Christians. She said a novena, which ended on the Feast of Our Lady Help of Christians. She wrote:

> On that day it struck me that this illness has been sent me as the means of making with glad and ready acceptance, the sacrifices that would have cost me most if I had been free, and called to religious life – to cease to pray in the churches I love, to see only at rare intervals my spiritual father, not to see my brother's children growing up in his house, to have friends who will never be able to come and see me – some of my greatest – not to look on the varied beauties of earth and sky.... Everything assumed a new aspect, when any of these 'never again' make my heart ache, the pain is superseded by the joy and the conviction that, according to Dom Bosco's prayer, that kind of health is granted me which will be the best for my soul.[24]

When *Ellen Middleton* was first published it was read by the daughter of the Rector of Stoke Rochford in Lincolnshire, Mary Taylor. She read it again and again. 'I thought the writer must have a most beautiful mind, and great genius, and I enshrined her in my heart as one of my chief heroines.' In the summer of 1846 Mary Taylor was walking in London with her sister when she was told that Lady

Georgiana Fullerton had submitted to the Church of Rome.

> I stood rooted to the spot – I was stunned. I can see the exact spot now, and the trees waving in the sun. I never felt the same about the Church of England afterwards – vague doubts used to come to my mind, but I was too young to understand the question.[25]

Mary Taylor later met Lady Georgiana in 1867 and with her help established a congregation of Sisters of the Poor Servants of the Mother of God, discovering the religious life to be 'far sweeter than any earthly joy'.[26] She visited Poland in 1869, returning to set up equivalent houses in London, the main convent being in Streatham. In this venture she was helped by the Duchess of Buccleuch.

The Duchess of Buccleuch, the Duchess of Argyll, the Duchess of Norfolk and the Duchess of Newcastle were all powerful figures in the revival of nineteenth century Catholicism – as was the American Duchess of Leeds. The Duchess of Newcastle had married the sixth Duke in 1861 and became a Catholic in 1879, the year the Duke died. The following year she married the Anglican Rector of Winstone and Colesborne in Gloucestershire. He died in 1892 and the former Duchess entered upon charitable works in London, among other things setting up a Girls' Club in Tower Hill with the support of Archbishop Vaughan. She had been received into the Church by the Cardinal's Jesuit brother, Father Bernard Vaughan, later renowned in Mayfair for his series of sermons on 'The Sins of Society', one given on what he called the First Sunday after Ascot.

> It is the misfortune of fast Society not to recognise that it is not by mere chance that it finds itself here in the midst of the good things of this world. It will not see that it has been sent here, charged with a mission, deputed to a work; and not only so, but that it is more-over sent here equipped efficiently, splendidly, by our indulgent Father for its work.[27]

He preached scathingly about high society: 'If Herod and Herodias were to re-visit the earth and appear in London, they would be flooded with more invitations than ever had been theirs during their reign at Tiberias.' Old Catholic families did not escape his opprobrium.

> I sometimes wonder how their easy-going children can look up at the old family portraits in their dining-rooms or read the old mottoes of chivalry crossing their coats of arms, or pass into the domestic chapel where their parents prayed, or peruse the old documents which tell of their love of Christ and of their country. Why this boast of heraldry, if it does not make us lift up the feeble knees and stretch forth the drooping hands and call us to action as Catholic English citizens?[28]

The Duchess of Newcastle, new to the Faith, responded as her confessor would wish, helping to relieve spiritual poverty in the West End as much as material poverty in the East End. By the sixth Duke she had had two sons and three daughters, one of whom, Lady Beatrice Pelham-Clinton, married Cecil Lister-Kaye. When Beatrice and Cecil's daughter Christine later became a Catholic she quarrelled with her parents and went to live with her Catholic grandmother, the Duchess, helping with her charitable works. Many of the poor from the East End were invited to Westminster Cathedral for Christine Lister-Kaye's wedding in 1908, when she married Charles Vaughan, the Archbishop of Westminster's nephew. Dressed in exquisite satin, she wore a headdress which had been in the Newcastle family for five generations. After the nuptial Mass the Duchess gave a reception at the Ritz for five hundred. The young couple lived in Essex with the Duchess, the house having been purchased at Cardinal Vaughan's instigation. Here the Duchess built a church, a Franciscan friary and schools.[29]

Cardinal Vaughan's mother was a convert who had become a Catholic four months after she married John Vaughan of Courtfield in Herefordshire. For an hour a day she had prayed in front of the Blessed Sacrament at Courtfield, pleading that her children spend their lives serving God. Six of her sons became priests, of whom three became bishops, and four daughters became nuns. After breakfast she went in to the chapel, knelt at the prie dieu, and fixed her eyes on the Tabernacle, reminding all her children that in the Tabernacle 'One who loved us more than even she did was always abiding, ever ready to greet us when we want to see Him.'[30]

> She made Heaven such a reality to us that we felt that we knew more about it, and liked it in a way far better than our home, where, until she died, her children were wildly, supremely happy. Religion under her teaching was made so attractive, and all the treasured items she gathered from the lives of the Saints made them so fascinating to us, that we loved them as our most intimate friends, which she assured us they most certainly were.[31]

Herbert Vaughan, her eldest son, was ordained in 1854, having made a retreat at the Passionist Retreat at Lucca. The future Cardinal of Westminster having forged his link with St. Paul of the Cross, celebrated his first Mass in Florence where the Marchioness of Lothian, Lady Henry Kerr and the Scott-Murrays were among the congregation.[32] This was while the Crimean War was raging, under the War Minister, Sidney Herbert. Thirteen years later, Cardinal Vaughan was to become the spiritual director of his widow, Lady Herbert of Lea. She became a Catholic soon after her husband's death. The Cardinal's guidance of Lady Herbert 'down a path of thorns as well as spiritual roses was a masterpiece of prudence and piety not without the rays which only martyred souls can emit or reflect.'[33]

Lady Herbert was left a beautiful widow with seven children of whom one, the Hon. Mary Herbert, became a Catholic, marrying the Catholic apologist Baron von Hügel. Her two sons subsequently became thirteenth and fourteenth Earl of Pembroke, one daughter married the fourth Earl of Lonsdale, while another married the

Marquess of Ripon's heir, Lord de Grey. But the earldoms of Pembroke, Lonsdale and de Grey, 'so closely connected with her hopes, evaded the Papal possibilities.' Indeed, the confirmations, communions and marriages of her children in another church were 'as ashes to her soul'.[34] In 1867 Lady Herbert sailed for the West Indies. Father Vaughan prepared her for the spiritual journey she was about to undertake.

> You will spend some of those calm, pure, clear nights you get in the tropics up on deck. How alone you will feel with God! Those great waters washing and embracing in their arms every shore, every isle; the great highway all over the world containing an infinity of life and beauty within its bosom; connecting us all together. What a picture of the great mercy of God to man! It will make you pray for the salvation of poor unhappy souls; it will fill you with sadness at man's indifference to Him; with hope and confidence; with immense love and tenderness to Him who suggests such thoughts to us. My love for Foreign Missionary work, my little zeal I feel for the salvation of the *whole world,* as contrasted with the narrow insular limitation of zeal which is so common, was nurtured by contemplations on the goodness and love of Our Lord suggested to my mind at sea.[35]

Lady Herbert followed Cardinal Vaughan's missionary lead by devoting her life to the Mill Hill Missionaries. 'While Miss Nightingale became the Lady of the Lamp in British sentiment, Lady Herbert lit the lamp that hung in the chapel at Mill Hill in love and fear and trembling hope.'[36] To this mission she gave her dowry, her jewels and many of her possessions. Shane Leslie, a relation of the Duke of Marlborough, wrote:

> Her high altar and her lamp, garlanded with cherubs, still adorn Mill Hill Chapel. Even the old curtains still hang where she placed them in her hero's room. Her gifts are worn and fading, but her remembrance is

carried by missionaries, who never saw her or knew
her, unto the ends of the earth.[37]

Notes

[1] S. Leslie, *Cardinal Manning. His Life and Labours*, Dublin, Clonmore and Reynolds, 1953, p. 42.

[2] H.C.G. Mathew, 'Gladstone and Manning', *The Allen Review*, no. 6, Hilary 1992, p. 17.

[3] A.O.J. Cockshut, *Anglican Attitudes. A Study of Victorian Religious Controversies*, London, Collings, 1959, pp. 39, 58.

[4] R. Gray, *Cardinal Manning. A Biography*, London, Weidenfeld & Nicolson, 1985, p. 29.

[5] D. Quinn, 'Manning as Politician', *Recusant History*, vol. 21, no. 2, Oct. 1992, pp. 267, 268.

[6] T.J.McCann, 'A Bumping Pitch and a Blinding Light: Henry Manning and the other religion', *Recusant History*, vol. 21, no. 2, Oct. 1992, p. 287.

[7] Ibid., p. 291.

[8] D. Newsome, 'Cardinal Manning and his influence on the Church and Nation', *Recusant History*, vol. 21, no. 2, Oct. 1992, p. 136.

[9] Gray, op. cit., p. 119.

[10] Ibid., p. 120.

[11] Ibid.

[12] Ibid., p. 153.

[13] S. Leslie, *Cardinal Manning. His Life and Labours*, Dublin, Clonmore and Reynolds, 1953, p. 50.

[14] N. Mitford, *The Stanleys of Alderley. Their Letters between the years 1851–1865*. London, Hamish Hamilton, 1939, p. 124.

[15] F.C. Burnand, *Records and Reminiscences, Personal and General*, London, Metheun, 1905, p. 201.

[16] H.J. Coleridge, S.J., *Life of Lady Georgiana Fullerton. From the French of Mrs Augustus Craven*, London, R. Bentley & Son, 1888, p. 3.

[17] Ibid., p. 4.

[18] Ibid., p. 33.

[19] Ibid., p. 75.

[20] K. Jaeger, 'Lady Georgiana Fullerton', University of King's College, Halifax, Nova Scotia, Ph.D., p. 113. Coleridge, op. cit., pp. 165, 168.

[21] Coleridge, op. cit., p. 174.

[22] Ibid., p. 250.

[23] J. Baker, *Lady Georgiana Fullerton. A Bournemouth Benefactor*, Bournemouth Local Studies Publications, 1991, p. 8.

[24] Coleridge, op. cit., p. 429.

[25] F.C. Devas, D.S.O., O.B.E., S.J., *Mother Mary Magdalen of the Sacred Heart*, London, Burns, Oates & Westbourne, 1927, p. 40.

26   Ibid., p. 46.
27   B. Vaughan, *The Sins of Society*, London, Kegan Paul, Trench, Trübner & Co., 1906, p. 105.
28   Ibid., p. 219.
29   M. Vaughan, *Courtfield and the Vaughans*, London, Quiller Press, 1989, pp. 144, 145, 149. 'Dowager Duchess of Newcastle', *The Times*, 9 May 1913, p. 9.
30   J.G. Snead-Cox, *The Life of Cardinal Vaughan, Vol. I*, London, Herbert & Daniel, 1910, p. 24.
31   Ibid., p. 25.
32   Ibid., p. 57.
33   S. Leslie (ed.), *Letters of Herbert Cardinal Vaughan to Lady Herbert of Lea 1867 to 1903*, London, Burns Oates, 1942, p. viii.
34   Ibid.
35   Ibid., p. 33.
36   Ibid., p. x.
37   Ibid., p. xiv.

Chapter Fourteen

It cannot all end here

The correspondence between Cardinal Vaughan and Lady Herbert of Lea was discovered during the second world war by Shane Leslie. In spare moments from his duties with the Home Guard during the worst bombing of London, he copied out their letters by hand. The son of an Irish baronet, Shane Leslie's mother was Leonie Jerome, an American heiress whose sister Jennie was married to Lord Randolph Churchill. Shane Leslie was a convert to Roman Catholicism. So too was Lord Randolph Churchill's brother, the ninth Duke of Marlborough.

In 1895 the Duke of Marlborough had married the American heiress Consuelo Vanderbilt. They had two sons and were divorced in 1921. Consuelo then married a Frenchman, Jacques Balsan. Soon afterwards the Duke married a second American heiress, Gladys Deacon. This marriage took place in Paris, the ceremony being conducted by the rector of the Scottish Presbyterian church in Paris, 'a tall, lanky Scot, in rusty clerical garb'.[1] Back at Blenheim the Duke was forced to ponder his new status when the Bishop of Oxford publicly requested the Duke not to attend any meetings of the Oxford Diocesan Conference in his capacity as Lord Lieutenant for Oxfordshire, declaring that his divorce did not give him full status as a communicant.[2] Meanwhile Consuelo wanted to marry her French husband with the full approval of the Roman Catholic Church and started annulment proceedings. Her parents had agreed to give evidence to show that

they had forced their daughter into marrying the Duke.
The lengthy procedure of questioning by priests in order
to ascertain if the marriage was null resulted in the Duke
becoming increasingly interested in the teachings of the
Roman Church. He approached Father Martindale for
instruction, visiting the famous Jesuit at Campion Hall in
Oxford. In 1926 the Duke's marriage to Consuelo
Vanderbilt was annulled. At a private ceremony at
Archbishop's House at Westminster the Duke of
Marlborough was received into the Church by Cardinal
Bourne on 1st February 1927. Present were the Duke's
second wife Gladys, who was a lapsed Catholic; Lady
Gwendoline Churchill, married to Winston Churchill's
brother John and a Catholic herself (being the daughter of
the Earl of Abingdon, a convert in 1858); the Countess of
Abingdon and Lady Lovat. Winston was deeply attached to
his cousin the Duke 'whose mystical sense had cut him off
from most of his friends and family'.[3] When in 1934 the
Duke was buried at Blenheim and his son and heir spoke
without appreciation of his father's spiritual qualities, he
was rebuked and enlightened by Churchill, who perceived
clearly in the late Duke the 'strong strain of the spiritual
and the mystic in his being'.[4] Churchill observed of the late
Duke:

> The need of contact with the sublime and supernat-
> ural of which he was profoundly conscious, led him to
> the Church of Rome. He asked for sanctuary within
> that august and seemingly indestructible communion,
> against which his ancestor had warred with formi-
> dable strength. The shelter and protections were
> accorded, and the last years of his life were lived in a
> religious calm which fortified him against the troubles
> of the world and the errors we all make in travelling
> through it.[5]

The Duke's spiritual director Father Martindale, an old
Harrovian convert to Rome, had conversations with the
Duke over a period of three years. For the last ten days of
his Instruction Father Martindale stayed at Blenheim –

probably the first Jesuit to do so. The priest was helped in his task by the Duke's innate sense of 'Authority and of Hierarchy and of Discipline, and, indeed, of the pageantry with which our human instinct always surrounds these things'.[6] For him a name, a palace and a rank were not instruments for self-indulgence but 'earthly reflections of the spiritual hierarchy of the Church, through which God revealed infallibly to man immutable truth and unchanging moral law'. After Holy Communion the Duke was dazed by the mystery to which he had been admitted. He now withdrew from both his second marriage and from society and set about to revive some of the glories of Blenheim that had been lost by his extravagant father. He came across Bernini's *modello* for his river-gods fountain in the Piazza Navona in Rome, given to the first Duke of Marlborough by the then Papal Nuncio. The long-mislaid marble was placed in a fountain on a new terrace designed by a French architect; a part of Rome was reconstructed on the edge of Oxfordshire. When the sculptor Epstein, whose bronze bust of the ninth Duke stands in the hall, asked to see the chapel at Blenheim, he said that he could see no evidence of Christian worship. 'The Marlboroughs are worshipped here', was the Duke's reply.[7] When the Duke came to be buried in the same chapel, Latin stanzas from the Spanish Carmelite St. John of the Cross were read out by Father Martindale. A 'few wreaths of incense floated over the sepulchral vault, and sniffing it suspiciously the Churchills withdrew into the living rooms of the Palace.'[8]

The Churchills had followed the cortège through the park through the long avenues of trees planted by the Duke. In the shadow of Blenheim Winston became expansive, and talked to his Catholic cousin Shane Leslie of the survival of the soul. 'Yes,' he said several times, 'the spirit must continue. It cannot all end here.' Father Martindale walked behind the coffin. As it was lowered into the vault the words of St. John of the Cross were a mystery to all those present except Lady Gwendoline Churchill and Shane Leslie, who both 'made feeble Signs of the Cross'.[9]

When a Requiem Mass was said at the Jesuit church of the Immaculate Conception in Farm Street, Protestant relations of the Spencer-Churchills packed the pews and tried to follow the Latin. Bewildered by the candles they were given to hold, some dared not blow them out. A Low Mass of Requiem was later said at the altar of St. Ignatius Loyola, attended by a few Catholic peers and friends. During his last illness the Duke had refused medication, telling the priest, 'I have joined the religion of which the centre is the crucifixion.' Before the onset of his illness the Duke had arranged through his friend the Duke of Alba to retire as a layman into a Spanish Benedictine monastery.[10]

Shane Leslie expressed the view that the Protestants present at the ninth Duke's Requiem Mass at Farm Street might have been more comforted hearing hymns such as 'Lead kindly light' or 'Abide with me', than ancient Gregorian chant. As an Etonian, his memories of chapel were of a daily draught of song, yet Leslie was convinced that the Jesuits who sang at the Mass at Farm Street had been far more successful than the masters at Eton at imposing the idea of the supernatural on English schoolboys. Not far from Eton the Jesuit school of Beaumont fulfilled the function of what Eton had done long ago, as a school for Catholic gentlemen. One of Beaumont's pupils, Sir Mark Sykes of Sledmere in Yorkshire, had become a Catholic as a child. It was Shane Leslie who wrote his biography.

☙❦❧

Winston Churchill said of Sir Mark Sykes that surrounded by every luxury and every temptation to lead an idle, pleasant country life he turned to the desert rather than the Yorkshire moors, to 'some piece of Imperial service single-handed in the unknown East' rather than the home duties of a country gentleman.[11] The only son of Sir Tatton Sykes, Mark's mother Jessica Cavendish Bentinck collaborated with her husband in his quest to build Gothic churches in the East Riding. On a visit to Vienna, Sir Tatton was so taken with the elaborate and ornate Votivkirche that he wanted to reconstruct the same church in the East Riding. Jessica corresponded with Manning about the Vicar of Sledmere, who did not share Sir Tatton's enthusiasm for his plan, thanking the Cardinal for sending him an exposition on conversion to Roman Catholicism. After their visit to Vienna in 1882 Lady Sykes travelled to Rome with her husband. As Sir Tatton came closer to the Eternal City he became increasingly reluctant to follow his wife's spiritual journey. She however took the final step, and was received into the Church by Manning, taking her four year-old son Mark with her. So it was that the future squire of Sledmere was sent to Beaumont, completing his education at an Italian Jesuit school in Monaco, the Institute de St. Louis in Brussels, and Jesus College Cambridge.[12]

In the library at Sledmere Mark became absorbed in the rare medieval and Renaissance manuscripts which remained from the sale of books by an earlier Baronet who had invested in horses. Then as an undergraduate he travelled to Palestine, returning to Jesus Lane to sit 'cross-legged, frequently, in some Eastern headdress and smoking a hookah'. He wrote books about his travels and gave lectures. In Cambridge he met the daughter of the local Member of Parliament, Edith Gorst, a recent convert. Going to Mass in order to gaze at her, he wrote to her as 'Honourable and Well-Beloved Co-religionist'. The young couple married at St. Wilfrid's church near York Minster and went to Jerusalem for their honeymoon.

Meanwhile Lady Sykes had moved to Grosvenor Square, attending daily Mass at Farm Street. She danced late into the night and rose early the next morning to do charity work in the East End. When she died in 1912 Requiem Masses were said for her in Farm Street, Hull and Jerusalem. At Sledmere a Requiem Mass was said for her in a marquee set up outside Sledmere church and she was interred in the churchyard. Sir Tatton died the following year, his funeral being inside the church. Turning from the graveside Sir Mark loudly criticised the Anglican service he had just witnessed, convinced that his father was in his heart of hearts a Catholic. The night before he had got hold of the keys of the church and with his friend Captain Bagshawe had lighted candles around the coffin. They then recited the Office of the Dead, prayers from the Requiem and the Absolutions.[13]

As soon as Mark inherited Sledmere he had the Blessed

Sacrament reserved in the house, before which a lamp perpetually flickered. Inside the church at Sledmere he set aside a small upper room for devotional reading and meditation, from where he looked out on Sledmere's green park and magnificent beeches. On his death English Catholics mourned him in Westminster Cathedral. In Aleppo and Jerusalem his Solemn Requiem was sung. At Sledmere the Benedictine monks of Ampleforth recited the Office of the Dead amid flickering tapers. It so happened that on the Eleanor Cross, one panel remained unfilled. Sir Mark's figure was blazoned in brass, armoured and sworded, a Muslim lying under his feet, 'Laetare Jerusalem' in a scroll above his head and the Holy City of Jerusalem in the background. The twentieth century Crusader had been laid to rest. A life of scholarship and travel, in which he found the Universal Church in every country he visited, Sir Mark always carried with him books of devotion. He also considered writing a novel, and sketched the plot. A Duke discovers that his son has sold the family estates and given the proceeds to a Portuguese Benedictine recluse; eventually the Duke himself enters a Carmelite monastery as a lay brother. Not directly inspired by the ninth Duke of Marlborough, the style of the novel was nevertheless directly inspired by the novels of Robert Hugh Benson, son of the Archbishop of Canterbury and a convert to Roman Catholicism in 1903. The ninth Duke of Marlborough had been received into the Church by Father Martindale, who happened to write a biography of the remarkable R. H. Benson.

⊚⊕⊚

Benson was brought up to be 'reverent, sober-minded, anti-Roman; to believe in the Real Presence without defining it'. He acknowledged the absolute mystery of his later being brought to Rome.

> Faith, after all, is a divine operation wrought in the dark, even though it may seem to be embodied in intellectual arguments and historical facts; for it is necessary to remember that two equally sincere and

intelligent souls may encounter the same external evidences and draw mutually exclusive conclusions from them.[14]

He went to prep school at Clevedon, where the church contained a dark sanctuary, the clergy wore coloured vestments and there was Gregorian chant. At Eton he found himself in 'the familiar academic atmosphere of plain dignity, beautiful singing and indefiniteness of dogma'. From Eton he went to Cambridge, dropping in once to High Mass at Our Lady and the English Martyrs, 'but it made no impression on me, except one of vaguely mingled contempt and awe'. He remembered an agreeable sense of shock when at the *Asperges* he felt a drop of water on his face. A friend lent him Challoner's *Garden of the Soul*.[15]

Following in the footsteps of his father, it seemed inevitable that Benson would become a clergyman, with a garden, a choir and a scholarly bachelor existence. He became a Deacon in 1894 and not long afterwards went on a retreat given by one of the High Anglican Cowley Fathers from Oxford. Two years later Archbishop Benson died, his last written words being a letter to *The Times* on the declaration by Pope Leo XIII that Anglican orders were null and void. Travelling in Italy, Benson was next struck by ignorance of the Church of England throughout Catholic Europe. In Cairo the Coptic Patriarch had not even answered his request to receive Communion and in Jerusalem and the Holy Land his discomfort increased. 'Here again in the birthplace of Christendom, we were less than nothing.' Not allowed to use the Greek altar, a table was wheeled in. Watched by curious Greeks, Benson celebrated what he 'believed to be the divine mysteries, and felt a deep sense of loneliness'.[16] Reading *The Guardian* in Damascus he discovered that his Anglican spiritual director had become a Catholic. Returning to England, Benson entered the Anglican clerks regular of the Resurrection at Mirfield. He began to realise that it was increasingly impossible to believe that for a thousand years the promises of Christ had failed.

> When a Soul reaches a certain pitch of conflict, it
> ceases to be absolutely logical; it is rather a very
> tender, raw thing, with all its fibres stretched to agony,
> shrinking from the lightest touch, desiring to be dealt
> with only by Hands that have been pierced.[17]

He read Newman's *Development of Doctrine*. This, like a
magician, waved away the last floating mists of doubt. He
felt drawn to a vantage point from where he could look out
and see the facts as they were, and it was Newman who
'showed me how the Church stood upon the unshakeable
foundation of the Gospel and soared to Heaven'.

> I saw the mystical Bride of Christ, growing through
> the ages from the state of childhood to adolescence,
> increasing in wisdom and stature, not adding to but
> developing her knowledge, strengthening her limbs,
> stretching out her hands; changing, indeed, her
> aspect and her language – using now this set of
> human terms now that, to express better and better
> her mind; bringing out of her treasures things new
> and old, which yet had been hers from the beginning,
> indwelt by the Spirit of her Spouse, and even suffering
> as He had done.[18]

After his reception into the Church Benson visited St.
Winefride's Well at Holywell. It was crowded with pilgrims.
Dressed in a grey suit and a bowler hat, he accompanied Sir
Piers and Lady Mostyn's chaplain to the shrine. He was some-
what perturbed when a priest on seeing the chaplain greeted
him loudly with the news of Benson's conversion.[19] As a
priest, Benson returned to Cambridge as University
Chaplain, and started a Motor Mission around East Anglia.
He turned a gipsy van into a mobile chapel with an altar,
harmonium, kneeling stools and a large crucifix and a
banner of the Blessed Virgin Mary. When met with the cry of
'No Popery' he merely replied 'Know Popery'. Long-hidden
Catholics emerged from the villages and towns of a part of
England which the Irish had never reached. But Benson's
real mission was to retire from the world.

He wanted to purchase the little island of St. Margaret off Caldey Island, where he would build a hermitage in which he could write and pray with only the seagulls for company.[20] Instead he found his haven in Hertfordshire, in the tiny village of Hare Street, where he purchased a dilapidated grand old house with frescoes. Here he turned his hand to making tapestries, painting pictures, cataloguing the library, clearing and planting the garden. His brother returned to the house and found the chapel had originally been an old brew-house with a timbered roof, the sanctuary separated from the rest of the chapel by an open screen of old oak. Benson's devotional retreat was filled with carved and painted statues, embroidered hangings, stained glass, hanging lamps and emblems.[21] The house was approached through wrought iron gates in which were fashioned the Sacred Hearts of Jesus and Mary, surmounted by a Monsignor's hat with tassels. The son of the Archbishop of Canterbury died at the age of 43 on 19th October 1914, eleven years a priest. His brother, Master of Magdalene College Cambridge, recalled:

I passed over the smooth lawn, under the leafless limes, through the yew tree walk to the orchard, where the grave lay, with the fading wreaths, and little paths trodden in the grass; by the hazel hedge and the rose garden, and the ranked vegetable rows with their dying borders; in to the chapel with its fantasy of ornament, where the lamp burned before the shrine; through the house, with its silent panelled rooms all so finely ordered, all prepared for daily use and tranquil delight.[22]

A Mr Benson was at Oxford with the Cowley Fathers when Francis Burnand, then an ordinand at Cuddesdon, later a barrister and Editor of *Punch*, approached the Community with doubts about the oath of Royal Supremacy which he had to take. Benson left him to browse in the library where a particular book attracted Burnand's attention. It was Newman's *Development of Doctrine*. Never having read Newman he opened the book

and immediately thought it dull and dry. Putting it back on
the table he turned to the treatises set out for him by Mr
Benson and replaced each one. He was still intrigued by
the Newman book and took it and several others back with
him to the inn where he was staying. He settled down by a
fire and began to read Newman, pausing only for a short
break for supper. Mr Benson came to the inn in search of
him and seeing the book warned Burnand of Newman's
errors and the serious consequences of adopting his
'theory of development' and following it to its logical
conclusion. The more Benson argued against Newman and
Rome, the more Burnand was convinced that Newman was
right. Benson apologised for his outburst the following
morning. By this time Burnand had decided to leave
Cuddesdon theological college.[23]

Burnand faced opposition on all fronts. When his father
learned of his decision to become a Catholic he was disinherited. He knew there was something wrong when his
suitcase was not taken up to his room but left in the hall.
After an interview with his father, it was the butler who
showed him out with some kindness. He immediately went
to see an old Catholic friend from Cambridge. Arriving at
his house he found a note to say that dinner had been
prepared for two and he would be back after Mass in Farm
Street. Waiting inside the warm room, so welcoming after
the coldness of his father's establishment, Burnand
noticed in the corner of the room a statue of the Blessed
Virgin Mary in a niche under a canopy. A light flickered at
her feet and flowers were placed close by. Suddenly the
door opened and in came his host, beaming with delight.
Hearing the news of Burnand's decision to become a
Catholic he was overcome with joy and heartily shook his
hand. He had had a presentiment that this would happen
and that it would occur on or about the Feast of the
Immaculate Conception. And so it did.[24]

Notes

1   H. Vickers, *Gladys, Duchess of Marlborough*, London, Weidenfeld and Nicolson, 1979, p. 178.

2   Ibid., p. 197.

3   S. Leslie, *Long Shadows*, London, John Murray, 1966, p. 237.

4   P. Caraman, *C.C. Martindale*, London, Longmans, 1967, p. 162.

5   *Charles, IXth Duke of Marlborough, K.G. Tributes by Rt. Hon. Winston Spencer-Churchill and C.C. Martindale, S.J.*, London, Burns, Oates & Washbourne, 1934, pp. 9–10.

6   Ibid., p. 13.

7   D. Green, *The Churchills of Blenheim*, London, Constable, 1984, p. 146.

8   Leslie, op. cit., p. 239.

9   Ibid., p. 238.

10 Ibid., p. 238; *The Times*, 11 July 1934, Caraman, op. cit., p. 162.

11 S. Leslie, *Mark Sykes: His Life and Letters*, London, Cassell, 1923, p. v.

12 R. Adelson, *Mark Sykes. Portrait of an Amateur*, London, Jonathan Cape, 1975, p. 46.

13 Leslie, op. cit., p. 43.

14 R.H. Benson, *Confessions of a Convert*, London, Longmans, Green & Co., 1913, p. 4.

15 Ibid., pp. 16, 24.

16 Ibid., p. 47.

17 Ibid., p. 90.

18 Ibid., p. 108.

19 C.C. Martindale, *The Life of Monsignor Robert Hugh Benson, Vol. I*, London, Longmans, 1916, p. 255.

20 Martindale, Vol. II, p. 427.

21 A.C. Benson, *Hugh. Memoirs of a Brother*, London, Smith, Elder & Co., 1915, p. 10.

22 Ibid., p. 195.

23 Sir Francis Burnand, *Records and Reminiscence. Personal and General*, London, Methuen, 1905, p. 188.

24 Ibid., p. 199.

Chapter Fifteen

A want of harmony and of beauty

R. H. Benson was received into the Church on 11th September 1903 in the Dominican priory at Woodchester in Gloucestershire. The tomb of another Old Etonian, William Leigh, with its sculptured effigy in the robes of a Knight of Malta, had rested in the church of the Annunciation close by since 1873. The church, set in a beautiful remote and steep valley on the edge of the Cotswolds near Stroud, was of a Gothic design built in thanksgiving for Leigh's conversion in 1844. Alongside the church Leigh had also built the priory. Married to the daughter of Sir John Cotterell of Garnons in Herefordshire, Leigh had been cold-shouldered by his wife's family on becoming a Catholic and had sought refuge in another county.[1] The priory and church were built by the architect Charles Hansom and Leigh invited Dominic Barberi to set up a Passionist community there. For a while Leigh had been living in Little Aston in Staffordshire when Barberi had first established his Passionist Retreat at Aston Hall.

Another Old Etonian, the Hon. George Spencer, had begun his novitiate at Aston to which he brought 'no earthly riches, but an unearthly spirit – humility, docility and burning zeal'. Revisiting Eton not long afterwards Spencer 'ruminated sadly over the scenes of forty years before, and the parting of friends ...'[2] For many converts, Eton was common ground. Lord Braye was particularly conscious of the influence of Spencer, the holy Etonian.

Who knows but that at some far-off date, when at length Anglicanism shall have been deprived of its supreme dominion in the land and Eton may have accustomed herself to the presence of Catholics, a memorial in some shape or form may be placed to this Etonian, forgotten now, but brought back to the admiration and gratitude of a future generation?[3]

Catholics were admitted to Eton for the first time in 1875, the closest Catholic church being at St. Edward's in Windsor. In 1915 Lord Braye founded a small chapel dedicated to Our Lady of Sorrows. Every day in the summer Etonians passed its open doors on their way over South Meadow to the river. 'Thus, after 400 years' exile the Blessed Sacrament had been brought back to Eton and a Catholic Church was ready to welcome the boys of the saintly Founder's Faith.'[4] But the Headmaster Dr Lyttleton declared the church out of bounds, making it an offence punishable by flogging or expulsion not merely to hear Mass or receive Communion, but even to enter the church. For five years Etonians were denied the liberty of worship which Catholics in England had enjoyed since the close of penal days.[5]

It is a mystery that Eton's long history of anti-catholicism, publicly enforced between 1915 and 1920, should have produced so many converts to Rome. If the Faith thrived under persecution, then Eton played its part in its revival. Lord Braye recalled that the school's 'thin religious atmosphere' was 'elusive and curiously unsatisfying'.[6] The Hon. Gilbert Coleridge was confident that 'much of the irreligion of our youth & after life was due to the intolerable boredom of these long services in chapel'.[7] When Dr Warre, Headmaster in the 1870s and the first to allow Catholics into the school, preached in chapel 'he stirred nobody, he was merely a headmaster doing his duty ... with round phrases that rolled away to the roof un-noticed till he came to an end'.[8] R. H. Benson recalled that chapel services at Eton were 'rather artistic, very academic'. They represented 'the same kind of official language to Almighty God as cheering the Queen when she came to see us'. Benson's preparation for confirmation comprised some talks from his tutor on morality with no mention of doctrine.[9]

The only preparation for confirmation Lord Halifax could remember was copying out certain devotional passages and hymns into a notebook and being told that it would be more of a disgrace to be whipped after he was confirmed than before.[10] Halifax's tutor at Eton was William Cory who described himself as a reverent agnostic. He said of Newman that he was 'the greatest man that ever tried, and he made the noblest effort ever made, to change the character of a nation; it was a splendid and beneficent failure'.[11] When one of his pupils became a Catholic, Cory observed that Baroque Catholic churches like the London Oratory 'were as much like the real thing as the tropical houses at Kew were like the tropics'.[12] When C. A. Alington was Headmaster he admitted that there would always be those impressed by the majesty and unity of Rome; 'but we believe we serve a higher ideal' being 'not only more true to the Christian standard in our definition of things doubtful and things necessary', but exhibiting 'a larger charity to those who disagree with us'.[13] Exercising such charity, Alington would doubtless have welcomed Alfred Verney-Cave's thoughts when he gazed out of his room at Eton.

> There rose Windsor in the majesty of morning, against the unclouded sky, mantled, as it were, with the dissolving mist of all the chronicle of English Catholicism. To the west loomed the glory of perpendicular architecture, St. George's Chapel, and I could realize that it was at once a shrine and a ruin, for within the walls lay the bones of the two Henrys – the Good and the Infamous. Here were the two terrible powers associated with material memorials, with bones and dust – powers which are in utmost antagonism even to this day, and will be till days are no more; the rebelling Human Will. And the calmness of the prospect to which the every leaf of the forest and the every eddy in the Thames gave tranquil consent

was consonant to the spirit of quiet Anglicanism in our land – our England.[14]

The Hon. Alfred Verney-Cave asked his parents long before he went to Eton why every Sunday they said they believed in the Catholic Church. No answer was forthcoming. It was not until he was eighteen that he realised that such a proclamation by Anglican tongues was misleading. The observance of saints' days at Eton he found to be a curious relic of the college's Catholic past. Then in conversations with a pious contemporary, Verney-Cave became interested in Tractarianism. Slowly he moved beyond the theory that the Church of England was a branch of the Church founded by Christ, 'a branch unfortunately in antagonism with the two other "branches" – all Three God's appointed Teachers of the Nations – a trinity of schism as it were'.[15] Next he came across a Benedictine breviary. 'There was something, then, beyond the Book of Common Prayer, and Elizabethanism did not embrace the entire Christian system.'[16]

Elizabethan services did not seem to hold the attention of Verney-Cave's fellow Etonians, despite the pompous entry of the Provost and Headmaster, preceded by the boys of the Sixth Form, walking 'with immense majesty up the centre of the chapel, a study in cuffs and collars and immaculate costumes'. There was a full choral service before each half-holiday, the effect of which on the minds of boys thirsting to be free for the river and cricket field meant that worship was somewhat distracted. Against the text of every anthem was written 'corrected and tested by generations of impatient listeners, the *time* taken in its performance'. Such was the unseemly rush to leave the chapel that masters regulated the departure 'after the manner in which the police now regulate the congested traffic in our streets'.[17] What awaited Etonians as they surged out?

Great trees of broad shade, great spaces of golden light, and the splendid River winding about us and washing our coast ... summer mornings on Fellows'

Eyot, the sparkling of the weir-stream, the softness of
mist and shade beneath the huge rampart of the
Castle on its height: and then the noble poise and
outline of the vast mass itself; grey and dim in the
morning freshness ...'[18]

Rising early, 'when all the mighty heart of the school was
lying still in the summer dawn' Alfred Verney-Cave
pursued his quest for Truth in prayer, lighting candles in
front of a triptych in his room. After a June sunset the
Round Tower of the castle assumed an extra halo of
romance when the Royal Standard was hauled down and
lay in profuse folds. Later, as a Catholic, Alfred Verney-
Cave introduced to Queen Victoria the idea that she, in the
papal tradition, should celebrate her Jubilee.[19]

Queen Victoria's attitude towards Roman Catholicism
moved back and forth from antipathy to reluctant acceptance. Her novelist Prime Minister Disraeli described
himself as a blank page between the Old Testament and
the New, while Melbourne entertained a healthy disregard
for any sort of intrusion by religion. 'Things have come to
a pretty pass when religion is allowed to invade the sphere
of private life' was his response to a clergyman expressing
concern about the effects of sin.[20] In drafting the Queen's
announcement of her forthcoming marriage, Melbourne
had neglected to specify that Prince Albert was a Protestant
prince. Rumours spread that Albert was a Roman Catholic,
a number of his cousins having converted and his Uncle
Leopold having married a Roman Catholic. But Albert
fully supported his Queen's Royal Declaration against
Transubstantiation, the Sacrifice of the Mass, and the
Invocation and Adoration of the Saints, declaring all superstitious and idolatrous. She repeated all this after the Lord
Chancellor in a 'clear voice and with great feeling'.[21]
Following their wedding Albert and Victoria celebrated
Easter with the German custom of withdrawing completely
from society for twenty four hours before receiving
Communion. Albert played Mozart's Requiem on the
piano, read passages from a German devotional work and
quietly walked with Victoria in the garden. They did not

receive Communion again until Christmas; Victoria thought twice-yearly Communion sufficed.[22] Prince Albert became her spiritual adviser. She became troubled by such Tractarian practices as veneration of the saints, the Sign of the Cross, chanting of the liturgy and Confession. To her, Puseyite clerics were 'snakes in the grass ... in fact the hidden Jesuits of the country'.[23] When in 1852 Lord Derby became Prime Minister she asked him not to recommend 'Puseyites or Romanisers' as Bishops. Twenty years later she was writing to her daughter that flowers, crosses and vestments all meant something most dangerous. The service at Osborne she thought to be rather advanced because the clergyman preached in a surplice rather than a gown. She came to regard Presbyterianism as 'the real and true stronghold of Protestantism' in the British Isles, giving instructions to her Court Chamberlain that on future state occasions the Moderator of the General Assembly of the Church of Scotland be given precedence over peers and privy councillors. She went into Anglican churches only for funerals. When after Prince Albert's death a clergyman consoled her with the thought that henceforth Christ would be her heavenly bridegroom she replied 'That is what I call twaddle.'[24]

Regarding the Puseyites with increasing disdain, Victoria developed a certain sympathy for Newman and Manning because of their willingness to sacrifice social position for religious principles. In 1858 she used her influence to end the official Anglican service commemorating the failure of the 1603 Gunpowder Plot.[25] By 1869 she still had grave reservations about ennobling Roman Catholics, writing to Gladstone that 'to treat them with perfect equality is an impossibility. Other countries show this clearly.' To her daughter she wrote that Roman Catholics 'will not be conciliated and wish to persecute and, by foul means or fair, to obtain the upper hand'.[26] She observed Mass for the first time in France visiting the Abbey at Haute Combe in Provence. She arrived by steamer, where the Prior of the monastery and an English-speaking brother were introduced to her by Sir Henry Ponsonby. The Queen slowly climbed the hill to the monastery where she visited the chapel and lunched with the community.[27] The following year the Pope sent a Papal Envoy to London in recognition of her Jubilee, who brought with him a costly mosaic depicting the English and Papal arms. To return the papal compliments the Duke of Norfolk was sent to Rome as an Envoy Extraordinary, bringing with him a gold ewer. The Pope said he would use it at his Jubilee Mass.

Despite a softening of her attitude towards Rome in her later years the Queen preferred the stark atmosphere of Presbyterianism at Crathie church far away from the glorious splendours of Rome. Her chaplain observed that it was a sight 'truly beautiful' when 'the mightiest Sovereign of the mightiest realm upon earth, literally and strictly, so mingles with the humblest peasants in the most sequestered part of her Empire'.[28] Yet still she felt drawn to the exotic 'in Disraeli's flowery oratory, in the traditions of continental Roman Catholic monasteries, in the customs and costumes of the exotic East'. As Empress of India she had in the Marquess of Ripon a Roman Catholic Viceroy. But she deplored his conversion in 1874. 'It is a complete surrender of your intellect – and individuality to another – when one thinks of what the confession is ... one can't understand anyone who has been a Protestant ever submitting to this.'[29]

❦❦❧

The Marquess of Ripon was born in 1827 at 10 Downing Street, his father, Viscount Goderich then being Prime Minister. He went neither to school nor university, but read much in the libraries of his ancestral homes at Nocton and Studley Royal. Following his father's political footsteps he entered Parliament at the age of 24, serving his first government under Palmerston, and by the end of his life sharing ministerial portfolios with Winston Churchill. He had no definite religious convictions until the age of seventeen, when he found an old breviary in a bookshop at Ripon, and began to recite the Office daily. This early fervour did not continue, but in 1870 he was brought back with a jolt when his brother-in-law was assas-

sinated by brigands in Greece. He went into St. George's
Cathedral in Southwark, heard Mass for the first time in
England and his desire returned to become a Catholic. He
started to read Newman. In a state of uncertainty he went
to Brittany to be in quiet communion with God. 'Heaven
was silent and his mind a blank.'[30] He entered into correspondence with his cousin, Lady Amabel Kerr, married to
Lord Walter Kerr, later Admiral of the Fleet. Lady Amabel
Kerr wrote in 1874 when Ripon was on the verge of conversion that she appreciated his feelings of not feeling quite at
home in the Church. 'But I am jealous for the inside of the
Church – and I will protest against any hopes you may have
of expecting to see the full beauty of the "painted
windows" till you are really inside'.[31]

> ... You have been led so much more clearly than so
> many – God has given you a faith without difficulty in
> all the supernatural parts of the Church. Even where
> you are, outside, you look and see and feel that the
> Sacraments are there as they are nowhere else; and if
> that is the case you must be out in the cold anywhere
> else.[32]

Two months later she wrote to the still struggling
Marquess:

> I never believed in grace till I was a Catholic. It is a
> sort of balm which God deigns to apply to one's daily
> struggles and wrenches and isolations in a way which,
> did one not feel to be so divine, one might be inclined
> to call too minute for God's Hand.[33]

On 16th September 1874, the Marquess having become a
Catholic, he received spiritual advice from Father
Dalgairns, an Oratorian priest, before his first Communion.

> Do not be over-anxious; men often spoil their commu-
> nion by undue activity of the soul and a certain
> tumultuous fear lest they should not receive it as well
> as possible. It is even recommended at the moment of

reception to honour our Lord by an adoring silence, simply remembering that He is there and bidding Him work His own will in the soul, only afterwards have recourse to your book to help you to thank Him for His great love. The best preparation is a good confession, which will cleanse your soul and clothe it in a wedding garment to receive Him. Our Lord has a peculiar love for the soul which He has reconquered after it has wandered from Him and which comes to him with a strong desire to dedicate and sacrifice all its future to His service. In that great act, as in every other, it is God Himself who does the greatest part, and the soul has only to present itself to Him with an earnest desire of doing His Holy Will. I shall say Mass for you when you communicate, and I trust that our Lord will help you to receive him as you should.[34]

As a Catholic, the Marquess's spiritual life was devout. Waking at six he spent an hour in prayer, spiritual reading and saying the rosary before his valet appeared at seven. He went to daily Mass, weekly confession and had a particular devotion to prayer in front of the Blessed Sacrament. He took great pleasure in carrying the canopy during a Eucharistic procession. At Studley where he had a private chapel dedicated to Our Lady of Fountains, he followed the Stations of the Cross every Friday. He had particular devotions to St. Bernard, St. Philip Neri, his patron St. George, St. Raphael, on whose Feast Day he was born, St. Francis of Assisi, St. Vincent de Paul and St. Clare. He used to light candles in front of the statue of the Blessed Virgin Mary in St. Wilfrid's Chapel in Ripon. Anyone entering the church would often see the Marquess bowed in prayer in front of the statue. On his becoming a Catholic in September 1874 *The Times* declared that a statesman who became a convert to Roman Catholicism at once forfeited the confidence of the English people.

Such a step involves a complete abandonment of any claim to political or even social influence in the nation at large, and can only be regarded as betraying an irreparable weakness of character. To become a Roman Catholic and remain a thorough Englishman are – it cannot be disguised – almost incompatible conditions.[35]

The Duke of Argyll wrote to Sir James Lacaita:

Lord Ripon's conversion is a deal in my mind ... There are many cells in the great madhouse of the world and there are many forms in which the all-pervading disease of breakdown manifests itself. One becomes an R.C. Another becomes a raving maniac, a third commits suicide, and so on ... I would give much, very much, to know the inner commencement of Ripon's turn, for it is a painfully interesting case to me. There is an air of tragedy and mystery about it.[36]

The Marquess, former Grand Master of the English Freemasons, had resigned from the government in 1873, ostensibly because of his disagreements with the government's proposals to extend the suffrage to the counties. Six years later he returned from the political wilderness and was created Viceroy of India, by which time Gladstone's anti-Catholic views had mellowed. He became one of the best-loved Viceroys through his efforts to improve the lives of Indians.[37] On his journey out to India Father Henry Kerr, S.J. said daily Mass in his cabin. Mass was said in the library at the Viceroy's residence. Three-quarters of the Christian community in India were Roman Catholic but it seemed all of India turned out to say farewell to the departing Marquess. At Amritsar he was nearly smothered with roses, the whole of Calcutta was illuminated and lined with a hundred thousand people in the streets. The journey to Bombay turned into a triumphal procession. Bombay was 'be-flagged and decorated, priests blessed him and merchants hung out garlands of pearls and diamonds'.[38]

The Marquess of Ripon died in 1909 and was buried in the family vault of St. Mary's Ripon. Solemn music was played in Ripon Cathedral and muffled bells tolled. Mass was said at Studley Royal and at St. Wilfrid's Ripon. There

was a Solemn Requiem at Westminster Cathedral.
Archbishop Bourne, preaching at the church of the Holy
Redeemer in Chelsea likened the Marquess to Thomas
More. 'He too left us an example of unswerving obedience
to whatever cost. Thirty-five years ago he became
convinced of the claims of the Catholic Church upon his
faith and obedience, and without hesitation he submitted
himself to her authority.'[39]

Once Grand Master of the English Freemasons, the
Marquess spent the last years of his life visiting the poor as
a Brother of St. Vincent de Paul.[40] It was his cousin Lady
Amabel Kerr who had guided him over the final obstacles,
resolved his nagging doubts and suggested further spiritual
reading. In 1897 she published what she called her
Unravelled Convictions. Her quest for the Truth had been a
solitary one. Not once during her eight and a half years of
spiritual struggle did she speak with a Catholic about the
Faith until a month before her reception into the Church.
Her chief source of searching originated in dissatisfaction
with the Church of England, which she likened to a piece
of tracing paper laid on foundations and incorrectly
copied. When taken away the tracing paper made no sense.
She asked if such an entirely national institution could be
the universal Christian system? Could an institution similar
in character but with variations to suit a particular people
flourish? The grace of conviction which she received influenced a statesman whose example of devotion long
outlived him. This conviction she stated simply:

> The more I look at all other Christian creeds beside
> the Catholic creed, the more do I see the finger of
> man in them and the finger of God in her; and if for
> any moment my faith in her gets shaken I feel cold
> and dismal, small and cramped, as if the Most High
> were suddenly diminished. Outside her there is a
> sense of unrest and incompleteness, a want of
> harmony and of beauty.[41]

Notes

1   D. Verey, 'Woodchester Park, Gloucestershire', *Country Life*, 6 February 1969, p. 285.

2   U. Young, *Life of Father Ignatius Spencer, C.P.*, London, Burns Oates & Washbourne, 1935, p. 142.

3   Lord Braye, *Fewness of My Days. A Life in Two Centuries*, London, Sands & Co., 1927, p. 59.

4   *Catholics at Eton. A Reasoned Petition*, London, St. Vincent's Press, 1920, p. 6.

5   Ibid., p. 10.

6   Braye, op. cit., p. 12.

7   Hon. Gilbert Coleridge, *Eton in the Seventies*, London, Smith, Elder & Co., 1913, p. 37.

8   P. Lubbock, *Shades of Eton*, London, Jonathan Cape, 1929, pp. 12–13.

9   R.H. Benson, *Confessions of a Convert*, London, Longmans, Green & Co., 1913, pp. 17, 21.

10 J.G. Lockhart, *Charles Lindley Viscount Halifax, Part One 1839–1885*, London, Geoffrey Bles, 1935, p. 40.

11 B. Holland, 'An Eton Master', *National Review*, vol. xxx, February 1898, p. 870.

12 F. Compton Mackenzie, *William Cory. A Biography*, London, Constable, 1950, p. 81.

13 Rev. C.A. Alington, 'Christian Outlines' in A. Lunn (ed.), *Public School Religion*, London, Faber & Faber, 1933, p. 73.

14 Braye, op. cit., p. 61.

15 Ibid., p. 56.

16 Ibid., p. 57.

17 O. E., *Eton under Hornby. Some Reminiscences and Reflections*, London, A. C. Field, 1910, p. 85.

18 P. Lubbock, *Shades of Eton*, London, Jonathan Cape, 1929, p. 115.

19 'Obituary. Lord Braye', *The Times*, 3 July 1928, p. 18.

20 Lockhart, op. cit., p. 75. G.W.E. Russell, *Collections and Revelations*, ch. 6.

21 W. Walsh, *The Religious Life and Influence of Queen Victoria*, London, Swan, Sonnenschein & Co., 1902, p. 11.

22 W.L. Arnstein, 'Queen Victoria and Religion' in G. Malmgreen (ed.), *Religion in the Lives of English Women, 1760–1930*, Bloomington and Indianapolis, Indiana University Press, 1986, p. 93.

23 Ibid., p. 99.

24 Ibid., p. 108.

25 Ibid., p. 117. The 1793 edition of the Prayer Book contained prayers for November 5th: 'O God, Whose Name is excellent in all the earth, and thy glory above the heavens; Who on this day didst miraculously preserve our Church and State from the secret

contrivance and hellish malice of Popish Conspirators; and on this day also didst begin to give as a mighty deliverance from the open tyranny and oppression of the same creed and bloodthirsty enemies: we bless and adore Thy glorious Majesty, as for the former, so for this Thy late marvellous loving kindness to our Church and Nation, in the preservation of our religion and liberties.'

[26]   Ibid., p. 118.

[27]   Walsh, op. cit., p. 195.

[28]   Ibid., p. 66.

[29]   Arnstein, op. cit., pp. 118, 122–3.

[30]   L. Wolf, *Life of the First Marquess of Ripon K.G., P.C., G.C.S.I., D.C.L., Etc.*, London, John Murray, 1921, p. 324.

[31]   Ibid., p. 324.

[32]   Ibid.

[33]   Ibid., p. 332.

[34]   Ibid., p. 344.

[35]   *The Times*, 15 September 1874.

[36]   C. Lacaita, *An Italian Englishman. Sir James Lacaita, K.C.M.G., 1813–1895, Senator of the Kingdom of Italy*, London, Grant Richards, 1933, p. 19.

[37]   A.F. Denholm, 'The conversion of Lord Ripon in 1874', *Recusant History*, vol. 10, no. 2, April 1969, pp. 112, 118.

[38]   S. Gopal, *The Viceroyalty of Lord Ripon, 1880–1884*, London, Oxford University Press, 1953, p. 215.

[39]   'The Late Lord Ripon', *The Times*, 12 July 1909, p. 11.

[40]   J.P. Rossi, 'Lord Ripon's Resumption of Political Activity', *Recusant History*, vol. 11, no. 2, April 1971, p. 62.

[41]   Lady Amabel Kerr, *Unravelled Convictions*, London, Catholic Truth Society, 1897, p. 89.

Chapter Sixteen

The fullness of time has come upon us

Lady Amabel Kerr was in Paris when first she appreciated how isolated England was in its Faith. Entering Notre Dame she felt as if on the threshold of Rome.

> As I travelled south through Catholic countries, a feeling of comfort came over me, and something filled my soul which made me aware how empty it had been before. I felt as if Jesus Christ had not quite left the earth, and, feeling this, I began for the first time to love Him ...[1]

It was such journeys by English men and women from England to Rome which eventually brought about the arrival of Italian priests on England's shores. The man who brought all this about was Sir Harry Trelawney, a Cornish baronet who commenced his studies for the priesthood in Rome at the age of seventy. Sir Harry had introduced Father Dominic Barberi to the Hon. George Spencer, who in turn introduced Barberi to Ambrose Phillipps De Lisle and Cardinal Wiseman. These central figures who dedicated their lives to England's conversion first met each other in Rome. Under the auspices of Wiseman, then Rector of the English College, the Italian mission to convert England was started. Dominic Barberi had been dedicated to England's conversion since he had first joined St. Paul of the Cross's Passionist Order, itself dedicated to prayers for the conversion of England. Added to this strong current of spirit of reparation, taken up with such vigour by the Hon. George Spencer, was another stream of Italian fervour in the figure of Antonio Rosmini-Serbati, founder of the Institute of Charity, whose priests were known as Rosminians.

All this long preceded the conversion of Newman, who was received into the Church by Barberi in 1845. And yet there were parallels. Rosmini, the last heir to an ancient noble family of the Italian Tyrol, was born in 1797, four years before Newman. In 1823, Newman went to Oriel and Rosmini first went to Rome. In 1827 Rosmini first became aware of his vocation to found a religious order. In that same year Newman was 'rudely awakened from his dream'. In 1830 the Institute of Charity was begun in Domodóssola. Three years later Newman's *Tracts for The Times* first appeared. In 1835 priests from the Institute of Charity visited Oxford for the first time, the same year in which Newman started to ponder his *via media*. 'At such a moment the two providential streams of agency, the one from without, the other from within the Church, met on English soil.'[2]

Antonio Rosmini-Serbati was born at Rovereto in a palazzo 'more massive than elegant' where the servants grew old with the family and lived in retirement in the palazzo. Antonio's sister Gioseffa had joined the Daughters of Charity, founded by Maddalena di Canossa. Their first house had been opened in Verona, dedicated to looking after poor children and orphan girls. In 1820 Antonio introduced his sister to the much-loved and well-connected foundress of the Daughters of Charity. Antonio also corresponded with the Marchesa di Canossa, at one point expressing his concern about people's understanding of the missal, breviary and martyrology, saying there was not sufficient teaching about the sacrifice of the Mass or the Latin. Antonio then met Count Carlo Giacomo Mellerio, who also knew the Marchesa. The Count had inherited a huge fortune, of which he had resolved to spend half helping the poor. It was at the Count's house in Milan that Antonio Rosmini met a missionary from Lorraine called Abbé Jean Loewenbruck. This French priest had long wanted to found a society with the object of reforming the clergy. Just at this time another member of this devout group returned from saying Mass in the church of San Celso. He had been praying in front of the statue of the Blessed Virgin Mary and had felt a direct calling that the place destined for any new foundation of this kind was the Calvario at Domodóssola, a deserted sanctuary dedicated to the Passion of Christ. On hearing this Rosmini remembered that Maddalena di Canossa had once expressed a hope that his Institute 'should be born on Calvario between Jesus Crucified and Our Lady of Sorrows'.[3] Mellerio was delighted that his native valley should be selected for the new enterprise and Loewenbruck immediately thought of the missionary work among the Protestant Swiss.

Domodóssola was in the Piedmont, surrounded by mountains through which the Ossola valley guided the fierce Toce river in its wild course to Lake Maggiore. Rosmini's sanctuary was on the top of a spur that rose steeply from the valley floor. The little hermitage was attached to a church built in the seventeenth century and dedicated to the crucifixion. On the way up to the sanctuary was an incomplete series of chapels representing the Stations of the Cross, each with rococo groups of stucco statues. Rosmini first climbed the steep hill on 30th July 1827. The following February Rosmini, the sole heir to his family's fortune, settled in his meagre cell, where the walls, which ran with damp, the cold stone floor, the ill-fitting window, 'provided the worst possible lodging for the sickly patrician to whom all austerities had been forbidden by his doctor.' The 'pale sun, with so tiny and jagged a horizon, rose late and set early as it floated over the small domain ...'[4] Early in Lent he began to write the Constitutions for the new Society. Soon he became ill. While he was recovering he was visited by Luigi Gentili. Rosmini wrote to Mellerio 'I am like a man who watched a procession from a balcony: Providence provides the spectacle. We cannot know what God wants from this young man.'[5]

Luigi Gentili had spent his youth as a much loved entertainer of English society in Rome. A tall and handsome young lawyer with startling blue eyes and a vivacious manner he had made a conscious effort to become part of the élite English society who wintered in Rome. Abandoning his career in law he bought a piano and learned to accompany his rich baritone voice in Rossini arias. He gave lessons to English visitors and took them on tours of Rome. He then discovered that Duke Sforza Cesarini had the privilege of creating Knights and Counts of the Golden Spur and he soon appeared in society wearing the Order. He bought a vineyard on Monte Mario and persuaded his father to buy the adjoining land. He fell in love with an English woman who turned him down. His thoughts began to turn to God. How would he atone for his wasted years?[6]

In March 1830 Luigi Gentili started training for the priesthood in the Irish College in Rome. In July the following year Ambrose Phillipps travelled to Milan. He heard that Rosmini was visiting Count Mellerio at his palace there and went to meet him. Phillipps later wrote to the Hon. George Spencer that from this encounter there started a friendship which he hoped would never cease. 'He is no ordinary being I can assure you – depend upon it God has raised him up for some grand purpose in the Universal Church.'[7] When Rosmini returned to Domodossola Gentili visited him in his hermitage. Rosmini's friendship with Ambrose Phillipps had turned his thoughts towards England. So it was that, when Gentili climbed to the top of the hill sanctuary at Calvario on 31st August 1831, Rosmini met for the first time the fervent and well-connected seminarian who spoke perfect English.

Two years later Sir Harry Trelawney also made the long trek to Calvario. He had decided to start a Catholic mission on his Cornish estate centred on Trelawney Castle. He wanted permission from Rosmini for Gentili to be the first chaplain. Gentili himself had sought the prayers of his friends, of Rosmini and of the Institute of Charity houses at Domodóssola and Trent. He prayed in front of the Blessed Sacrament, fasted more religiously and took on additional penances. His knowledge of the English was such that he knew that by settling in England the Institute of Charity would receive more opposition from the

Catholic clergy than from Protestants. In 1835 Gentili and two companions set sail for England. Before they did so Pope Gregory XVI came on board the steamship and blessed them, a privilege not even granted to St. Augustine and his companions by St. Gregory the Great. A month later the three Italian priests arrived in England and made their way to London. Gentili wrote to Rosmini:

> We seemed to be entering the very city of Pluto; black houses, black ships, dirty sailors, – all was covered with filth – the waters of the Thames were a dirty yellow and emitted a highly offensive stench. On land, all was noise and confusion; horses, carriages, men of every condition running and crossing one another's paths – in short, the devil is here seen enthroned, exercising his tyrannical sway over wretched mortals.[8]

Gentili arrived at Trelawney Castle to discover that Sir Harry Trelawney had just died. Though the estate was passing to his Protestant heir, the will had provided for a Rosminian foundation. This will was successfully contested and the mission closed. In September 1835 Gentili wrote to Laetitia Trelawney saying how he wished his English was better. 'I would then be free to run from one point of this spiritually desolate land to another to shake it from this frightful lethargy or spiritual death in which it lives so wretchedly.'[9] Gentili went to Prior Park, a magnificent Palladian mansion overlooking Bath and then a seminary. Under the direction of Gentili sixty seminarians dressed in cassock and cotta undertook a three day retreat based on Ignatian spirituality, with its detailed timetable, silence and darkened chapel. In the same year Gentili moved on to Oscott and after three years ventured out into the country-side to make his first public mission in England. The following year in 1840 Gentili became Ambrose Phillipps's chaplain at Grace Dieu. From here he wrote to Rosmini that nothing he had seen in the Papal States or in the Ossola mountains approached the destitution and wretchedness of Leicestershire. Nevertheless in the Leicestershire villages of Shepshed, Belton and

Osgathorpe Gentili made many converts, despite being
pelted with mud wherever he went. At Osgathorpe his
effigy was burned and thrown into a stream. The following
day Gentili returned to the same spot with his converts
where they sang the Litany of the Holy Name. He was
beginning to find the intricacies of Ambrose Phillipps's
liturgical demands wearisome and was anxious to extend
his missions further afield. It was in the heart of the
Leicestershire countryside at Grace Dieu that he first met
Dominic Barberi:

> Gentili, refined, cultured, aristocratic in manner, a
> linguist and born orator, handsome and of impressive
> presence, had all the social graces; Dominic, though
> by no means lacking in true refinement and tact ...
> had none of the superficial social graces and could
> hardly express himself in English. Dominic was
> already too sensitively aware of his natural limitations
> to be depressed by the contrast, and these two great
> apostles of England were friends from the start.[10]

From Grace Dieu Gentili moved to Loughborough from
where he again travelled the country preaching in the
same style as Barberi. He was the first priest to wear a
Roman collar and cassock in public. He conducted
missions and retreats and public solemn renewal of
baptismal vows. He introduced processions of the Blessed
Sacrament, public recitation of the rosary and hymns to
the Blessed Virgin Mary during the month of May, contin-
uous silent prayer for forty hours in front of the Blessed
Sacrament exposed in a monstrance, the distribution of
scapulars and holy medals, the Easter blessing of houses;
all unknown in England since the time of the
Reformation. Catholic Emancipation having been granted
only six years before Gentili's arrival in England, Gentili's
prediction that such overt practices would antagonise the
Catholic clergy accustomed to maintaining a low profile,
proved correct. His Rosminian biographer thought he was
probably the first priest to convert an Englishman on a
train. Then on 26th September 1848 Gentili died suddenly

in Dublin. *The Tablet* said:

> The fullness of time has come upon us, and God once
> more sends us the heralds of his faith from the same
> land, across the same mountains, from the same city,
> from the same See from a Pope bearing the name and
> swelling with the thoughts of him who twelve hundred
> years ago laid the first stones of the English
> Apostolate.[11]

Someone said of Gentili, 'Our Lady cannot forget that he
was the first to carry her in triumph through the streets of
England.'[12]

It was thanks to Cardinal Wiseman that Gentili had been
given the opportunity to undertake his great but short
apostolate to England between 1835 and 1848. Of Irish
descent, Wiseman's grandfather had left Waterford for
Seville, where his mother had laid him on the altar of the
cathedral to consecrate him to the service of the Church.
Thus Wiseman's upbringing in Spanish Catholicism was
entirely in accordance with Gentili's introduction of
Roman practices into England. Educated in England at
Ushaw seminary and St. Edmund's College Ware, Wiseman
then went to the English College in Rome when it was first
re-opened in 1818 after the Napoleonic wars, having been
closed for a generation. The young seminarians who
arrived at the deserted college found lofty vaulted corridors, a long staircase leading up to high halls, a garden
with orange and lemon trees, a library with its contents in
disarray, a refectory with walnut panels and a chapel illuminated with the saints of England.

Wiseman recalled '... we made it, after years of silence,
re-echo to the sound of English voices, and give back the
bounding tread of those who had returned to claim their
own.'[13] Wiseman was ordained in 1825 and was Rector of
the Venerable English College between 1828 and 1840. He
was a scholar and a linguist; Newman said of him that he

could speak with readiness and point in half a dozen languages, without being detected for a foreigner in any of them, and at ten minutes notice address a congregation from a French pulpit or the select audience of an Italian academy. In 1830 the Hon. George Spencer arrived at the English College and the zealous nobleman found in Wiseman his first convert to the cause of England. He immediately told Wiseman that he should apply his mind to something more practical than Syrian manuscripts or treatises on geology. Wiseman was then visited by Newman and Froude on their visit to Rome in 1833. Wiseman recalled: 'From the day of Newman and Froude's visit to me, never for an instant did I waver in my conviction that a new era had commenced in England ... to this grand object I devoted myself ... the favourite studies of former years were abandoned for this aim alone.'[14]

Wiseman came to England in 1835 and delivered a series of lengthy lectures which had an electrifying effect on fashionable London. Five years later he became President of Oscott College. In 1850 he became the first Cardinal of Westminster on the restoration of the hierarchy. Addressing the Catholic Congress at Malines in 1863 Wiseman mentioned a small catholic chapel which had sprung up close to York Minster, as if the Cathedral had struck roots underground.

> Yes, gentlemen, the Catholic Church is springing up again; it had left its tap root under the religious soil of England, from which new suckers are now shooting upwards; the sap which was believed to be drained out is rising in them once more. The old plant scents again the waters, and revives, enclosed with a marvellous fertility.[15]

Born on Spanish soil, Cardinal Wiseman was nurtured in a land once conquered by Muslims who took Christians as captives. In the thirteenth century two Orders for the Redemption of Captives from the Moors were founded: Our Lady of Ransom (de Mercede), known as Mercederians, and the Trinitarians. The Ransomers devoted themselves to the release of Christians who were in slavery in the hands of the conquering Moors, and ransomed them, either through the collection of alms or by taking their place. The only other way that captives could be granted liberty would be if they renounced Catholicism and embraced Islam. Five hundred years later the Guild of Our Lady of Ransom was founded in England. 'We were out for the redemption of captives from heresy; also those in danger of apostasy, and we added the forgotten dead in the captivity of purgatory'.[16] The founder of the Guild was the Hon. Lister Drummond, grandson of the second Baron Ribblesdale and a descendant of Lord Strathallan, the Jacobite leader killed at Culloden in 1745. Drummond became a Catholic in 1875 at the age of nineteen and his mother the Hon. Adelaide Drummond became a Catholic in her seventieth year. Father Bernard Vaughan wrote of Drummond on his death:

> There had been, by his going hence, a fall in the spiritual thermometer; they could ill afford to lose so genial, bright, and tactful a son of the Church. He was such an enthusiastic Catholic, so simple and childlike in his piety, so zealous a worshipper of the Blessed Sacrament, and so ardent a client of our dear Lady. Getting near to Drummond was like drawing close to a blazing fire. He charged your soul with enthusiasm for the Faith, and made you feel that you yourself, like him, ought to be getting busy, without delay, for God's interests among your fellows.[17]

Drummond was a barrister who used his debating powers at Hyde Park. Handsome and refined he became a well known figure, known as the 'Escaped Protestant'. He was urbane and courteous in the face of any hostility. 'When once we recognise that those who trample on our sacred dogmas are metaphorically blind, it is impossible to be angry, and to excuse them becomes a positive duty.'[18] He left Catholic Truth Society pamphlets on railings, in railway carriages and on omnibuses, and in railway station waiting rooms. He would walk down a street and with a gesture of contempt throw down a tract to watch it being picked up by someone else. He once said the rosary alone, walking along the Martyrs Way from Newgate to Tyburn, which later became a crowded annual pilgrimage. He practised at the Old Bailey, close to Newgate, and brought many converts to the Faith. One such was a boy whom he defended for murder who was convicted on circumstantial evidence and condemned to death, like the martyrs of the Reformation before him. Before his execution the boy was received into the Church. The boy wrote his last letter to the Hon. Lister Drummond.

> In answer to your most kind and instructive letter, for which I beg to thank you, and for all your kindness to me and my dear parents, by God's grace and your help I have borne my trouble bravely. I feel that God has already given me relief to my sufferings and it is Our Lord's Will that I should serve him in Heaven. My ordeal has been a blessing and I firmly believe God has strengthened me through His teaching in our Church. I am praying earnestly to make a good Confession to my priest, and praying for you so as we can meet in the joy of Heaven. As I have not been confirmed, Bishop Butt will confirm me on Monday. On Tuesday the priest will say Mass in my cell and give me Holy Communion. It will be the first Mass I have served, and the last principal act of my life, so that God is very good to me. I cannot in words tell you what a consolation my religion brings me and it is giving me help and strength to meet my death. Do please pray for me. You can be sure I shall pray for you.[19]

Notes

1   Lady Amabel Kerr, *Unravelled Convictions*, London, Catholic Truth Society, 1897, p. 3.
2   Very Rev. Dr. Casartelli, *A Forgotten Chapter of the Second Spring*, London, Burns & Oates, 1895, p. 6.
3   C. Leetham, *Rosmini. Priest, Philosopher and Patriot*, London, Longmans, Green & Co., 1957, pp. 1, 39, 58, 73, 80, 82.
4   Ibid., p. 88.
5   Ibid., p. 112.
6   C. Leetham, *Luigi Gentili. A Sower for the Second Spring*, London, Burns & Oates, 1965, p. 15.
7   E.S. Purcell, *Life and Letters of Ambrose Phillipps de Lisle*, London, Macmillan, 1900, p. 51.
8   Leetham, *Gentili*, op. cit., p. 61.
9   Ibid., p. 65.
10   A. Wilson, *Blessed Dominic Barberi. Supernaturalized Briton*, London, Sands & Co., 1967, p. 221.
11   Casartelli, op. cit., p. 24.
12   Leetham, *Gentili*, op. cit., p. 214.
13   Cardinal Wiseman, *Recollection of the Last Four Popes*, London, Hurst & Blackett, 1858, p. 10.
14   Ibid., pp. 100, 109.
15   H.E. Cardinal Wiseman, *The Religious and Social Position of Catholics in England, An Address Delivered to the Catholic Congress at Malines, August 21, 1863*, Dublin, James Duffy, 1864, p. 16.
16   P. Fletcher, *Recollections of a Ransomer*, London, Sands & Co., 1928, p. 55.
17   R.E. Noble, *Lister Drummond K.S.G., Barrister-at-Law*, London, Catholic Truth Society, 1922, pp. 1–2.
18   Ibid., p. 9.
19   Ibid., p. 15.

Bibliography to Part I

M. Baring, *The Puppet Show of Memory*, London, Heinemann, 1922

R.H. Benson, *Confessions of a Convert*, London, Longmans, Green & Co., 1913

Countess of Blessington, *The Idler in Italy Vols. I & II*, London, Henry Colburn, 1839

Countess of Blessington, *The Idler in Italy. Vol. III*, London, Henry Colburn, 1840

J.E. Bowden, *The Life and Letters of Frederick William Faber, D.D.*, London, Thomas Richardson & Son, 1869

A.M. Brown, *Wintering at Menton on the Riviera. A Compagnon de Voyage with hints to invalids*, London, J. & A. Churchill, 1872

Rev. John W. Burgon, *Letters from Rome to Friends in England*, London, John Murray, 1862

B. Camm, 'Memoirs of a Benedictine monk', in *The City of Peace by those who have entered it*, Dublin, C.T.S., Sealy, Bryers and Walker, 1903

Northampton Record Office, D. Cary-Elwes, *My Journal Volume III*, Jan. 15, 1888

Mrs Winthrop Chanler, *Roman Spring. Memoirs*, London, Williams & Norgate, 1935

Lt. Gen. Sir George Cockburn, *A Voyage to Cadiz and Gibraltar up the Mediterranean to Sicily and Malta in 1810 & 11, Vols. I & II*, London, J. Harding, 1815

J.G. Cox, *Jubilee-Tide in Rome*, London, Burns & Oates, 1888

M.S. Crawford, *Life in Tuscany*, London, Smith, Elder & Co., 1859

W. Davies, *The Pilgrimage of the Tiber, from its Mouth to its Source: with some account of its tributaries*, London, Sampson Low, 1873

E. Dicey, *Rome in 1860*, London, Macmillan, 1861

W. Elwes, *The Feilding Album*, London, Geoffrey Bles, 1950

Rev. John Chetwode Eustace, *A Classical Tour through Italy*, London, J. Mawman, 1819

F.W. Faber, *Sights and Thoughts in Foreign Churches and among Foreign Peoples*, London, J. G. F. & J. Rivington, 1842

M. Graham, *Three Months passed in the mountains East of Rome, during the year 1819*, London, Longman, Hurst, Rees, Orme and Brown, 1820

Mrs G. Gretton, *The Englishwoman in Italy. Impressions of Life in the Roman States and Sardinia, during a ten years' residence*, London, Hurst & Blackett, 1861

Lady Elizabeth Grosvenor, *Narrative of a Yacht Voyage in the Mediterranean during the years 1840–41*, Vol. *I*, London, John Murray, 1842

N. Hall, *The Land of the Forum and the Vatican; Or, Thoughts and Sketches during an Easter Pilgrimage to Rome*, London, James Nisbet, 1854

A.J.C. Hare, *The Story of My Life. Vol. I*, London, George Allen, 1896

Lady Herbert, *Cradle Lands*, London, Richard Bentley, 1867

Lady Herbert, *Impressions of Spain*, London, Richard Bentley, 1867

Rev. B. Hill, *Observations and Remarks in a journey through Sicily and Calabria, in the year 1791*, 1792

G.S. Hillard, *Six Months in Italy*, Vols. *I & II*, London, John Murray, 1853

Earl of Ilchester (ed.), *The Journal of Elizabeth Lady Holland Vol. I 1791–1811*, London, Longmans, 1908

C. Kerr (ed.), *Cecil, Marchioness of Lothian*, London, Sands & Co., 1922

I. Ker, 'Newman and the Mediterranean' in M. Costell (ed.), *Creditable Warriors 1830–1876*, London, Atlantic Highlands N.J., The Ashfield Press, 1990

Rev. W.I. Kip, M.A., *The Christmas Holydays in Rome*, London, Longman, Brown, Green & Longmans, 1847

Greater London Record Office, Papers of Hon. Edward Legge, F/LEG/902

S. Leslie, *Mark Sykes, His Life and Letters*, London, Cassell, 1923

University of Nottingham, Department of Manuscripts, Ne C 12, 983 'Lord Lincoln's journal of Mediterranean Cruise and tour, 1850', 4 May.

Marchioness of Londonderry & H. M. Hyde, *More Letters from Martha Wilmot. Impressions of Vienna 1819–1829*, London, Macmillan, 1935

Lady Lovat, *The Catholic Church from Within*, London, Longmans, 1901

M. Lutyens (ed.), *Effie in Venice. Unpublished letters of Mrs John Ruskin written from Venice between 1849–1852*, London, John Murray, 1963

Hon. Mrs Alfred Montgomery, *On the Wing: A Southern Flight*, London, Hurst and Blackett, 1875

H. Morton, *Protestant Vigils, or Evening Records of a Journey in Italy in the years 1826 and 1827*, Vols. *I & II*, London, Seeley and Burnside, 1829

G.M. Musgrave, *The Parson, Pen and Pencil: or, Reminiscences and Illustrations of an Excursion to Paris, Tours and Rouen, in the Summer of 1847; with a few memoranda on French farming. Vol. I*, London, Richard Bentley, 1848

G.M. Musgrave, *A Pilgrimage into Dauphiné; comprising a visit to the monastery of the Grande Chartreuse; with anecdotes, incidents and sketches from twenty departments of France*, Vols. *I & II*, London, Hurst and Blackett, 1857

G.M. Musgrave, *Ten Days in a French Parsonage in the Summer of 1863,*

Vols I & II, London, Sampson, Low, Son & Marston, 1864

G.M. Musgrave, *A Ramble through Normandy; or Scenes, Characters and Incidents in a sketching excursion through Calvados*, London, David Bogue, 1865

B.W. Noel, M.A., *Notes of a Tour in the Valleys of Piedmont in the Summer of 1854*, London, James Nisbet, 1855

Marquis of Normanby, *The English in Italy*, Vols. *I & II*, London, Saunders and Otley, 1825

'Olinthus', *Reminiscences of Rome: or, a religious, moral and literary view of the Eternal City; in a series of letters addressed to a friend in England, by a member of the Arcadian Academy*, London, Paternoster Row, 1838

J. Pemble, *The Mediterranean Passion. Victorians and Edwardians in the South*, Oxford, Clarendon Press, 1987

J.M. Robinson, *The Dukes of Norfolk. A Quincentennial History*, Oxford, O.U.P., 1982

H.J. Rose, *Untrodden Spain, and her Black Country; being sketches of the life and character of the Spaniard of the interior*, Vols. *I & II*, London, Samuel Tinsley, 1875

Dame Mary Francis Roskell, O.S.B., *Memoirs of Francis Kerril Amherst, D.D. Lord Bishop of Northampton*, London, Art and Book Company, 1903

T.U. Sadleir (ed.), *An Irish Peer on the Continent (1801–1803). Being a narrative of the tour of Stephen, 2nd Earl Mount Cashell, through France, Italy etc.*, London, Williams & Norgate, 1920

G.A. Sala, *Rome and Venice, with other wanderings in Italy, 1866–7*, London, Tinsley, 1869

G.A. Sala, *A Journey Due South. Travels in Search of Sunshine*, London, Vizetelly & Co., 1885

W.F. Stead, *The Shadow of Mount Carmel. A Pilgrimage*, London, Richard Cobden-Sanderson, 1926

Lord Teignmouth, *Reminiscences of Many Years. Vol. I*, Edinburgh, David Douglas, 1878

C. Thomas, *Love and Work Enough. The Life of Anna Jameson*, London, Macdonald, 1967

G. Townsend, D.D., *Journal of a Tour in Italy, in 1850, with an account of an interview with the Pope, at the Vatican*, London, Francis & John Rivington, 1850

M. Trappes-Lomax, *Pugin. A Medieval Victorian*, London, Sheed and Ward, 1932

Rev. M. Vicary, B.A., *Notes of a Residence at Rome in 1846*, London, Richard Bentley, 1847

W. Ward, *Aubrey De Vere. A Memoir*, London, Longmans, Green & Co., 1904

C.R. Weld, *Auvergne, Piedmont and Savoy: A Summer Ramble*, London, John W. Parker, 1850

C.R. Weld, *A Vacation in Brittany*, London, Chapman & Hall, 1856

C.R. Weld, *Last Winter in Rome*, London, Longman Green, 1865

Cardinal Wiseman, *Recollections of the Last Four Popes*, London, Hurst and Blackett, 1858

Rev. J.A. Wylie, *Pilgrimage from the Alps to the Tiber or the Influence of Romanism on Trade, Justice & Knowledge*, Edinburgh, Shepherd and Elliot, 1855

Bibliography to Part II

R. Addington (ed.), *Faber, Poet and Priest. Selected Letters by Frederick William Faber*, London, D. Brown & Sons, Ltd., 1974

R. Adelson, *Mark Sykes. Portrait of an Amateur*, London, Jonathan Cape, 1975

Rev. C.A. Alington, 'Christian Outlines' in A. Lunn (ed.), *Public School Religion*, London, Faber & Faber, 1933

L. Allen, 'Ambrose Phillipps De Lisle, 1809–1878', *The Catholic Historical Review*, April 1954, Vol. XL

W.L. Arnstein, 'Queen Victoria and Religion' in G. Malmgreen (ed.), *Religion in the Lives of English Women, 1760–1930*, Bloomington and Indianapolis, Indiana University Press, 1986

Dowager Duchess of Argyll (ed.), *George Douglas Eighth Duke of Argyll, K.G., K.T. (1823–1900). Autobiography and Memoirs*, London, John Murray, 1906

J. Baker, *Lady Georgiana Fullerton. A Bournemouth Benefactor*, Bournemouth Local Studies Publications, 1991

A.C. Benson, *Hugh. Memoirs of a Brother*, London, Smith, Elder & Co., 1915

R.H. Benson, *Confessions of a Convert*, London, Longmans, Green & Co., 1913

J.E. Bowden, *The Life and Letters of Frederick William Faber, D.D.*, London, Thomas Richardson & Son, 1969

Lord Braye, *Fewness of My Days. A Life in Two Centuries*, London, Sands & Co., 1927

Sir Francis Burnand, *Records and Reminiscences. Personal and General*, London, Methuen, 1905

E. Butler, *An Autobiography*, London, Constable, 1922

P. Caraman, *C. C. Martindale*, London, Longmans, 1967

J. Cartwright, *Journals of Lady Knightley of Fawsley, 1856–1884*, London, John Murray, 1915

Very Rev. Dr. Casartelli, *A Forgotten Chapter of the Second Spring*, London, Burns & Oates, 1895

Rev. James Cassidy, *The Life of Father Faber, Priest of the Oratory of St. Philip Neri*, London, Sands & Co., 1946

Catholics at Eton. A Reasoned Petition, London, St. Vincent's Press, 1920

R. Chapman, *Father Faber*, London, Burns & Oates, 1961

A.O.J. Cockshut, *Anglican Attitudes. A Study of Victorian Religious Controversies*, London, Collins, 1959

Hon. Gilbert Coleridge, *Eton in the Seventies*, London, Smith, Elder & Co., 1913

H.J. Coleridge, S.J., *Life of Lady Georgiana Fullerton. From the French of Mrs Augustus Craven*, London, R. Bentley & Son, 1888

J. Davies, *Cardiff and the Marquesses of Bute*, Cardiff, University of Wales Press, 1981

'The late Earl of Denbigh', *The Times*, 17 March 1892

F.C. Devas, D.S.O., O.B.E., S.J., *Mother Mary Magdalen of the Sacred Heart*, London, Burns, Oates & Washbourne, 1927

O. E., *Eton under Hornby. Some Reminiscences and Reflections*, London, A. C. Field, 1910

A.F. Denholm, 'The conversion of Lord Ripon in 1874', *Recusant History*, vol. 10, no. 2, April 1969

B. Elliott, 'The Return of the Cistercians to the Midlands', *Recusant History*, vol. 16, no. 1 (1982–83)

W. Elwes, *The Feilding Album*, London, Geoffrey Bles, 1950.

W. Elwes and R. Elwes, *Gervase Elwes. The Story of his Life*, London, Grayson & Grayson, 1935

Warwick Record Office, CR2017/F170. Facts and Correspondence relating to the admission into the Catholic Church of Viscount and Viscountess Feilding by Right Reverend Bishop Gillis, Edinburgh, Charles Dolman, 1850

P. Fletcher, *Recollections of a Ransomer*, London, Sands & Co., 1928

J. Gillow, *A Literary and Biographical History, or Biographical Dictionary of the English Catholics from the Breach with Rome, in 1534, to the present time*

S. Gopal, *The Viceroyalty of Lord Ripon, 1880–1884*, London, Oxford University Press, 1953

R. Gray, *Cardinal Manning. A Biography*, London, Weidenfeld & Nicolson, 1985

D. Green, *The Churchills of Blenheim*, London, Constable, 1984

A. Guinness, *Blessings in Disguise*, London, Hamish Hamilton, 1985

D. Gwynn, *Lord Shrewsbury, Pugin and the Catholic Revival*, London, Hollis & Carter, 1946

A.J.C. Hare, *The Story of My Life Vol. III*, London, George Allen, 1896

Lady Herbert, *Impressions of Spain in 1866*, London, Richard Bentley, 1867

B. Holland, *Memoir of Kenelm Digby*, Sevenoaks, Fisher Press, 1992

B. Holland, 'An Eton Master', *National Review*, vol. xxx, February 1898

Right Rev. Sir David Hunter-Blair, *John Patrick Third Marquess of Bute, K.T. (1847–1900)*, London, John Murray, 1921

Right Rev. Sir David Hunter-Blair, *A Medley of Memories. Fifty Years'*

Recollections of a Benedictine Monk, London, Edward Arnold, 1919

K. Jaeger, 'Lady Georgiana Fullerton', University of King's College, Halifax, Nova Scotia, Ph.D.

Lady Amabel Kerr, *Unravelled Convictions*, London, Catholic Truth Society, 1897

C. Kerr (ed.), *Cecil, Marchioness of Lothian*, London, Sands & Co., 1922

Lady C. Kerr, *Edith Feilding. Sister of Charity*, London, Sands & Co., 1933

Warwick Record Office, Letter from Lady Alice Kerr to Lord Feilding, 22 Jan. 1854; CR2017/C448.

C. Lacaita, *An Italian Englishman. Sir John Lacaita K.C.M.G., 1813–1895. Senator of the Kingdom of Italy*, London, Grant Richards, 1933

C. Leetham, *Rosmini. Priest, Philosopher and Patriot*, London, Longmans, Green & Co., 1957

C. Leetham, *Luigi Gentili. A Sower for the Second Spring*, London, Burns & Oates, 1965.

S. Leslie, *Mark Sykes: His Life and Letters*, London, Cassell, 1923

S. Leslie (ed.), *Letters of Herbert Cardinal Vaughan to Lady Herbert of Lea 1867 to 1903*, London, Burns & Oates, 1942

S. Leslie, *Cardinal Manning. His Life and Labours*, Dublin, Clonmore and Reynolds, 1953

S. Leslie, *Long Shadows*, London, John Murray, 1966

J.G. Lockhart, *Charles Lindley Viscount Halifax, Part One 1839–1885*, London, Geoffrey Bles, 1935

P. Lubbock, *Shades of Eton*, London, Jonathan Cape, 1929

R. Macdonald, 'The Catholic Gaidhealtachd' in D. McRoberts (ed.), *Modern Scottish Catholicism 1878–1978*, Glasgow, Burns, 1979

F. Compton Mackenzie, *William Cory. A Biography*, London, Constable, 1950

Charles, IXth Duke of Marlborough, K.G. Tributes by Rt. Hon. Winston Spencer-Churchill and C. C. Martindale, S.J., London, Burns, Oates & Washbourne, 1934

C.C. Martindale, *The Life of Monsignor Robert Hugh Benson, Vol I*, London, Longmans, 1916

C.C. Martindale, S.J., *Mother Stuart*, London, Catholic Truth Society, 1933

H.C.G. Mathew, 'Gladstone and Manning', *The Allen Review*, no. 6, Hilary 1992

Hon. Mrs Maxwell-Scott, *Henry Schomberg Kerr. Sailor and Jesuit*, London, Longman, 1901

T.J. McCann, 'A Bumping Pitch and a Blinding Light: Henry Manning and the other religion', *Recusant History*, vol. 21, no. 2, Oct. 1992

N. Mitford, *The Stanleys of Alderley. Their letters between the years 1851–1865*, London, Hamish Hamilton, 1939

M. Monahan, *Life & Letters of Janet Erskine Stuart, Superior-General of the Society of the Sacred Heart, 1857–1914*, London, Longmans, 1934

J. Morris, *The Life of Mother Henrietta Kerr, Religious of the Sacred Heart*, Roehampton, 1887

K.L. Morris, *The Image of the Middle Ages in Romantic and Victorian*

Literature, London, Croom Helm, 1984

K.L. Morris, 'The Cambridge converts and the Oxford movement', *Recusant History,* vol. 17, no. 4, Oct. 1985

M. Napier and A. Laing, *The London Oratory Centenary, 1884–1984,* London, Trefoil, 1984

'Dowager Duchess of Newcastle', *The Times,* 9 May 1913

J.H. Newman, *Lectures on the Present Position of Catholics in England,* London, Burns Oates & Company, 1851.

D. Newsome, 'Cardinal Manning and his influence on the church and nation', *Recusant History,* vol. 21, no. 2, Oct. 1992

R.E. Noble, *Lister Drummond K.S.G., Barrister-at-Law,* London, Catholic Truth Society, 1922

R. O'Donnell, 'Roman Catholic Architecture in Great Britain and Ireland 1829–1878', University of Cambridge Ph.D., 1983

R. Ornsby, *Memoirs of James Robert Hope-Scott of Abbotsford, D.C.L., Q.C.,* Vols. I & II, London, John Murray, 1884

J. Patrick, 'Newman, Pugin & Gothic', *Victorian Studies,* Winter 1981

Rev. Father Pius, *Life of Father Ignatius of St. Paul, Passionist. (The Hon. & Rev. George Spencer.) Compiled chiefly from his Autobiography, Journal and Letters.,* Dublin, James Duffy, 1866

Rev. Father Pius, *The Life of St. Paul of the Cross: Founder of the Congregation of Discalced Clerks of the Holy Cross and Passion of Our Lord,* London, P. J. Kennedy & Sons, N.Y., 1922

A. Pollen, *Mother Mabel Digby. A Biography of the Superior-General of the Society of the Sacred Heart 1835–1911,* London, John Murray, 1914

E.S. Purcell, *Life and Letters of Ambrose Phillipps de Lisle,* London, Macmillan, 1900.

D. Quinn, 'Manning as Politician', *Recusant History,* vol. 21, no. 2, Oct. 1992

The Rambler, 1855

J.M. Robinson, *The Dukes of Norfolk. A Quincentennial History,* Oxford, O.U.P., 1982

J.P. Rossi, 'Lord Ripon's Resumption of Political Activity', *Recusant History,* vol. 11, no. 2, April 1971

G.W.E. Russell, *Collections and Recollections,* ch. 6.

C. Ryder, *Life of Thomas Edward Bridgett. Priest of the Congregation of the Most Holy Redeemer, with Characteristics from his Writings,* London, Burns & Oates, 1906

Rev. Joseph Smith, C.P., *Paul Mary Pakenham, Passionist,* Dublin, M.H. Gill & Son, Ltd., 1930

P. Smith-Steinmetz, *Life of Mother Janet Stuart,* Dublin, Clonmore and Reynolds, 1948

J.G. Snead-Cox, *The Life of Cardinal Vaughan, Vol. I,* London, Herbert & Daniel, 1910

J. Vanden Bussche, C.P., *Ignatius (George) Spencer Passionist (1799–1864),* Leuven, Leuven University Press, 1991.

B. Vaughan, *The Sins of Society,* London, Kegan Paul, Trench, Trübner & Co., 1906

M. Vaughan, *Courtfield and the Vaughans*, London, Quiller Press, 1989

J. Vereb, C.P., *Ignatius Spencer Apostle of Christian Unity*, London, CTS, 1992

D. Verey, 'Woodchester Park, Gloucestershire', *Country Life*, 6 February 1969

H. Vickers, *Gladys, Duchess of Marlborough*, London, Weidenfeld and Nicolson, 1979

W. Walsh, *The Religious Life and Influence of Queen Victoria*, London, Swan, Sonnenschein & Co., 1902

W. Ward, *The Life and Times of Cardinal Wiseman, Vol. I*,
Warwick Record Office CR2017/C415/3, 5

A. Wilson, *Blessed Dominic Barberi. Supernaturalised Briton*, London, Sands & Co., 1967

H.E. Cardinal Wiseman, *The Religious and Social Position of Catholics in England, An Address Delivered to the Catholic Congress at Malines, August 21, 1863*, Dublin, James Duffy, 1864

Cardinal Wiseman, *Recollection of the Last Four Popes*, London, Hurst & Blackett, 1858

L. Wolf, *Life of the First Marquess of Ripon K.G., P.C., G.C.S.I., D.C.L., Etc.*, London, John Murray, 1921

U. Young, C.P. *Life of Father Ignatius Spencer*, C.P., London, Burns, Oates and Washbourne, 1935

Index